Jan. 18, 2025

To God be the
glory ~

A LIGHT SHINING
IN THE DARK

Anne G. Lang

D1713429

A LIGHT SHINING
IN THE DARK

A Memoir

By

Anne G. Lang

ISBN: 979-8-321-94804-0 (paperback)
ISBN: 979-8-218-57038-5 (hardcover)

DEDICATION

For my Heavenly Father, the Ancient of Days; You know all from the beginning of time. This book is only a surprise to me. To God be the glory for the great things He has done. I thank You Father for protecting me. I thank the Holy Spirit for guiding me when I had no clue what to do. I thank Jesus for setting me free.

For all those clinging to the light in the darkness, hold on, dawn has risen.
His name is Jesus.

For Paul, you are my best friend and just as adventurous as I am, which means we have a lot of fun together. Thank you for allowing me to heal not only through tears but also through laughter. Our laughter with each other is life-giving and healing to my soul. You gave me the time and the space for the Lord to take me on a healing quest. Thank you for encouraging me to write my story and walk in truth. God had you waiting just for me, and I am grateful you were, and you are my future. I love you with all my heart. God bless you.

For Bryan. It has been a wide open adventure since the moment you were born. You have kept our family life exciting, and you have brought us joy and delight. I am amazed to see the man of God you have chosen to be every day. God has gifted you in powerful ways, and He will continue to show His glory through you. I see discernment, leadership, and strength in you. It makes me proud that you are my son. I love you with all my heart. God bless you and your children through all generations.

For Laurel Anne. You have brought us joy and laughter since the moment you were born. Our family would be boring without you and your sense of humor. I am in awe of the woman of God you have become and continue to choose to be daily. It is thrilling to see all the gifts God has specifically given to you. I see great faith, strength and determination in you, and it makes me proud I get to be your mama. I love you with all my heart. God bless you and your children through all generations.

AUTHOR'S NOTE

What I tell you in the dark, speak in the daylight; what is whispered in your ear, proclaim from the roofs.
—*Matthew 10:27*

I have held a story in my heart for over twenty years now. I think I have been a bit traumatized, and I honestly did not want to talk about it or deal with it myself. On September 4, 2021, I was on a walk, and I felt the gentle voice of the Lord say, "It is time. What you learned in the darkness, I want you to share in the light. I want to heal you and my people. Write your story of darkness—and I will make it a light."

So here we go.

Yikes.

Some of the names of the people and places in this memoir, as well as some of the dates, have been changed to protect privacy.

PREFACE

We also have the prophetic message as something completely reliable, and you will do well to pay attention to it, as to a light shining in a dark place, until the day dawns and the morning star rises in your hearts.

—2 Peter 1:19

In Him was life, and that life was the light of men. The light shines in the darkness, and the darkness has not overcome it.

—1 John 1:4–5

In reading this story you will have a glimpse of a portion of my personal life. I have written this for you to be encouraged about the God we serve, and for you to know how He can use the dark times of our lives to bring us into His glorious light by the power of Jesus who died for our sins, and by the power of the Holy Spirit who is the counselor and guide for believers in Christ.

Anything is able to be conquered and healed through the light. Please read this without condemnation for any sins you might be involved in now or in the past. My intent is not to produce shame, but to illustrate how walking with God is truly walking in the light, as He is the light. We all sin and have fallen short of the glory of God. Praise the Lord; He walks with us, and in us. He who lives in us is greater than he who lives within this world.

Here is a warning: my testimony might be a lot to take in, so take your time. As you read, please take time if you need to pray and to even put this down and walk away for a little while. It is to be an encouragement and a reminder of who is fighting our battles for us. Until the day dawns, and the morning star rises in your hearts.

Please pray with me:

Dear Heavenly Father,
We come before Your mighty throne, and ask you to speak to each heart that reads this testimony of who You are. Jesus, open the eyes of our hearts and reveal the glorious light you walk in with us. We ask You to wash away our sins, through the blood of Jesus. Fill our minds with Your thoughts, Holy Spirit of truth, our counselor, and do not let the enemy discourage any reader of this text in any way. Let this be a light to this dark world, and shine to heal hearts across the land. All the glory goes to You, our God.

In the mighty name of Jesus, we pray in faith,
Amen.

CHAPTER 1
SUMMERTOWN

Train up a child in the way he should go, and when he is old he will not depart from it.

—Proverbs 22:6

I was born and given the name Anne Gillespie Powell. My parents called me Anne G., as a double name. My siblings called me Angie, but my mother pronounced my name, Anne, with a pause, G.

Growing up as the youngest of five children was an exciting life. I grew up on Signal Mountain in Southeast Tennessee on property handed down through the women of my mother's side of the family. My parents, Dugg and Eleanor Powell, were Bible-believing Christians who loved God and loved people. They called me "the baby," since I was fourteen years younger than my oldest brother, Happy, twelve years younger than Frank, ten years younger than Bill, and eight years younger than my sister, Mary Lee. My siblings still refer to me as "the baby," and I like that. I liked my place in the family. I was a big surprise to my parents, and there were not many secrets in our family. My mom said she cried for nine months when she found out she was having number five, but that I was a joy to my parents in their old age.

My parents were exhausted by the time I came along. As a result, from a young age I had the freedom to explore our family's fifty-acre property as I pleased, which was in the country on Walden's Ridge, in a small community called Summertown. Before air conditioning, families would ride up from the city of Chattanooga by horse and buggy to "summer" in their cabins, escaping the city's heat and yellow fever because the mountain springs, known as Mabbitt Springs, were thought to have medicinal advantages.

My great-great-great-grandparents purchased our family's original property in Summertown in 1873. Then in 1905, my great-grandparents—who owned the Coca-Cola bottling company in Savannah, Georgia—purchased the property I grew up on as their summer retreat, to be near her parents. Then my grandparents built their own summer home on the property. When my mom was twelve, they stayed for a winter, and after that, they never moved off Signal Mountain again.

I grew up surrounded by family—we all lived next door to each other. Our property included my grandparents' house, my family's house (which was the original home of my great-grandparents and the home where my brother Bill and his family now live), my aunts and uncles' family homes, two summer homes of my aunt and uncle who lived in Savannah, and two smaller homes for workers that are now used as guest houses. My cousins were more like siblings, and my siblings and I were closer than most families are. Today my older siblings' families make up the eighth generation to live in Summertown.

As a child, I was able to come and go as I pleased on our family property of open fields and old-growth trees. I would take off on my own, many times disappearing for the whole day to our barn to take care of our animals— puppies, my horse Black Jack, new litters of pigs or goats— whatever happened to be there at the time. I found deep peace and joy in taking care of our animals. If I wasn't tending to them, I was probably covered in dirt playing in Mabbitt Springs. As a result of my freedom to explore God's magnificent creation, I grew to be fiercely independent and wild at heart.

I was a good child, except I seemed to get quite a few spankings. Mostly, according to my daddy, because of my sassy mouth. I knew he was right, and I probably deserved twice as many spankings as I got. My daddy was always my hero.

My parents both had wonderful senses of humor and did not take themselves too seriously. Honestly, they were the reason I wanted to walk with the Lord from an early age. They were not perfect and did not pretend to be perfect, and it made me desire to have the peace they had, through a relationship with the Lord.

Our house was constantly bustling with friends and neighbors who were always popping in. The doors were always open, and people of all ages were always welcome. When I would walk in the door, I never knew who'd be sitting at the kitchen table talking to my mom (and daddy if

3

he was home from his work as a stockbroker). Our kitchen was where everything happened in our house; it was the hub of all the family excitement. And while happenings around our kitchen table were almost always like a spontaneous party, the atmosphere was much more formal at my grandmother's house. Granny lived next door and was always dressed beautifully in the latest fashion. When the family came to the dining table at her house, we were served in the dining room on lovely bone China with way too many forks and knives to choose from. At her table we were expected to dress appropriately, sit like ladies and gentlemen with straight backs, and use all the silverware properly. "Yes ma'am" and "Yes sir" were part of our everyday vocabulary growing up. Granny would correct us and would occasionally even correct PawPaw at the table. I got tickled when PawPaw got in trouble because he would secretly make funny faces. Even with the vast differences between the short distance from my parents' home to my grandparents' house, I knew my boundaries, and I was happy with them. Especially since most of the time I had complete freedom.

I had two best friends, Denise, who I met at age three, and Holland, who moved into the neighborhood the next year. We grew up walking to each other's homes. I had an almost picture-perfect childhood, looking back. My parents were always open to hosting Sunday school parties, Campus Crusade meetings, or any other Christian meeting or event at our house. My parents loved me, and they disciplined me and my siblings. We had plenty of chores, a garden to work in, animals at our barn to take care of, and there was always housework and yard work to do.

Life was good. Very good.

For God so loved the world, that He gave His one and only Son, that whoever believes in Him shall not perish but have eternal life.

—*John 3:16*

I asked Jesus Christ to come into my life at age five. My mom would soak in the tub and read her book to relax. One day, I walked straight into her bathroom and told her I wanted to ask Jesus to come into my heart. She immediately put her book down, and we prayed right there while she was soaking in the bath.

I knew from that moment, I was saved.

From a young age I was fiery for the Lord. Holland's mother, Mary Sue Haverty, called my mom one day when we were six years old and said I had Denise and Holland trapped from going down the stairs, telling them both if they didn't accept Jesus Christ into their heart and believe in Him, they would go to hell and burn for eternity when they died. So, they should go ahead and do it right then. Holland's mother was a strong Catholic, and a good friend with my mom. She told my mom I was preaching hellfire and damnation from the steps, so she had to intervene, and she wanted my mom to know. At the dinner table that night, my mother asked me about my "sermon on the steps," and I told her I wanted Denise and Holland to be in heaven with me one day. She and daddy got a big kick out of that.

I had the desire to read the Word of God from an early age. I would grab my Bible by my bed and read a little many nights before going to sleep. I had a good relationship with my earthly father, which made it easy for me to understand that my heavenly Father loved me. In elementary school I became involved in my church youth group, which led me to join Campus Crusade in junior high, and then Young Life in high school. I fell in love with Young Life immediately and felt like I had found my people. It was a perfect fit for my personality. Having fun in the presence of God Almighty. That was my bottom line.

A good name is more desirable than great riches; to be esteemed is better than silver or gold.
—Proverbs 22:1

Growing up, I wanted a good reputation. After all, I heard my older brothers talk about the girls with bad reputations at the dinner table and *everything* they had done. I wanted to make sure I was never talked about at anyone's family dinner table. There were no topics off limits at our dinner table. That is where I learned all the answers to my questions in life—listening to my older siblings. I have always adored my siblings, who were (and are) some of my closest friends despite our large age gap. They each have been pillars of support to me in different seasons of my life. Because I had good relationships with my family, and because I knew my parents loved me, I always felt extremely secure in who I was. Sometimes, maybe too secure. Being the baby of five, I never worried about doing any of my schoolwork; in fact, I never worried about much of anything. I would have much rather been at our barn taking care of the baby pigs. My life was an adventure, and I enjoyed each new day.

I knew I was loved, and joy filled my spirit to the brim.

CHAPTER 2
MISSIONARY BOY

So in Christ we, though many, form one body, and each member belongs to all the others. We have different gifts, according to the grace given to each of us. If your gift is prophesying, then prophesy in accordance with your faith; if it is serving, then serve; if it is teaching, then teach; if it is to encourage, then give encouragement; if it is giving, then give generously; if it is to lead, do it diligently; if it is to show mercy, do it cheerfully.

—Romans 12:5–8

My parents had a gift that God had given them. They loved people. They loved people right where they were, not where they should be or were going to be one day. They loved them where they were. Because of that, people of all ages were drawn to them. They counseled people in our home all the time. One example was a group of single mothers who met at our house and brought their children to play in our yard or house while my parents taught a Bible study of hope from the Word of God. My parents were often asked by our church and many Christian organizations in town to allow people to stay with us for a night, a week, a month, or even a year at a time. They were asked to host new Campus Crusade staff moving to town, missionaries from the mission conference at church, or missionary kids coming to college in the United States. We had children from Bethel Bible Village, an orphanage home for children who had a parent in prison or a parent(s) who had died, or adults who had hit a hard time in life from alcohol or gambling. They came, my parents loved them for a season, and then they went on their way. Yes, they came at different times and at different ages, and my parents just loved them. Christmas, Thanksgiving, and every other holiday usually involved someone not in our family who joined our table and festivities. Our house was a soft landing, and our guests were drawn into our family and all the chaos. That was the gift the Lord gave my parents, and He used it for His glory.

Growing up, I was a wildly active younger child with lots of energy. As a teenager, I was still very active and always doing something adventurous, but I never got into any real trouble. I never had the desire to drink or experiment with any drugs. Although to be honest, I did go to the parties with the people who did. I never wanted to miss a good party.

One day, during my sophomore year of high school, my mother told me we were going to have a missionary boy from our church who was born and raised in Tanzania, East Africa, come live with us to go to college for the year. His name was Caleb Sharp. His parents were white Americans who had moved to Africa before having their children. So, he was coming with his father to get settled into the community college in the nearby city of Chattanooga. His father planned to stay several weeks with us also, and then head back to East Africa.

I did not think twice about these new guests. They arrived on a hot Sunday afternoon at the end of August. My extended family had Sunday family lunches which, most of the time, were at my mom and dad's house. Everyone brought food, and it was like Thanksgiving after every Sunday church service in the summer. After lunch, I drove my mother to pick up our newest house guests from the Chattanooga Airport, about thirty minutes from our house. We met at the curbside of the airport and had quick greetings and introductions with Caleb and his father, Jason.

Caleb was very attractive, I thought, in an untamed way. His light brown hair was a little wild, sticking straight up in a long buzz cut and a little longer in the back. He had on faded Levi blue jeans, a light colored t-shirt, dark tan skin, and he wore a tough piece of leather as a necklace around his neck, which I found out later was from a hippopotamus he had killed. Caleb was about 5'10" with an athletic soccer player build. He was cordial but cool in his demeanor, which honestly came across as arrogant. I was summing him up in my mind, not sure what to think. I noticed when he spoke, he sometimes referred to himself in the third person. He looked around and said with a smile, "Caleb might have a hard time driving on the opposite side of the road. In Africa, Caleb drives on the left side," which I found amusing. I thought, *This guy really is straight out of the bush.*

The two guests loaded all the luggage up into the car. I got behind the wheel and my mother slid into the passenger's seat. As Caleb and his father got into the back seat,

Caleb immediately said, in his thick African accent, "In Africa, women do not drive."

So I rammed the car in drive and purposely pressed down hard on the gas to take off quicker than I usually would and said, "Well, welcome to the United States," in a very spicy tone.

My mom, who was riding beside me, pretended, like a good Southern woman, that she did not hear my saucy comment, and she started asking the two new house guests about their trip. I casually made eye contact with Caleb in the rear view mirror as he smirked at me as I zipped up the W Road—a road up the mountain many were afraid to drive because of its sharp switchback curves. Because of his comment, I made sure to drive extra fast around the switch-backs to prove I was confident in my skills.

I would say that was a good description of our relation-ship from day one. He was arrogant, and I was sassy. There was no sugar coating it on either side.

Caleb enrolled in college, and his father went back to Tanzania. I was busy with my high school social life and time went by. As the year went on, we became friends. I began to see his kindness to me beneath the hard exterior. He became part of our family, and we would sit down every night to dinner at 6:00 p.m. Whoever was in our house was expected to be at the dinner table whether they lived in the house or were visiting. During dinner, I saw that Caleb was not as arrogant as I thought; he was alone in this new coun-try, and I started to soften to him. My parents also began to love Caleb, which made it easy for me to see his heart. He knew we accepted him as part of our own family, and he loved us, so he started to open up to us about his lifestyle growing up in Tanzania and attending boarding school in Kenya. Around the dinner table, he began to tell us of his hunting adventures and of demonic spirits and witchcraft in Tanzania. We would question him and begin to hear of a world we could not understand.

That fall, Caleb bought a used, light blue Pontiac Sunbird to drive himself to school, and to work at our church. One afternoon we were in the kitchen discussing his new car, and he asked if I knew how to drive stick shift. I said, "No, I have never learned."

He told me, "Everyone should know how to drive a stick shift. In Africa that is what almost all the cars are. What if you are in an emergency situation where that was the only car available to drive?" Then he asked me if I wanted him to teach me.

I am very independent and what he said made a lot of sense to me—and challenged me. I rarely turned down a challenge. So, I said with a big smile, "Of course I do."

We loaded up in his car. As Caleb tried to teach me on the mountain backroads, we laughed so hard we had tears in our eyes. He teased me as the car jerked and the engine died under my beginner's hand and foot. Something happened when he was teaching me to drive that car. As his hand was on top of my hand teaching me the gears, my heart began to see him in a new way. Caleb was gentle with me, and caring—he wanted me to succeed. From that day on, our relationship began to grow beyond the realm of friendship, and we started to occasionally flirt with each other playfully.

That spring, near the end of the school year, he asked me to go to the movie *Dirty Dancing* with him. In the darkness of the theater, he held my hand. I remember thinking, *What–is–happening?* I knew I liked him and the feelings between us had been building for months. Then one night, in April, he kissed me. Caleb had a bad-boy image; although he was a Christian, he had an edge to him. He had a cool and confident exterior. And I was a good girl who was very attracted to his bad-boy edge. He was always good with me. He never drank or cursed or was inappropriate with me in any way. He treated me like a lady and respected me, and I liked it. I remember going to bed wondering, *Will he ever do that again?* I did not tell my parents because I knew they would not approve with him living in our home.

Caleb left to go back to Tanzania for the summer soon after our kiss. His parents and sisters were coming as a family for furlough the next school year, and he would live with them. So I was not sure what was going to happen. Caleb started sending me letters from Africa after he left, and I wrote letters back. My mother quickly caught on that something had changed in our relationship, and needless to say, my parents were not pleased. However, they liked Caleb.

So, my parents set some guidelines to dating when Caleb got back from Africa. However, I was not sure if we even wanted to date; neither of us knew what we wanted. I think both of us were surprised we ended up liking each other. I was way too sassy, and he was way too arrogant, and both of us were extremely strong-willed. And yet, here we were, wondering how this would turn out.

CHAPTER 3
FLAMES

Trust in the Lord with all your heart, and lean not on your own understanding; in all your ways acknowledge Him, and He shall direct your paths.

—Proverbs 3:5–6

During that summer, while Caleb was back in Tanzania, we both dated other people. I figured when he came back with his parents, we would see where our hearts were. After all, we had not discussed anything before he left, just that we would see each other when he came back. His first night back, his whole family came up to my house to visit my family. He told us all about his adventures over the summer in Tanzania and Kenya.

It was awkward being around him for the first time in three months, especially with both of our families being there. I was wondering, *What is he thinking after being away for so long?* I was sitting on the kitchen counter to the side, and he was in the center—at the table with his family. He caught my eye in the crowd of people and quickly raised his eyebrows and smiled at me, letting me know he was thinking about me. It was an affectionate little thing he would do that made me feel special. When I looked at him, I was smitten, and he looked at me the same way back. There was lots of chemistry between us that had built up over the last few months he had lived in our house. In our letters we had gushed about how we missed each other. In fact, he had poured his soul out in his letters, confessing he was falling in love with me and telling me all about his hunting adventures.

Realistically, I did not know what was going to happen with us being apart for so long, and now we would not be living in the same house. I wondered, *Will our relationship just fade away?* If we had never lived in the same house, I don't think we would have ever been interested in dating.

Later that night once the sun had gone down, his parents left to go back to where they were staying. Caleb stayed at my house and asked me if I would like to go on a walk. My heart jumped. As we walked toward our family barn in the hot August summer night heat, I got so nervous, my teeth started chattering. He asked me, "Are you cold?"

I said, "I guess so," but it was all nerves. He took me in his arms and started trying to warm me up. Then he gently kissed me. It rocked my entire world. It was as if we were having our first kiss all over again. He held me in the moonlight of the summer night and poured out his guarded heart. He told me he had all summer to think about us. He did not want to rush our relationship, but wanted to think through everything clearly. He had realized in Africa that summer—he had fallen in love with me. Typically, he was mysterious, and here he was being completely transparent with me, which made me feel amazing. He confessed he had dated another girl while he was in Kenya, and I told him I had also dated two boys over the summer. I was pleasantly surprised at his honesty. I did not tell him I was in love with him at that time. I was not sure what I was feeling at that moment, but I knew I was very attracted to him. We kissed again, he told me that he was in love with me, and he asked if we could date. I laughed about how we were complete opposites and who would have ever thought we would be so attracted to each other. Then I smiled, "Yes, I would love to date you." We kissed again, and declared how much we missed each other beneath the Southern stars.

Caleb came to visit me again the next day and we sat down with my parents and told them we wanted to start dating. My parents agreed that would be okay, but they set up some rules. We were allowed to go on a date once a weekend, the other night I would go out with my friends, and then Caleb could come visit me at my house throughout the week. That seemed to work well for us. All of my siblings were married and not living at home anymore. My parents and my grandparents, who lived next door, loved Caleb as if he were one of their own. They spent time with us while we dated, and he was always coming up to visit me at our house for dinner and to spend time with my family.

While dating, we had Bible studies together, during which we discussed our Christian faith and our hopes for our future. I was strong in my faith with the Lord and in my convictions to not drink or be promiscuous before marriage and because of that, Caleb was strongly drawn to me; he was challenged because of my strength. We both wanted to live Christian lives and to raise our children in the church. Caleb knew his Bible from going to a Christian boarding school in Africa much better than I did. In fact, he knew the lineage of the heroes in the Old Testament and all the stories and names from Genesis to Revelation. Sometimes we played Bible trivia, and Caleb rarely got a question wrong. I was amazed at his knowledge and wanted to know my Bible the way he did. He even knew the books of the Bible in order. I still don't know the books of the Bible in order. I was drawn to him.

He was aloof to other people, but privately he shared his thoughts with me, and his dreams. As we fell in love, he would pour his heart out to me and declare his love for me, often sending me love letters, thoughtful little gifts, or flowers as I fell completely head over heels in love with him, and he also fell more in love with me. Caleb was protective over me while we dated, and I liked it. He worked hard on the morning shift at UPS, and made good money while going to college. He paid for all of our dates and meals, and he usually opened the door for me and treated me like a lady. I felt safe with him; Caleb was manly and quietly strong.

I was never attracted to boys who were not strong. My mother and my father were both alphas, and my grandmother and my grandfather were alphas too. In fact, all of my siblings and all of my cousins were alphas; all fifteen of us. That is the only type of boy I would ever be attracted to. I liked that Caleb let me be strong, but he was quietly just as strong and would tell me if he did not agree with me. We loved being together, but because of our independence, we actually didn't need each other. Ironically, this magnified our attraction.

As we dated, he began to tell me and my parents more stories of witchcraft in Africa, and how he stayed away from all that. There were dark spirits he spoke of that had the power of evil. The witch doctors could place voodoo spells on people and people would die or have horrible things happen to them. I could tell it was not a joke; when he spoke, it was very real. And I wondered about all these things I did not understand. Once, he told me a story of when he was a child in Tanzania, riding with his sisters in the back of his parents' truck one afternoon. They passed an African man riding a bicycle who suddenly burst into flames as Caleb watched. Then the man and the bicycle disappeared. Caleb and his sisters discussed what had happened afterward and all agreed on what they had seen. I knew he was telling me the truth, but I would just laugh because I didn't know what else to do with it. However, I wondered about all the stories.

There were many times Caleb told me several different stories about a large black panther that followed him growing up, from the time he was twelve years old until he was in high school. While he was hunting in the hunting grounds, he would see this panther stalking him for years and years. The odd thing is, there are no large black cats in Tanzania, only lions, leopards, and cheetahs.

We talked about it, and he believed it was some type of dark spirit. I would listen, but I had never experienced anything like what he was describing. I think he thought I didn't believe him, but actually it made me unsettled. So, I would laugh nervously and say: "Caleb, are you sure?"

He also told me a sad story about an African man who was a poacher that he shot and killed when he was in high school while he was working with the government rangers patrolling for poachers in the hunting grounds. Everything had happened quickly, and he lived with remorse. I was sorry to hear that story. I could tell it bothered him deeply, and he wanted to confess it to me. As we continued to date, Caleb began to share more experiences from growing up in East Africa. He had to leave his family and his home in Tanzania and go to boarding school in Kenya, another country away, at the young age of twelve. That made him have what I would describe as a hard outer shell. Almost like walls of defense he had around his heart. His attitude was that it was him against the world. He would hold grudges against people and say he would get them back one day. I would laugh and tell him, "Oh Caleb, that's silly. You need to let it go."

We were growing up together, and we were best friends.

We were completely in love, and we had no secrets—or so I thought.

CHAPTER 4
AFRICA

Place me like a seal over your heart,
like a seal on your arm;
for love is as strong as death,
its jealousy unyielding as the grave.
It burns like a blazing fire,
like a mighty flame.
—Song of Solomon 8:6

Five months into dating, Caleb broke up with me. He started seeing a girl from the community college he went to. Caleb was totally into her, and I was completely devastated. My parents told me I needed to stop acting so heartbroken, that I was too young to act like that. My pain was very real then, and it is still real. Heartbreak is a heart break, no matter what age you are. So I poured my heart out to my older brother. He told me the way he got over his ex-girlfriend was to fall in love with someone else. His advice was to start dating and have fun. He said I was young and pretty and that was how I could get over my broken heart.

What he said made sense to me, so I decided I needed to start having fun. It was before Christmas, so I lined up some outings and started to enjoy going out to some Christmas parties. I went on a few dates with one of my boy cousin's friends. As soon as word got out I was going out on some dates, Caleb got jealous and came to visit me and told me he wanted to take me out on a date. We went out on that date, and he broke things off with the other girl. I was happy to be dating Caleb again. We were broken up for less than two months.

As we continued to date, Caleb's family invited me to Tanzania for the summer after graduating my senior year of high school. They wanted me to see the country where Caleb had grown up to gain a better understanding of him. Denise's mother, Mrs. Marie Helen Boehm, told my parents she thought it was a good idea. She was from Switzerland and knew how vastly different other cultures could be. Much to my surprise, my parents thought we were getting serious, and they decided it would be a good idea for me to see if I could live in Africa. So, this became the plan: I would fly to East Africa with Caleb and stay with his family for five weeks, then fly by myself to Paris to meet Holland, Denise, and Denise's mother for a month-long tour of Europe. Mrs. Boehm spoke several languages and would be our chaperone. This would mark my first time to travel out of the United States. I was excited and ready for a new adventure.

That June of 1990, I flew with Caleb to Nairobi, Kenya, where Caleb's father, Jason, picked us up at the airport, and then we headed to Tanzania in their Land Cruiser. It was over a twelve-hour drive to his parents' house outside of Shinyanga, Tanzania. Half tarmac and half dirt roads made for a bumpy ride to his parents' home, so there was not much sleeping possible. It was late at night, and I was in the middle of the front bench seat, next to Caleb.

We came upon an African man riding a bike down the dirt road. I braced myself as we got closer, wondering if he was going to move so we could drive by, or if we were actually going to hit him. Then I blinked and he was gone. I was surprised to have seen this with my own eyes. I never knew what to think about Caleb seeing the man on the bicycle go up in flames. However, after seeing this myself, I was perplexed. I later told Caleb what had happened. He wasn't surprised and did not doubt me for a second. "I told you about the spirits in Africa," he said knowingly. "You'll see."

Caleb was very kind and protective of me on my first trip to his home country. His parents had moved to a hospital base outside of Zanzui, many hours away from the childhood home Caleb had grown up in on the shores of Lake Victoria, near Mwanza in a small village called Mabulugu. At his new home, red dirt roads ran through the small hospital compound that included a school for the local children, and also a soccer field perpetually being played on by the kids and the adults. This was Caleb's first time seeing his parents' new home, which was a small concrete house with three bedrooms and two baths that was neat and tidy. His mother had a way of making things nice and comfortable even though it was basic with concrete floors. It was decorated warmly and was spotless.

When I arrived, I was delighted. Sharing a bedroom and bathroom with Caleb's sister, who was there for the summer also, I was thrilled we had flushing toilets, even if we had to fill the back of the tank up with a garden hose before flushing it. I was especially thankful we did not have to bring water in from somewhere else. There was no hot water out of the faucets in the house, so we had to heat up a five-gallon bucket of water with a heating coil to bathe. It took about forty-five minutes, and if you heated it boiling hot, then you could add water from the bathtub faucet, which was cold, and have a little more warm water for your bath. After driving on dusty, dirt roads during the day, everyone needed a bath every night.

Most nights, Caleb would heat the water for my bath— two five-gallon buckets, one at a time—so I'd have a nice amount for bathing. While the water warmed, he would make us hot chocolate we would drink in the living room with his family. Then he would pour the water into the bathtub for me, and I would go bathe.

When I say he was kind, he was gentle and loving to me, and he treated me like a princess.

Caleb spoke Swahili just like a national from his country. If I closed my eyes, I could not tell the accent he had apart from a Tanzanian speaking. Everywhere we went, strangers were astounded and would ask, "How do you speak Swahili better than we do?"

"Please, I am just as African as you are," he would say. They thought that was really funny and treated him like a celebrity. And now I understood his arrogant attitude. If I had grown up like a celebrity, I'd probably have an inflated sense of self too. There were very few white people where he grew up, and even fewer who grew up in the culture and understood it completely the way Caleb did.

I realized he was a Tanzanian in spirit.

While in Tanzania that summer, we drove all over in Caleb's parents' Land Cruiser. He also took me on his Honda dirt bike on the dusty roads pocked with potholes. He would fly down the roads zigzagging, dust dancing up behind us, to avoid the deep ruts.

When inside Caleb's house, I could wear my shorts. But outside the house and in public, I had to wear either one of the long dresses my mom had made me, or a kanga. The traditional apparel of East African women, kangas are long thin garments decorated with bright colors and bold prints. Caleb drove me on his dirt bike into town to shop for my kangas, my wild blond hair flying all over while holding on behind him. The African children wanted to touch my hair everywhere we went, and I got a taste of what it felt like for him growing up, being different from everyone around.

We went hunting in the hunting grounds of the Maswa Game Reserve, where he grew up hunting. Caleb always wanted me to try a hippo burger, which was one of his favorites. So he took me hippo hunting where he grew up on the beautiful Lake Victoria, in a canoe made out of a hollowed-out tree trunk that, to my despair, leaked. There were five of us in that hollowed-out tree trunk. Caleb's three Tanzanian friends paddled us out for about thirty minutes until we came upon a slough. The men paddled us quietly up the slough, lush with thick greenery on each side, and not a person in sight. Caleb explained we were looking for little bubbles popping up from the bottom. Hippos run on the bottom of the river, so Caleb would shoot the animal when it came up for air. When we finally found one, Caleb's friends paddled slowly after the bubbles while Caleb stood in the boat with his .375 rifle ready to shoot. Both Caleb and his friends wanted the meat, and not an ounce of meat was ever wasted from our hunts. I prayed the hippo wouldn't come up for air, and that I would be able to get out of that boat alive. Hippos were known to kick boats upside down in the water and break the boats in half. In fact the year before, a missionary kid we had heard about had died this way. I thought I might not make it out alive and prayed silently, *Oh Lord, if you get me out of this, I will never be so stupid to get in a leaky tree trunk and go hippo hunting again.* We did not kill a hippo that day. Later, Caleb said it was because he knew I prayed we would not be successful. Smiling, I quietly agreed. Needless to say, I learned my lesson and never got in a small canoe to go hunting again.

But I loved the experience—once it was over.

Then we went a short distance down the road and visited the primary boarding school his parents ran all of his life and had just recently moved several hours away from. He showed me the lifestyle and the freedom of his childhood that he loved. He had the same kind of freedom to roam the way I did as a child, and I understood his love for his home.

Our adventures lasted five weeks. Many of them were with Caleb's family. We rode in their bright blue Land Cruiser packed down with our supplies on the roof rack. We camped as we went to the Ngorongoro Crater and the Serengeti, along with several other national parks where we saw all the amazing animals, including the Big Five: lions, leopards, rhinos, buffalos, and elephants. We saw the Serengeti grasslands burning, and the great migration of wildebeest and zebra, which was like a dream. The scenery of East Africa blew me away—the plains, lakes, and high mountains. Seeing all Caleb had to share with me, my eyes and my heart were full of beauty.

One night while camping in the Serengeti with Caleb's family, a leopard came right up to our campsite and climbed the tree above our tent. It was so loud it sounded like a chainsaw. I stopped breathing for as long as I could, with wild thoughts racing through my mind. I prayed long and hard as my heart raced. My body felt so heavy with fear; I couldn't move a muscle. Luckily, the leopard lost interest and left after what had seemed like an eternity. It took me a while to fall back to sleep that night. Many nights, as we slept in our tent, we heard the deep throaty growls of lions in the distance, or the haunting laughs of hyenas close by in the dark. Hearing the lions sent a chill down my spine, and the hyenas just creeped me out. I was especially thankful we were all packed in the tent together on those nights, and I was glad I was not sleeping on one of the sides of the tent, in case an animal came to attack us.

At the end of my trip, we headed to Kenya so I could fly to Europe. Once we arrived in Nairobi, Kenya, we found ourselves in a riot over an election and drove down the streets that were filled with burning cars turned upside down, buildings with storefront glass broken out, and people vandalizing the stores. We fled out of Nairobi, in the dusty packed-down Land Cruiser to Caleb's old boarding school up in the Rift Valley outside of town to stay the night for safety.

Caleb loved and yet resented Rift Valley Academy because they had kicked him out right before graduation, and did not let him walk for his graduation diploma. He had not done much to get kicked out. I can't remember the details, but it seemed over-the-top as a punishment. I heard the resentment in his voice when he spoke about it, but he also loved the school and told me stories of the wonderful memories and people from there. He always vowed he would get them back for kicking him out one day. I could sense the inner war inside him between love and hate for his alma mater. I would say, "You need to let it go."

For our struggle is not against flesh and blood, but against the rulers, against the authorities, against the powers of this dark world and against the spiritual forces of evil in the heavenly realms.

—Ephesians 6:12

I brought the book *This Present Darkness* by Frank Peretti to Africa with me, and I finished the book during the five weeks I was there. The book is about the demonic force of evil in the heavenly realm, which we have to deal with on this earth: demons and angels. It is biblical that there is a full spiritual world we do not see; Ephesians 6 tells us about it. I would talk to Caleb about the book, and he would agree with what the Bible said of demons and angels. He would tell me there was a whole spiritual world I was too naïve to see because I grew up in the United States. As I read the book, I knew he was right. To be honest, I did not want to know too much about that world because it gave me the heebie-jeebies.

All in all, my trip to Tanzania and Kenya was an exhilarating adventure. Caleb showed me his heart through the land and life he loved, and I fell even more in love with him. He took good care of me in Africa, and I saw how he was protective of me, and could lead me well. He was a confident, strong person, who could sit back and let others talk and be comfortable doing that. He could be mysterious—sometimes I wondered what he was thinking. But ultimately, he was open with me, and once we were alone together, he shared his heart freely with me. He was quiet until you knew him, and then he talked as much as me. He treated me with respect and love, and I treated him the same way back.

After spending five weeks in Africa, I was finally leaving Kenya to fly to Paris, France, to meet my friends Denise and Holland. As I got ready to leave Nairobi, Kenya, Caleb drove me to the airport, and we started to say goodbye. As we embraced, Caleb started crying. It was the first time I had seen him cry, and it touched me deeply. Then he told me he loved me and he wanted to marry me. I told him I loved him too, and I thanked him for sharing his beautiful Africa with me. It was lovely.

Shortly after, I left Africa.

CHAPTER 5
HAVING TO CHOOSE

*There are three things that are too amazing for me, four that
I do not understand: the way of an eagle in the sky, the way
of a snake on a rock, the way of a ship on the high seas, and
the way of a man with a young woman.*

—Proverbs 30:18–19

After that summer, I started my freshman year of college
as a student at University of Tennessee, in Knoxville, a
couple of hours away from home. Caleb returned to school
in Chattanooga, and I realized we were getting serious. I
was involved in Young Life, and I wanted to be able to date
and see what dating other people was like because I was
not convinced he was the one for me. I didn't want to hurt
Caleb the way I was hurt when he had broken up with me
for another girl, but I told him I did not want to date one
person. I wanted to be able to date casually. He tried to
talk me out of it, but I was determined to spread my wings a
little and experience life.

I started spending more time with my Young Life college group. In the group there was a boy named Tim Finnegan. He was very different from Caleb. Tim was very handsome and athletic in an all-American boy way. He was outgoing, a straight-A student, a strong leader, and a people person. He was entertaining, full of energy, and I was drawn straight to him. We mostly spent time with a big group, and then we started spending some time alone together. Tim was from Knoxville, and he took me on many adventures around the area, like hiking to the Chimney Tops in the Smokies in the middle of the night to watch the sunrise, and caving at night in the-middle-of-nowhere East Tennessee. We visited the Lost Sea, which is an underground lake, and we went horseback riding at my daddy's farm, in the nearby town of Sweetwater. We had so much fun together, and I never knew what our next adventure would be. That said, I was honest with Tim about Caleb, and honest with Caleb about Tim.

One night, at the beginning of our relationship, Tim and I were sitting on a bench on campus, away from any students in a little bit of a dark area where some class buildings were. My cousin Tony, who also went to school at University of Tennessee, drove by. We did not see each other all the time, but we were friends, and I did ride home with him on the weekends that he and I were both going home to Signal Mountain. He lived on the family property next door, and he knew Caleb well. He passed us in the dark, then he put his car in reverse and slowly backed up and stopped. He rolled his window down, and I smiled.

He said, "Anne G., what are you doing out here?"

I said, "Hi, Tony, we're just talking."

He replied, "It's dark." I sat there.

"Why are you over here where no one is around?" Tony asked.

I laughed, "We are just talking. This is Tim. Tim, this is my cousin, Tony."

Tony said, "Hey."

Tim said, "Hey, it is nice to meet you."

Then Tony looked at me and said, "Do you need a ride back to your dorm?"

"No," I replied, "but thank you." Tony sat there for a few awkward seconds not saying anything.

"Where's Caleb?" Tony asked.

I said with a defiant tone, "I guess in Chattanooga."

"Oh," Tony said. He knew I was fiery and was not going to be thrown off my game. Again, he sat there in the dark. So, I waited.

Then he casually said, "Okay, be careful."

"Okay, I will, thanks." I said.

Tony drove off, and I apologized to Tim. "My cousin's a year older than me and is just watching out for me," I said. I actually liked that Tony was keeping an eye out for me; we were pretty tight.

Understanding, Tim said, "Your older cousin *should* be watching out for you, especially sitting with some boy he did not recognize on campus." I was so attracted to Tim; his laid back attitude and confidence made me more attracted to him. He was strong and independent, and I liked it. I ended up falling completely in love with Tim. In fact, when I was with Tim, I never even thought about Caleb.

Caleb gave me space for a little while, and I got more serious with Tim. Then I stopped seeing Caleb completely, and he started sending me roses and proclaiming his love for me through letters. Several times he surprised me and drove up to the University to take me to dinner or to just see me, and those same nights, drove back to Chattanooga two hours away.

I knew I had broken Caleb's heart. That was the last thing I wanted; I remembered how it felt when he broke up with me. I got very confused.

Around that time, Caleb told me he promised God if he could marry me, he would live his life honoring God and would be the spiritual leader of our family. He was telling me all the things I wanted in my future. I did not know what to do. After several months of dating Tim, I went home for a visit. As I sat on the kitchen counter, I remember my mom and daddy sitting at the kitchen table telling me it was not fair for me to date two people. I needed to decide. I started crying because I honestly did not know what to do. I had broken up with Caleb, but he refused to take no for an answer and continued to pursue me. It was as if my heart was both Tim's and Caleb's. Through my tears, I asked my parents to decide for me. They said they could not make that decision for me. I was in agony. Once I was in love with two people, it was torture. My parents and my grandparents loved Caleb. He would visit them while I was away at school and tell them how much he loved me and that he prayed we would get back together. Although they loved him, they did not want to influence my decision. They would all tell me I had to decide, but they felt sorry for Caleb because his family was a world away, so he treated my family like it was his.

That spring, my parents came to visit me in Knoxville at college, and Tim joined us for the afternoon. When he walked away, my mother commented that she knew I would end up marrying Tim—She said she could see in my eyes that I was in love with him. I could see in her eyes it was hard for her, although she would not admit it. It made me wonder if I was making a bad decision because at that point I felt confident Tim was the one for me. I started to doubt my decision. Summer came, and I went home to Signal Mountain.

That summer, Caleb and I spent the long hot days together while I was home on Signal Mountain. He ended up talking me into transferring to the University of Tennessee in Chattanooga for the upcoming school year. He had already transferred there a few years before. He told me we needed to see what it was like going to school together.

So for my sophomore year, I attended college in Chattanooga and started being a Young Life leader. I still was very much in love with two people. Although now that Caleb and I were spending time together every day, Tim began to fade from my heart and mind.

In December, Caleb was going to go back to Africa because he was graduating from college, and he was going home to visit his parents. We had a very serious talk on the outdoor swing at my house about our future together and if there was going to be one. I told him, "I do not want to live in Africa. So you need to go to Tanzania and decide if you want to stay and make it your home, or come back to the United States." His dream was to be a professional hunter. I understood that was his dream, so I encouraged him to go. But I was very clear I would not be joining him if he decided on living in Africa. I was not interested in being a professional hunter's wife or living in Africa at all. That was not what I wanted in life, and he needed to figure out what he wanted, and then we would decide if we had a future or not. I was not emotional and told Caleb, "The only way I would go to Africa is if God called me, like on the phone and said, 'Anne G., go to Africa.' Besides God calling me, there is no way I will live there."

However, I was still not convinced Caleb and I were right for each other. I had prayed since I was a little girl for my husband, and I was still in love with two men. I did not know what to do. So I waited and continued to pray.

Caleb left for Africa for four months. I went on a Young Life ski trip to Breckenridge, Colorado, as a leader the week between Christmas and New Years, and I shattered my tibia and fibula in my right leg. I had been challenged on a dare from another leader to ski the Horseshoe Bowl, a double black diamond bowl, at the top of the mountain. My adventurous spirit had finally caught up with me. During the next six months, I went through two painful bone surgeries, but my leg was not healing. Desperate, my daddy took me to see a specialist at Campbell Clinic in Memphis. After my exam, the doctor broke the news, "Your X-rays look more like a broken leg from a motorcycle accident. There's a lot of trauma, and that's why it's not healing."

This resulted in months of me being in a wheelchair with an elevated leg, and my sweet mom waiting on me at home and driving me back and forth to my college classes. As I was recovering from a broken leg, Tim was busy in school in Knoxville and called me, but it was expensive because of the long distance, and not as often as a relationship needed to thrive. The truth was, he was not pursuing me the way Caleb was. Caleb sent me flowers after my surgery all the way from Africa; he was always wooing me. Tim was exciting, I loved him and I know he loved me, although we never said it to each other. Caleb, who wrote me letters almost every day and who called from Africa once a week to check in, made sure he was the perfect boyfriend. I got lots of attention from Caleb and once again my love for him grew.

Embarrassing as it is to admit, instead of addressing my relationship and being truthful with Tim about my heart—I simply disappeared. I ran from my feelings and ran from my problem of not being able to make a decision.

In April, after four months of being in Africa, Caleb came home from Tanzania, and we had a serious talk. He told me he had decided Africa was not for him. He loved growing up there, but it was too hard to go back and try to start a life and a career. He told me he loved me and wanted to marry me and live in the United States, and that we could travel to Tanzania and Kenya often so our children would know his home country. I was in complete agreement about traveling over there often. Traveling was one of my new favorite interests. It made me happy he decided to live in the United States and wanted to marry me.

Caleb proposed to me on the brow of Signal Mountain in June of 1992. It was night; the city lights in the Chattanooga valley below twinkled like gold stars. I said yes, wearing a full-length cast on my right leg up to my hip. I was on crutches, with no weight bearing on my leg—it was still not healing from my snow-skiing accident. I said yes, and for the first time in months, I did not notice my cast and crutches as we kissed.

Tim came to town and surprised me the week after I got engaged. He arrived at our house around midnight and brought a friend because they were traveling through Chattanooga on the way somewhere else. I spoke to them for a short time when they arrived, but it was late and my parents were already in bed, so we said good night.

The next morning, the boys came downstairs. I was in the kitchen with my mom, my broken leg propped up on a chair. Mom made breakfast, and the boys came to the table. We started eating and talking and after a little while my mom said, "Did you two hear Anne G.'s good news?" I froze.

I had not told Tim the night before because his friend was with him. I did not know what to do, so nervously I put out my hand and showed him my engagement ring.

It was undeniably one of the worst moments of my life. My heart was breaking for myself and for hurting him. At that moment, I honestly did not know if I was making the right decision or not. If Tim was not around, I was very happy with Caleb. If Caleb was not around, I was very happy with Tim. But Tim was never around. Tim was stunned. I was humiliated.

The rest of breakfast was uncomfortable, with my mom and Tim's friend carrying the conversation. I don't think I said another word. After breakfast Tim asked me if we could talk. He walked, I crutched on crutches, to the back of the house. He looked at me and said, "Is this what you want?" All I could do was nod my head yes.

My nod was not as convincing to myself as it was to Tim. He said tenderly, "Okay, I just want you to be happy." Then he left, and I went to bed crying. I knew I loved him, but I loved Caleb also. I thought Caleb would be the more attentive husband. I wanted an attentive, loving, best friend. They both were my best friends, they both loved the Lord, both wanted Christian families, and my daddy told me it was not fair for them or me to continue to not decide. I had to end it with one of them. So, I did. Well, actually, I didn't.

Immobile as I was on crutches, I had run from that decision.

But it got resolved. For better or for worse.

CHAPTER 6
CAUGHT

Wives, submit yourselves to your own husbands as you do to the Lord. For the husband is the head of the wife as Christ is the head of the church, His body, of which He is the Savior. Now as the church submits to Christ, so also wives should submit to their husbands in everything.
Husbands, love your wives, just as Christ loved the church and gave Himself up for her to make her holy, cleansing her by the washing with water through the word, and to present her to Himself as a radiant church, without stain or wrinkle or any other blemish, but holy and blameless. In this same way, husbands ought to love their wives as their own bodies. He who loves his wife loves himself.
—Ephesians 5:22–28

I was excited about marrying Caleb. We loved being together. He fit into my family well, and we spent lots of time with my parents and my siblings and their children.

He loved my nieces and nephews as much as I did, and he was playful so I thought he would be a good father.

Caleb was strong and confident, and he knew what he wanted. When he made his mind up he did not give up until he accomplished what he set out to do. I admire that about him. I was in his aim, and he got what he wanted. He pursued me the way any woman wants to be pursued: with passion and persistence. I was his top priority. We planned a wedding for November; it was June.

I prayed my leg would heal. It had already been six months since my skiing accident. Caleb assured me, "I don't care if I have to carry you down the aisle, we are getting married."

He made me feel loved.

Caleb and I did not sleep together before we married and we had dated for five years, so we were both excited about what marriage had to offer us. We married in November 1992, at First Presbyterian Church in Chattanooga. Caleb planned an amazing seven day honeymoon to Saint Thomas, Virgin Islands. It was fantastic, although my leg had still not completely healed eleven months after my accident. I had been determined to walk without crutches for my wedding day. So even though I wobbled down the aisle—it was a major answer to prayer. When I told my doctor the plans for mine and Caleb's honeymoon, he'd shown mercy on me by putting me in a removable prosthetic cast that they molded to my leg. I was able to take my first long hot bath in almost a year, which is one of my favorite things in the world to do, so I was thrilled. Because of my new waterproof cast, I got to go snorkeling with Caleb in the crystal blue waters of the Virgin Islands. After being bound in a cast for almost a year, it was exhilarating to be free from it. Not to mention the removable cast only went up to my knee. It felt like my life was starting fresh. I was very naïve when I married Caleb. We celebrated our new life as one, and we were very happy. So I would have never guessed what was about to happen.

After the honeymoon, we came back to Chattanooga and lived in a one-bedroom apartment off the mountain, close to town. I loved my life. I was still in college and Caleb had graduated and started a new job as a security person who watched for shoplifters on camera at a department store at the mall. During this time, Caleb applied for a job at the police department and some other places where he could put his criminal justice degree to use.

One day in December, less than a month after our wedding, Caleb received a large envelope in the mail from a hunting company in Africa. I asked him what it was. He opened the envelope and read the letter. Then he told me he had applied to be a professional hunter in Tanzania, and they were writing to tell him they had no positions available. The blood drained from my face as I stood there stunned at what he revealed to me. I asked why he would do that. We had talked before we married, I had made it very clear I did not want to go live in Africa, and he needed to decide if he wanted to live in Africa before we married. He told me not to worry about it, he did not get the job. I was furious, and I felt he had tricked me. We had a major fight. I fled to the bedroom in the back of the apartment and got into the bed crying because I was furious and hurt. I wondered, *What have I gotten myself into?* Caleb was all of a sudden acting indifferent to me less than thirty days after the wedding, and after dating for so many years. He was not apologizing about applying to be a professional hunter in Africa. He was stern in his response, and he was not remorseful for not being honest with me. I promise you, if we'd been dating, this would've been the end of our relationship. But we were married now, and neither of us was giving in. I could not believe he was the same boy I had dated for five years.

Two weeks later, Caleb received another envelope from another professional hunting company from Tanzania. Again I was shocked and asked, "Why did you lie to me again?" We had another explosive fight. I stayed mad for several days before confronting him in our apartment: "Why did you marry me, knowing you intended to go back to Africa after I made it very clear I did not want to go live in Africa, and that you needed to decide if you wanted to live in Africa *before* we got married?"

And finally he said the words I'll never forget: "I've caught you now. We're married. There's nothing you can do about it."

CHAPTER 7
DENIAL

May your fountain be blessed, and may you rejoice in the wife of your youth.

—*Proverbs 5:18*

Caleb's domineering declaration overwhelmed me and made me feel desperately out of control. Especially since he was right, there was nothing I could do. It was true, I'd finally given myself to him completely—my trust, my body, my future. And now I was seeing a side of him I'd never seen before in all the years we dated. I was crushed. I was also prideful and loyal to a fault. Not wanting my parents to know what was happening, ashamed, embarrassed and feeling like a fool, I didn't tell a soul. Instead, since Caleb didn't get the jobs, I decided to act like our disputes never happened. *His job applications and our fights had just been a bump in the road,* I told myself. I graduated college and began teaching school. But in the quietness of my heart, I prayed he would not get a job and move us to Africa. Or worse, my biggest fear was for him to leave me in the United States for months while he went on hunts overseas without me.

So Caleb and I moved forward with our life as husband and wife. Once our battle was over, we ended up settling into our first year of marriage beautifully. He immediately went back to being the boy I fell in love with. If there was a birthday for a family member, he was there. Any holiday, he was there. Every Sunday for church and lunch afterward, he never missed. Our little apartment and each other were all we needed. We were like two kids in a candy store without adult supervision, playing our music loudly while we practiced cooking together and doing the household chores around the apartment. We had very little money, but we felt rich, like we had the world on a string. Married life was a new adventure, and we were both thrilled about all of it. Again I felt his love and adoration for me. I loved my husband, and our marriage was a success.

After a year of being married, Caleb got the job with the Chattanooga Police, and we moved up on the mountain into a small guest house behind my parents' home.

The next year, in January, we bought our first house on Signal Mountain—an adorable three-bedroom, two-and-a-half-bath home in a cute neighborhood five minutes from my family's compound. We were both proud of our hard work that allowed us to purchase our home, and it seemed that all our dreams were coming true.

However, two and a half years into our marriage, I had noticed Caleb was growing hard toward me occasionally. I didn't know why—we had a great friendship, and we didn't argue much. We had a sweet romance; he gave me compliments and told me I was pretty. We spent all of our time off work together, I loved being married and having someone to come home to, and Caleb acted as if he loved being married too. But I began to notice he seemed to have two sides. He started to not be as loving and gentle. I was not sure why I was sensing these invisible walls between us.

One day, Caleb came home from work holding a cup from a fast food restaurant. Earlier, when I had spoken to him on the phone, he told me he had eaten lunch at a different fast food chain than what was advertised on his cup. So now I asked, "Why did you tell me you went to McDonald's when you're holding a cup from another restaurant?"

Blowing me off, he said, "Why does it matter? What's the difference?"

"Because," I said boldly, "it's not the truth."

Slowly over time the lying got worse, and I would always confront him, which would start a fight. Then I began to notice he started lying to other people in front of me. I would never confront him in front of other people because I did not want to disrespect him in public, but we would get into the car and I would say, "That was a lie, that was not true."

I remember thinking, *I cannot trust anything he tells me.* How in the world could I have dated him for so long and not know him at all? My mother and father were honest, how did this happen to me? And what happened to the boy who'd fallen in love with me and who'd pursued me with his all?

Caleb and I both knew that his new persona was out of my control.

Around this time, in June 1995, he and I traveled to

Africa together. I was excited because I love traveling, and Caleb had been so kind to me during my first trip to Tanzania before we were married, so I was looking forward to being together. This trip went very differently.

We stayed with his parents and had plans to go hunting and camping. A cute, young European couple lived and worked at the hospital where Caleb's parents lived. Caleb's father had told them we were coming and that they were welcome to join us camping in the parks, including the Serengeti and the Ngorongoro Crater.

Before we left the U.S., I told Caleb I really wanted to stay at one of the beautiful lodges in the national parks while we were in Tanzania now that we were married. We visited many of the lodges during my first trip to Africa with Caleb and his family. For a fun break we would go during the day for a nice cold Coke, and as I sipped the refreshing drinks, I would dream about how nice it would be to stay in one of these fancy places. Caleb agreed that sounded like a good way to splurge for our vacation. So before leaving on our two-week camping trip, I told Caleb I wanted to pay for us to stay a night in the beautiful Ngorongoro Lodge that overlooked the crater. I enjoyed camping and found it beautiful, but I knew that by this point in our trip—a week in—a long hot bath and nice bed to sleep in would be wonderful. I had a good job, and Caleb and I could easily afford the one-night stay. He agreed, and I was thrilled. So thrilled, I gushed about it to Caleb's dad and the young couple.

We had a great first week, and on the day we drove from the Serengeti to the Ngorongoro Crater, I told everyone in the Land Cruiser I was ready for my hot bath and bed. I was eager to get a room, so before we got to the conservation

area, I asked Caleb if he would drop me off at the lodge before he and the rest of our group went to the campground
to set up. He ignored me completely, something he had
started doing these days—just pretended like he didn't
hear me—but I and everyone else in the vehicle knew he'd
heard me loud and clear.

When we made it to the Ngorongoro Crater, I asked
Caleb if he would drop me off at the lodge again. He dis-
missed me and said we needed to get a good spot at the
campground first. I was very disappointed, and embarrassed he was treating me disrespectfully in front of everyone in the car. I was not going to fight in front of the other
people on the trip, but it was obvious we were fighting. I was
mad. We arrived at the campground, and I said, "Caleb, will
you take me over to the lodge?" It was a twenty-minute drive
away. He told me to first help them set up. It took well over
an hour to get the camp set up. I was furious at this point
and when we finished, I asked Caleb, "Are you going to take
me to the lodge or not?"

He said, "No. I am not. It's almost dark and there's no
reason for you to stay at the lodge when you can stay here in
the tent. Besides, we don't need to spend the money."

I was furious, embarrassed, and humiliated. He had allowed me for weeks to dream about something he had no
intention of letting me do. To make matters worse, over the
course of our trip, the young couple had heard all of mine
and Caleb's conversations about how excited I was to stay
at the lodge. If we had been in the United States, I would
have driven over there myself. But we were driving Caleb's
father's Land Cruiser, and I did not have a vehicle myself. I
was completely under his control, and he knew it.

Having heard Caleb's response, Caleb's father laughed nervously then said, "Oh, Caleb. You're so bad." It was almost as if he was delighted Caleb had put me in my place.

"Well, Anne G.," my father-in-law said, "Camp is set up. Just stay here with us if he's going to act like that."

I believe his father also knew Caleb was beginning to take control and play mind games with me. It was a slow, calculating process that started a month after we married; he very slowly began to control me in passive aggressive ways to take any power I had for myself away. It was so slow in fact, I did not see clearly what was happening. I look back twenty-five years later with more clarity. Clarity I wish I had then.

One day, after returning to Caleb's parents' house, I went out for a walk alone. On my walk I ran into the young couple who'd gone camping with us. Similar in age to Caleb and me, they were training to be doctors and volunteering at the hospital. I stopped on the dirt road behind the small hospital compound to visit with them and was asking about their recent surgeries when the woman looked at me with a great amount of sympathy in her eyes. Neither married nor a Christian, she asked me, "Are you happy in your marriage?"

Surprised by her question, I hesitated before saying, "Yes."

She looked at her boyfriend, then back at me, compassion in her eyes, and said, "We are both concerned about how Caleb treats you. You are very kind to him, and he treats you badly, without any respect. It's been bothering both of us, and we've been wanting to speak to you about it, but there has never been a good time. You are in a very unhealthy relationship, and we wanted to tell you it's been upsetting for both of us to watch."

Ouch. That hurt. It hurt because here was a couple I had just met who'd spent a lot of personal time with Caleb and me over the last two weeks, and who'd seen our everyday relationship more than most people.

I explained to them how Caleb and I had been married for two and a half years, how we dated for five years before that, and how he had never acted like that toward me when we were dating. The first sign of this controlling side of him started right after we married and recently it had gotten worse. During my first trip to Africa, before we married, he had treated me like a queen. On this trip I realized Caleb treated me much worse in Africa than when we were in the United States. I thought about how kind and attentive he was to me years earlier when we were dating. I had no control, and I had no idea what to do.

We left the conversation at that. The couple went on their way, and I went on mine. As I walked back to Caleb's parents' house, I realized the couple had also confirmed what I was contemplating in my own head. I was almost doubting myself that the situation was as bad as I thought it was. Caleb would tell me I was wrong in thinking he was trying to control me, that it was all in my imagination. After someone tells you that for a while, you start to think maybe they are right. *How did this happen? How did I date him for years before we married, and never seen this side of him?* I was spinning with my thoughts. I went back to his parents' house and mulled it over in my head. When I had the opportunity to talk to Caleb about it, I got feisty and we got in a big fight—immediately. I told him he treated me badly, was controlling and disrespectful to me, and complete strangers confronted me because they were worried about me. He told me they were trying to cause problems in our marriage, that for some reason they were jealous. I knew that was ridiculous and told him so. Caleb told his dad what had happened and Caleb and his dad agreed—they did not want us to spend time with that couple anymore, they were trying to cause problems and what they said was not true.

But I knew it was true, and that is why it upset me so much. Caleb knew it was true also, and so did his father. They tried to keep me away from that couple for the rest of the visit. I still saw the cute couple and spoke with them; I appreciated their honesty. Caleb did not speak to them again. Once he decided he did not want a relationship with someone, they were out; he pretended like they did not exist.

Unfortunately, confronting Caleb about the problem did not resolve anything. So, my choice was to dwell on it or move on and let it go. After a few days of being mad, I chose to move on. Caleb was good at making up and pretending like nothing happened. I was too. *That's what's needed to have a good marriage*, I figured. And with Caleb being such a master at making up after we fought, with how extra-loving and thoughtful he would be to me, it made me wonder if, all along, I had just been overreacting.

CHAPTER 8

NEW BEGINNINGS
AND FRESH LIES

*For I know the plans I have for you, declares the Lord,
plans to prosper you and not harm you, plans to give you
hope and a future.*

—Jeremiah 29:11

We returned to the U.S. and started back to work.
We spent lots of time working in our yard together,
stripping wallpaper and painting, and making our home
the way we wanted. Caleb and I were both hard workers
who enjoyed working together. However, in my daily life
as a teacher, I was miserable. I'd been teaching for almost
two years and felt trapped inside a building. I hated feeling
trapped more than anything in the world and just wanted
to be free.

One night after work, as Caleb and I recounted our
days, I started to tear up.

"Why are you upset?" Caleb asked, since it was unusual for me. Typically I tried to have a positive attitude about most situations, but it all came tumbling out. The truth. I confessed I hated my job. I loved my students, but I hated not being able to leave the building, and it was the same routine every day. I knew I had received my degree in education, but I was very unhappy.

I confessed, "I feel like I am trapped."

Caleb was so gentle with me. He had a sweet, tender spot for me. I could see it in his eyes and hear it in his voice; I knew how much he loved me. He asked me what I wanted to do. I said, "I want to try to sell real estate. I think I would enjoy it."

He said, "I think you would be a great realtor." He encouraged me to look into the opportunity of selling real estate. So, I went and spoke to the three real estate companies on Signal Mountain to see if I could get a job. The first company said they wanted me, and she would go with me to knock on doors to get business. That scared me.

An old man owned the second company and told me I was too young: "Twenty-four years old and not even two years out of college. No one will purchase a house from you, you're too young. What are you thinking? You have a good job and ought to appreciate it."

Disheartened and defeated, I got in my car and drove home, my eyes welling up with tears. Once there I pouted to Caleb that no one thought I'd be a good realtor.

"You'll be a great realtor," he replied. "Don't give up because of one grouchy old man's opinion."

So I made an appointment with the third real estate company, and it turned out to be the perfect fit. The broker even sent me daffodils, which are my very favorite flower. I hoped it would be my dream job and went to talk to my parents. They were not thrilled, saying I'd gone to college (which by the way, they had paid for), had graduated with a degree, and was now looking into a job that needed no degree and, more importantly, had no salary—at all.

I was discouraged. But Caleb stood next to me, encouraging me to go for it. He was the only one besides me who thought it was a great idea. He knew this job was what I desired in my heart, and he wanted me to do what I loved.

Caleb said he would pay our bills until I got going in my business. So, I quit my job. Yikes.

I received a phone call at 5:00 a.m. the very first morning after quitting. I woke up to answer it, and it was Caleb calling me to tell me he had been in a shooting and that he was all right. But he had killed the man who had fired a gun at him. The shooting was near my school. I asked if he was okay, and did he want me to come to him? He said, no, he would be home after some more paperwork with the police department. I had a confirming sense that I had made the right decision not to teach school anymore; God's timing was remarkable. I remember lying in bed thanking the Lord for protecting Caleb and for his perfect timing. I never doubted from that day forward if I was making the right decision to quit teaching.

Caleb came home around seven thirty that morning, which was the time I would normally be leaving to go to work. We talked about what had happened that morning. He was not as upset as I thought he would be, but I figured he was in shock. We continued talking in bed as the sun came up. This was his second shooting, the first one being the poacher he shot in the hunting grounds in Tanzania. The first time bothered him more than this one, probably because he wasn't being shot at first. In bed he told me about it again, what had happened and how he felt really badly about that shooting. It had happened quickly. He watched the man die and wished he had not killed him. I listened quietly and with compassion as he talked about it with a great deal of remorse. We also talked about the shooting that had just occurred and how the police department was giving him two weeks off for his mental health recovery, and also so the police could investigate. After the investigation we found out the old man who Caleb shot had dementia. Of course, he did not know that when he shot the man. It was very sad.

In April of 1996, three and a half years after Caleb and I got married, I went to real estate school, then started work as a realtor. My goal the first year was to sell enough to match my teaching salary. It seemed like a big goal. And since my parents did not think it was a good idea, I was determined to do everything I could to be successful at real estate. I exceeded my goal the first year, and I was thrilled and loved my new job. My new job was more flexible, allowing me to be with Caleb and travel. I was very thankful Caleb continued to stand by me. I don't think I would have had the nerve to do it without him. He was supportive to me, always believing I could do anything, and he was always on my team.

Teammates though we were, I did not enjoy being a policeman's wife. So together we decided to try to start a safari business where he would sell hunts from the United States, and we could travel together to Africa and other countries, but still live in Tennessee.

Around this time, Caleb started asking to have children. He mentioned he thought it would be good for our kids to live at boarding school the way he had been raised. I was not interested in that lifestyle and wanted to make sure our children would live at home with us. Therefore, I told him I wasn't ready to have children. I was the baby of five children and was used to compromising, so I was happy with him selling safaris from the United States—instead of going to Africa to be a professional hunter. He was happy too, and I was his biggest cheerleader, encouraging him to start his business, just like he had encouraged me to start real estate. I knew that was what he desired in his heart, and I wanted him to live his own dreams. We believed in each other and believed that we were both capable of doing anything we put our minds to, and we both thrived because of that. Caleb's safari company grew as we traveled to safari shows and he sold hunts. He encouraged me with real estate, and I encouraged him in his safari business.

We prospered, separate and together, and our individual businesses and our lives seemed to be flourishing. But at the same time, Caleb's lying continued to get worse. I loved him, but lies were starting to embarrass me in public because, as his business grew, his lies were becoming unbelievable, and I was embarrassed other people thought so too. He started lying about the animals he had killed, the size, the number, the countries he had hunted in, pretty much whatever came into his mind. He had never killed a lion or elephant, and all of a sudden, he had outlandish stories about his lion and elephant hunts. I would always confront him in the car on the way home or afterward when we were alone. "Why did you tell them you had been on a

lion hunt when you have never shot a lion? That was a lie."
He would blow me off and tell me to not worry about his
business, that I needed to take care of myself and not worry
about him.

I could feel his heart was also growing colder toward
me, a little more every day of every year. I asked Caleb to
work the day shift for the police department and not work
nights because I was alone at home, and I was afraid. His
captain told me Caleb now had the choice to work the day
shift, but Caleb said he enjoyed nights and was not going
to change his job. He then started working "extra jobs" occasionally, which policemen can pick up to subsidize their
pay. Dressed in his uniform, he would stand guard outside
of restaurants or bars that would pay him to discourage
any problems among the patrons. I would beg him not to
go work extra jobs. He would tell me he was going to; we
needed the money. I would say, "We have plenty of money,
why would you choose to be gone from me more than the
regular hours of your job?" We started fighting really badly
about his extra jobs and his choice to work the night shift.
I was working, we made good money together, and I even
had money in savings. I could not understand why he would
want to be away from me more than necessary.

My marriage was falling apart.

CHAPTER 9
INTRUDER

He reached down from on high and took hold of me; He drew me out of deep water. He rescued me from my powerful enemy, from my foes, who were too strong for me. They confronted me in the day of my disaster, but the Lord was my support.

—2 Samuel 22: 17–18

One night in early June of 1996, I was sleeping alone at home while Caleb was working with the police department. It happened to be his birthday. He left for work in normal clothes because he was working undercover, which he did sometimes. I woke up around three that morning because I had to go to the bathroom, and I felt someone in the room. I looked through my barely opened eyes so whoever I sensed could not see I was awake. There was a man standing at the end of my bed; he was tall and wore a hat and a trench coat. I was paralyzed with fear. I sensed with everything in me that he wanted to kill me. And I knew if I did not do something, I would be dead. So, I jumped out of bed, ran out the front door, and ran across the street and behind one neighbor's house to the next neighbor's back door, whose husband was a policeman for the county police department (Caleb was a city police officer). I frantically knocked on their back door thinking the man who wanted to kill me was probably following me. I was only wearing a silk nightshirt. My neighbor, Jill, came to the back door and opened it. I quickly told her what had happened. She let me in and locked the door. We were both panicked.

I tried to call Caleb from her phone, but he would not answer his cell phone. Then Jill called her husband, Tommy, who radioed the police. The police came immediately, and her husband called dispatch for Caleb's police department. They could not get in touch with him either. Tommy rushed home as the police went through my entire house, joining them to investigate. The police found no signs of a break-in or anyone there, so I thanked the policemen and they left.

Hours later, Caleb came home. It was still dark, but the sun was getting ready to come up. I was still at Jill and Tommy's house.

"I'm so sorry, Anne G.," said Caleb when he met me at our neighbors'. "I was undercover and didn't get the radio call."

I thought that was strange, but did not say much. I had nothing to say. I knew how unimportant I was to him since I had begged him to stop working nights, and he could choose when he wanted to work. I was also afraid because of what had just happened and was silenced by my fear. I had never been a fearful person, but I was rattled to the core.

Caleb thanked the neighbors and took me to our house. He apologized again for not answering my phone calls or the radio from dispatch. I was in a daze, and was not saying much, which was unusual. We got into bed, and he pulled me into his arms. He told me in the darkness of the morning he was sorry for not being a good husband, he wanted to start taking care of me, and he confessed he had not been doing that. He told me he was going to stop working nights and stop working extra jobs so he could be with me to sleep. He told me he should have been home to protect me that night. Then he confessed he knew he had not been thoughtful toward me, and I was a good wife and always tried to make our marriage the best it could be, and that I was his best friend and he loved me, and he wouldn't know what to do without me. We had one of those talks you have with your spouse that are truthful. Both people are being honest with their hearts. Open hearted and honest. I told him I had been waiting to hear those words for a long time. He hugged me, told me again how much he loved me, and promised he was making a change right then and would be a good husband to me; he was very convicted. I was stunned that this event had such a major impact on him. I had been praying for my marriage for years. I was very quiet and let him do most of the talking. It was beautiful to hear him acknowledge all the things I had tried to talk to him about. It was one of the most beautiful moments in our marriage. As we lay there in the dark, I felt safe and loved. There was tremendous joy in my heart at that moment, and I thanked the Lord. I did not care what had to happen to me to get us here, I had the boy I fell in love with back. Caleb was talking like the boy who wooed me when we dated. It filled my heart with hope. We were lying there close together in the dark, enjoying the moment, not speaking, just being together. After a little while I felt something. I can only describe it as a coldness, and it came in between us, like a division. I felt it clearly and there was a presence I cannot explain. The atmosphere completely changed. Then I felt Caleb change. I was startled and I said into the darkness, "What is that?"

Caleb said, "What?"

I said, "Caleb, we dated for five years, and we have been married over three years, I know you better than anyone, what was that? I felt you change, I felt it, you cannot lie to me. It was cold and you changed."

He was silent.

I am still not sure where this came from, it must have been the Holy Spirit in me, but I pressed. "Tell me what it is. We both know something is here. We were lying here in a beautiful moment and all of a sudden you changed, and I felt the coldness. What was it? It's scaring me."

After what had just happened to me with the stranger in my room, I was afraid and he knew it, hearing the fear in my voice. I was rattled.

He admitted quietly, "That is my dark side."

Looking back, I am surprised I didn't overreact. But I just laid there next to him. I said, very seriously, "What do you mean?"

He said, "Don't worry, you will never see that side of me, you are my good side."

I quietly asked, "Where did you get your dark side?"

"I don't want to talk about it. You will never see that part of me, I'll protect you from it," said Caleb.

I asked, "What do you mean you will protect me from it?"

He did not respond. "Does it have anything to do with

that black panther that followed you around the hunting grounds of Tanzania?"

"I am not going to talk about it anymore," he replied. I tried once more, but he had finished talking and had shut down. He took me back in his arms and held me protectively as I wondered, *What is he talking about? We just had this beautiful moment, he confessed his love for me and how he wants to be a better husband and protect me, and now this? What is his dark side?*

Caleb felt convicted and stopped working nights after the intruder. He cut back on the extra jobs too, after we compromised on him working one per month. Now with all the extra hours at home, he could sell more hunts and hopefully it would become a full-time job in the future. He was attentive toward me again, as the cold walls that had formed between us suddenly dissolved. I was surprised how powerfully that night had affected Caleb and our marriage. My husband was back, he was loving and respecting me, and I was extremely thankful. My business was thriving, and I did not have to sleep alone anymore.

The bizarre thing was, I started to have nightmares after I saw the man at the end of my bed. Each one had a different story, but they all had the same theme. Someone or something was always trying to kill me. Then over the next year, they slowly turned into night terrors. Sometimes once a month, sometimes every other week, sometimes once a week, but they were getting worse, and more violent, and I was suffering. I would pray for God to take them away and asked Caleb to pray with me. They were tormenting me, and I never knew when they would come. I would wake up screaming in terror. Sometimes jumping up out of the bed to run, sometimes stuck in place because I was being choked by whatever horror was in the dream. Caleb would wake up, comfort me by putting his arms around me and pulling me close, and we would return to sleep. My nightmares all started that night that I woke up with that man at the end of my bed. I was puzzled at what was causing these terrors, over and over wondering, *Why will they not go away?*

CHAPTER 10
HANGING ON

Now faith is confidence in what we hope for and assurance about what we do not see.

—Hebrews 11:1

Over the next two years, Caleb was involved in two more shootings while working with the police department's drug enforcement team. Caleb shot both men, who were drug dealers, on separate occasions, and they both died. It was upsetting to hear about these shootings, but Caleb resolved, "It's part of the job." Caleb's safari business had taken off, we had been married six years, and we decided together he should stop working as a policeman and sell safaris full time. When I started real estate, Caleb was sweet to me and told me he could support us for a while until I could make some money. So I told him it was my turn, we were a team. I was making enough to support us with my job alone, and he already had income from working part time selling safaris. We should be fine financially. We were both thrilled and full of hope. I thought the police department had almost destroyed our marriage, but good things were coming our way.

I was believing in faith for that.

However, my nightmares were wicked and continued to torment me. Caleb could be loving and thoughtful to me, and then turn and be indifferent quickly without any warning or argument. I was fighting to have a good marriage, and I was determined to do everything in my power to make it happen. As I continued to work on my marriage, it was clear to see there was a lot of good. I would say much more good than bad. So I focused on the good. Caleb and I always enjoyed spending most of our time together; at home or in public we were usually touching, either standing close together or Caleb would grab my hand or have his arm around me. At night we piled up on the couch watching TV. During our entire marriage, we always had a good physical life, we went 4-wheeling together, I went hunting wherever he went, and we traveled together. So even though he treated me with indifference and disrespect sometimes, he also had this attentive, loving, soft side toward me that he didn't have with anyone else, and that helped me hang on. It was almost like he was two different people, and it was confusing to me. *How can he act like he loves me so much and then be completely different so quickly without warning? Is it him or is it me? Is he right, is it my imagination?*

One day one of Caleb's good friends from the police force came up to visit. He told me while we were visiting, when Caleb had walked inside for a minute, that Caleb always talked about how much he loved me and what a good marriage we had. Caleb told his friend he could not wait to get home every day, because I would run to greet him with excitement when I saw him, and I did. I was always excited to see and spend time with my husband. Caleb had a very tender spot in his heart for me, and I knew it. Other people would tell me they could tell that Caleb adored me by the way he looked at me. It was strange, because I knew he adored me and had me on some type of pedestal. I was a strong Christian in my faith, I loved my husband and my family, and he admired that and told me all the time he was so proud I was his. I was proud he was mine too. But there was something off, and I was wrestling with it in my heart, praying the Lord would give me wisdom and help me.

In the fall, we flew to North Carolina for Caleb's high school reunion. It was for his boarding school in Kenya, and when we were there, he told me some of his school friends—two men and a woman who had traveled to the reunion together—were coming to stay at our house for two days after the reunion.

I asked about the girl.

"We dated in junior high," Caleb told me at the gathering, "but not in high school. And there was never any real romance between us in junior high. We just said we 'dated.' So there's nothing to worry about," he said. They were just friends who had not seen each other in years and wanted to catch up.

Her name was Amelia.

We flew back home that night while Caleb's friends drove the four hours from the reunion to our house. When they arrived at our house, the boys were in one car, and she was in a different car. I realized they had not traveled to the reunion together, as Caleb had told me they had. In fact, after speaking to the three guests that night, I discovered they were living in different states and had not spoken since high school, and she was married.

From the second she stepped in our home, Amelia was very flirtatious toward my husband in front of me, and it made me very uncomfortable. Caleb was enjoying it and was responding like a schoolboy. She looked at him like she wanted to eat him for dessert—right in front of me and everyone else.

I asked him to come to our bedroom at one point, where I confronted him: "Why did you bring her here? She's flirting with you right in front of me."

"Anne G., don't be ridiculous," Caleb said. "Why are you acting insecure for no reason? Do you really think I'd be interested in someone like Amelia? She and I are friends just like the guys and I are friends. You're being a little dramatic. Why are you acting so jealous for no reason? It's all in your mind."

It was the first time in our relationship I worried about Caleb cheating on me, and I was on high alert. I asked him to get Amelia to leave. I told him I didn't want her staying under my roof, disrespecting me by openly luring my husband.

"No," Caleb said. "It's my house too, and you won't tell me what to do. She's staying."

Not only did she stay, she was determined to win the battle for his attention. In fact, she liked the fact she had his attention and liked that I knew he was choosing her.

I was heartbroken. Over the next two days I didn't leave the house to go to work, afraid Amelia and Caleb would sneak off together. She would whisper in his ear as I was feeding the guests, pretending I had some respect, but I was humiliated in front of our house guests.

When the guests left after what had felt like an eternity, I was so relieved.

Lord, thank You she's gone, I prayed. *God, please help me.*

As Caleb's business grew, we started going to Africa more often with his company. Traveling had quickly become my favorite thing to do. I loved traveling to Africa, seeing all the new countries; the people from other places and the scenery of each country were so unique. Our safaris fulfilled my need for adventure and fed both of our desire for excitement and freedom. So I loved taking off across the world with my husband. However, I noticed when we would travel to Africa, my night terrors would get worse. One night on a trip to Zimbabwe, I was sleeping in a luxury tent. Caleb was at another camp close by, which was not typical; we were usually together. I woke up in the early morning dark and, as I was lying awake, I felt something evil entering my tent. I felt it move toward me and then I felt it as it crawled on top of me. It was big, dark, and heavy. This dark spirit came over me completely and started pressing down on my chest and pushing all the air out of me. It then started choking me at the same time. I could not breathe, and I could not get it off me. I struggled and fought. I panicked because I could not breathe at all and I was literally fighting for my life and I knew with everything inside me: my life was in danger. Finally, I was able to get a breath. I cried out loud, "Oh God, please help me!"

The evil spirit vanished.

Traumatized, I prayed, "Lord, Jesus, why won't this stop?"

I would beg God to protect me from these night terrors that tortured me. They were absolutely horrible, and I would wake up and they were sometimes still happening in real life. I felt a very dark evilness around me in my dreams, and I did not know what to do about it. I knew it wanted to kill me, that was always the theme of every night terror. It was bad at home, but worse when I traveled to certain countries. I continued to pray about them. As a couple, we prayed together every night before we would go to sleep, and Caleb would pray for my nightmares to stop. At our own house, I would wake up screaming and sometimes jump or fall out of bed. However, in some of these other places, occasionally, I would literally be picked up and violently thrown out of the bed onto the floor. One time when Caleb and I were in Mexico together, I ended up bruising my knee badly when I was thrown out of the bed onto the tile floor. My knee took over a week to heal. What is odd is that I never had anything happen during the day, only when I was asleep or just waking up from being asleep. Caleb and I would talk about how it was getting worse over time. I was discouraged, but was still trying to keep a good attitude about it. But let's be honest, it had been years of torment, and I was being worn down. He had no advice for me, and I had no idea what to do either. My friends and family knew about my night terrors and they had no advice for me either except to pray.

So I did. I prayed. Because, tortured though I was, I was still a strong believer who knew without a doubt God had a plan. Wondering why things seemed to be hard, but trusting that God would heal my marriage and my nightmares. As a couple, we went to church together every Sunday, and we also had a good Sunday school class that we both enjoyed.

But when I would ask Caleb to read the Bible with me, he would not do it. His pledge from when we dated to walk with the Lord and lead as the head of our family toward Christ was so far off from what it had been when we dated that I was in complete disillusionment. So I would pray and continue to read my Bible and wait. I would ask Caleb if he wanted a great marriage, but he seemed preoccupied. It was as if two plus two was equaling five, and I could not see where the extra number was coming from. Nothing added up. I remember asking Caleb one day, "Why did you pursue me so hard when we dated? You read devotionals and the Bible with me and now you do not do any of that."

Looking me straight in the eyes he said, "The chase is over, I've got you now."

I was completely overwhelmed at the honesty of his statement, and my mind swirled with how I could fix this issue before the truth sank in—I couldn't. After all, I'd tried fighting, being loving, being mean, being quiet, being funny, being entertaining...it didn't matter what I did. But because it wasn't my personality to give up, I continued to pray, read my Bible, and wait. Clinging to faith, I continued to hang on.

Nothing changed in my marriage.

CHAPTER 11
REFRESHED

I lift up my eyes to the mountains—
where does my help come from?
My help comes from the Lord,
the Maker of heaven and earth.
　　　　　　　—Psalms 121:1–2

In the summer of 1997, five years into our marriage, Caleb and I traveled to New Zealand's South Island on a seven day hunting trip for tahr and elk. We went with a company Caleb wanted to represent for selling hunts. As we flew into the South Island, I peered out the plane windows to the lush countryside. I had the distinct thought, *It feels like I am coming home.*

So I looked at Caleb, "I have the strangest feeling like I'm coming home," I confessed out loud as we prepared to land in Christchurch.

He said, "You have never been here."

"I know," I replied full of wonder. "I'm not sure what it is. I've never felt like this before."

The next week was glorious. We stayed at a five-star small, luxury resort named Lilybank Lodge that was straight out of a magazine. The resort staff fixed three meals a day for us, and we were the only guests there at the time. The views of the Southern Alps stood right beyond our room's window. The property encompassed a large ranch with glorious views in every direction. Growing up in the hills of Tennessee, I was familiar with beautiful mountains, but this was a spiritual time for me. I felt the presence of God in a way through seeing His creation that I had never experienced before. I had seen stunning things in my life, but the spectacular Southern Alps ministered to my soul and spirit, filling me up like living water.

We hunted the Southern Alps. A helicopter would drop us off, and we would hike along the ridgelines for tahr, which are a type of mountain goat. During the hunts I would look out and I could not believe what my eyes were seeing. The snowy peaks, bright skies, and turquoise-crystal lakes of the South Island—I drank it all in for the entire week while reflecting on my life. New Zealand is amazingly beautiful and the mountains and sky made me feel a closeness to God that opened my soul up.

I had never experienced something so stunning that touched me so deeply.

Our professional hunter for the week, Phil, quickly became my friend. A mountain man who was bearded and thin, Phil was quiet with a dry sense of humor. Once you connected with him though, he was a wonderful conversationalist. The first afternoon we were there, Caleb and Phil sighted in their guns. I was always along for the adventure, having never shot an animal on a hunting trip and not desiring to. The second day was a full, long day of hunting, which consisted of being dropped off by helicopter on the ridgeline of the mountain and walking on slate rocks that were sliding down the side of the mountain with each step you took. One slip and you could easily slide down twenty to fifty feet or more. It was like trudging up a Stairmaster for most of the day. When Caleb and I came back to the lodge, we were exhausted with shaky legs, whereas Phil acted like it was a walk in the park.

That morning we had eaten breakfast, but had skipped lunch that afternoon because we were hunting all day. Caleb and I showered and dressed for dinner. I was on my best behavior because Caleb was doing business and I wanted to act ladylike because, you know, I am a good Southern girl and it was a luxurious place.

In the lodge living room, Phil asked us what we would like for a cocktail before dinner. Caleb said he would like a screwdriver, which is a cocktail of vodka and orange juice. I was twenty-five and had only drunk alcohol a few times during celebrations like weddings. "I'll have what Caleb's having," I said casually, trying to act like an adult.

Over the next half hour, we visited with the lodge manager, his girlfriend, and Phil about our exciting day. I was starving and drank all of my orange juice and vodka. When dinner was nearly ready, the waiter brought us a refill of our cocktails, then led us into the dining room and sat us at a lovely formal table. I was trying my best to sit ladylike, knowing my Granny would have never approved of bad manners at the dining table. The manager sat at the head of the table. Caleb sat next to him and across from the manager's girlfriend, and I sat next to Caleb and across from Phil. As we continued to wait on our food, I sipped on my second cocktail, enjoying it after our long day. Pretty soon, I started to feel giddy and giggled at something that was said. Then Phil made a funny comment, and I started laughing so hard, tears spilled from my eyes. Phil started getting tickled with me, and now we both could not stop laughing. Caleb and the two others tried to carry on their conversation as if it were a normal dinner.

When I got a hold of myself I quietly said to Phil, "I think I'm in trouble."

"You should've told me you were a lightweight," he said. "Have you *ever* had a drink before?"

Well, that did it. Because it was true, I hardly ever drank—so I got so tickled it was as if a dam inside me broke. I could not stop laughing, and tears were falling from my eyes. And the more I laughed, the more Phil got a twinkle in his eye and made quick dry comments under his breath that made us both laugh even harder. My stomach hurt, I was laughing so hard.

Caleb was trying to ignore me, continuing to talk to the manager about work. Everyone knew I had only had one full drink. I guess the altitude, an empty stomach, and hardly ever drinking was why it hit me so hard. I am still not sure.

I remember looking at Phil across the table and confessing, "I do not drink often."

He said in his funny dry tone, "You really are a good little Catholic girl, aren't you?"

He assumed if you were a Christian, you were Catholic. And while I was really trying to be good, it was not working. I had no control over myself. I whispered to Phil, "I can't get it together." I crossed my arms and put my head down on the table, laughing in surrender. The server brought out soup and everyone started eating. I looked across the table at Phil, because he and I were obviously having our own private party. Trying to keep a straight face, but not succeeding, I looked to him to help me out. He picked up his spoon and showed it to me and said quietly, "Take a few bites of soup. It will be good for you," and gently smiled at me. I took a bite. He continued to talk to me and kept telling me to have some more soup between giggles. Something happened during that exhilarating dinner. Phil became a trusted friend. He was my support when Caleb was sitting right next to me. Phil was sticking with me, helping me out. While eating my soup, I didn't care about his past, present, or future. I was loyal to Phil and from that moment on, he was my forever friend. It was a done deal.

During the next week, the three of us spent all our time together. Caleb and Phil talked about hunting in New Zealand, and Phil and I talked about life and our faith.

On the last day of our trip, everyone was together in a field sighting in the guns, and I was marveling at the amazing Southern Alps. Caleb wandered off to talk to the manager of the hunting company, and I was casually talking to Phil. We were a good distance from Caleb so Phil, who was the kind of guy who didn't waste any words, and said what he meant, looked straight at me and said, "Caleb doesn't give you much attention, does he?" It was out of the blue. I was embarrassed, and a little surprised. We had a bond that was unspoken since dinner that night, and we had built a friendship over the past week. At that moment, I knew he said it because he cared for me. His words struck me to the core. Especially since he said it very matter-of-factly, with no sympathy in his eyes.

For some reason, I wanted to be truthful with someone, and I knew I would probably never see Phil again. So after the shock wore off, I admitted, "Yeah, you're right. I guess he doesn't." It was odd admitting the truth out loud. I was loyal to Caleb, so it was hard for me to be honest with anyone about our relationship, even myself. It had to be someone safe that I could be truthful with, someone who lived across the world from me. It made me very sad to admit this about Caleb. Yet, for five years I had prayed, tried to be the best wife I could be, and tried to cover up Caleb's bad actions toward me. It was like a cool breeze of honesty on that field that day. With almost a stranger. I shared the truth of my heart with Phil at that moment. We both knew it. Being honest with Phil allowed me to also be honest with myself. And it hurt.

He never said anything else about it during that trip and neither did I.

During our stay, I asked Caleb if we could extend our trip to do some traveling around the South Island. I was in love with New Zealand and wanted to see as much as I could. We could have easily stayed; we had the time, and the flights home would take two days. Caleb said no. "We can come back within the year to travel around New Zealand," he said. But since he tended to lie to me, I asked several times before we returned to the States.

"Caleb, do you promise we can come back within the year?"

"Yes," Caleb said every time. "I promise."

We talked to Phil all about what we should see and how long our trip back to the South Island should be. He agreed to help us find lodging, and he wanted us to come visit his hometown on the coast for part of the trip. I was so excited Caleb promised to come back with me that I told him I would pay for the entire trip. We exchanged contact information with Phil for our next trip to New Zealand. I was full of hope.

As we were boarding our plane to leave, I told Caleb I had never been to a place I wanted to explore and see as much as South Island, New Zealand. It was stunning. Once we arrived back in Tennessee, I spent the next several months studying where to travel in New Zealand and making notes and plans for all the places I wanted to see. Caleb listened to my every word for months of research, and never disagreed with my exciting plan. He knew how much I loved being there, and I was thrilled about our next trip. The next spring, a year later, I spoke to Phil on the phone, and we decided the best time to visit. That night, while we were talking in our living room, I was confirming with Caleb the exact dates for our travel and was getting ready to purchase the plane tickets. "I'm not going back to New Zealand," he said matter-of-factly.

His words felt like a punch to the gut. I asked, "What? Why would you let me plan our trip all this time, and tell me before we left New Zealand that you would come back with me within the year and then not stand by your word?"

"I never said I would go back to New Zealand," he said. "And I'm not going."

I was once again devastated. I was also tired of always being controlled by Caleb and set up for failure. He knew each time what he was doing, and he was slowly chipping away at my sanity. I was starting to lose who I was: my confidence, my spark for life, my joy. For the next two weeks I begged him to keep his word. The more I asked and tried to bargain, the more I saw he would not budge. His refusal to yield happened in the little everyday things in our life, but it was how he behaved toward the big things that delivered the most devastating blows. The way he treated the dreams I planned on and worked toward, like staying at the nice lodge on the Ngorongoro Crater, and the trip back to New Zealand, hurt the most. *Why would he tell me yes, when his answer was really no? Why did he want to pull the rug out from under me and watch me fall?*

I was livid. It had happened so many times and I was sick of being manipulated and I was weary from his control and constant mind games. *Everything* had become a game for him to control me. He wanted to drive me insane, and I had started to feel the effects.

I knew my parents would disapprove, I knew it was not what I thought was the right thing to do as a good Christian wife, but I told him I was going anyway. Yes, I was going across the world to New Zealand by myself if he did not want to go. Was I afraid? Yes. But I was mad enough to go without him. I told him I was finished with his mind games and lies. He said he would never play mind games with me, he just decided then it was not a good idea for either of us. We did not need to go back to New Zealand, we had seen it already. It was a waste of money, and we needed to go somewhere new that we had never seen instead. I saw red. I was over the games Caleb played; I was over him always controlling me without coming out and commanding. He never yelled or was violent. It was a constant, invisible battle for control: quiet and manipulative.

I called Phil and explained Caleb had decided not to come. Phil said I was welcome to come anyway, and he and his girlfriend would be happy to have me base my trip from their homes. Phil and I had talked deeply about our faith while we were hunting in New Zealand. I knew Phil was not a Christian so in a strange way, I felt relieved I did not need to explain why I was not being a good Christian wife to Caleb.

So I planned my trip, bought my ticket, and flew to New Zealand by myself. It was August of 1998, a little over a year since Caleb and I had been to the South Island. I went to stay with Phil and met his girlfriend Sheri' who I immediately bonded with. She and I got close and one day, as the two of us were cooking together at her house, I confided in her that Caleb had promised to come back to New Zealand with me within the year and had broken his promise as I was buying the tickets to come, so I decided to come without him.

Sheri' said matter-of-factly, "That sounds about right. Phil told me Caleb is a self-centered ass who treats you badly."

I laughed. It made me feel even closer to both of them. "Good," Sheri' said. "I'm glad you came on without him. Don't let him ruin your plans."

Something about that conversation and her words set me free. I no longer felt guilty about coming without Caleb across the world. And from then on, I loved her and Phil.

During my two-week trip, I did some traveling alone and stayed in a hostel in Queenstown where I met a forty-year-old teacher from California named Stephanie. She was cute and vivacious, and we hit it off right away. We went jet boating, explored the city, and met a couple in their early fifties from Australia on an excursion who we went out to dinner with. It was exhilarating to be on my own. I met people everywhere I went, most of them were traveling from Australia, and wow, the amazing people from New Zealand and Australia—with their funny sense of humor and laid back attitudes—were just what I needed.

During those fourteen days, I had some deeply profound moments by myself. I felt like I got a deep breath of air in my lungs and was getting some of my independence back. My spirit soared from the profound beauty, and my heart was filled with wonder as I gazed at the turquoise lakes and snow-capped mountains of the Southern Alps. It was as if I was seeing God Himself and it was holy. Awe filled me up like living water for my thirsty soul during this amazing trip. I was given a refreshed spirit, full and overflowing. I felt the profound peace of God, and my joy was refreshed.

I flew home feeling satisfied about my adventurous trip, and sad about my marriage. When I arrived home, Caleb met me at the airport, he expressed how thankful he was that I was his wife, and he showered me with compliments. Our marriage was his priority once again, and he decided I was the girl of his dreams. It was so good in fact, I thought to myself, *Was my marriage really as bad as I thought? Maybe this time, it will last.*

CHAPTER 12
TWO SIDES

For who knows a person's thoughts except their own spirit within them? In the same way no one knows the thoughts of God except the Spirit of God.

—1 Corinthians 2:11

After being married five years, Caleb started telling me more vehemently he wanted us to get pregnant and have babies of our own. We both loved children and had always spent tons of time with our nieces and nephews, playing soccer and baseball in the yard, jumping on the trampoline, and helping them tend to whatever baby animals were at our family barn at the time. We went to their sporting events and watched my nieces' performances they created just for the family, like dances, movies, and skits. There was always something going on, and Caleb loved being a part of it all as much as I did. My family was a major part of our lives, and Caleb loved my family as if it were his own. He and I were the fun, young aunt and uncle that my nieces and nephews wanted to be with, and we wanted to be with them just as much. He was a great uncle. So, I knew he would be an even better father. However, when it came to having children of our own, I would say I was not ready; I was too young. I would always make an excuse that I wanted to travel to a new country I had not yet seen yet. There was always a reason I had, and the truth is I had always wanted to be a mama more than anything, but God had taken the desire away from me. I had no peace about it. Since Caleb started regularly begging me to get pregnant, I bought a beautiful Golden Retriever puppy named Taz and told him this was our baby for now.

We sold our first house and bought a new beautiful house on two acres, closer to my family. Our new home had enough space to start a family and had a large office space for Caleb to expand the safari business. He hired a guy named Richard, who we knew from our church, to come work for him. Caleb was working full time selling safaris and started doing some professional hunting himself, and I was a full-time realtor. Our life seemed amazing on one hand. We both had great businesses and we had my large family we were always doing things with. Caleb could be attentive and loving towards me, but I was feeling like I was losing my mind. And I didn't know why.

My night terrors had been going on for over four years and I continued to feel like I was being controlled with mind games from Caleb. If I confronted him, he made me doubt myself and my own reality, and he would tell me it was all in my mind. That was simply not true. I lined up for us to go see a Christian counselor a handful of times that spring. We'd meet with her together and separately, and during one of my sessions alone, she told me everything seemed fine with Caleb, that she didn't see any problems. "Your husband seems to adore you," she said.

That was the problem. Caleb was two different people, and he could change on a dime. She saw the boy I fell in love with. He always told other people I was his life, and more than half of the time he acted like that, and yet other times I was dealing with someone completely different. Everywhere I went for help was a dead end, and it made me feel like I was crazy for thinking that I sensed there was a problem. Caleb would not acknowledge it.

That fall, after years of selling real estate successfully, I decided to splurge on a new BMW. I'd always been more of a saver than a spender, but when it came to something I wanted, I would save up and I didn't mind buying it no matter the price. I had saved up almost enough to pay cash for my new car, and Caleb went with me to the dealership to look at the BMW I had my eye on. As we test drove it he could tell how much I wanted it. Back at the dealership, Caleb looked at me with his smoky eyes. "Baby, if I buy you this new BMW, will you get pregnant?" he bargained.

I laughed. "Caleb...I do want to have children one day," I said, "just not yet." I kissed him and slipped away to look at the car again.

Smiling, Caleb followed me. He knew I was hard to pin down, and he liked it. I told him I didn't need him to buy me my new car, I almost had enough saved.

"I want to buy it for you," Caleb said. "I can tell you love it. And when you get this out of your system, you'll be ready to have children."

I just laughed and smiled. "Thank you! I love you, and I

love this car!" I said, purposely not making any promises to get pregnant.

Caleb paid for half of my car that day, and I drove home with it. He liked spoiling me with gifts, and I liked it too. I knew he loved me, and the car was a genuine gift, but in my spirit I stayed on high alert as Caleb continued to try to persuade me to have a baby. There was something inside me that had no peace about having a baby with him. Because deep down I knew that if I were to do so at this time, the child would become another way for Caleb to exercise his control.

CHAPTER 13
THE GOOD

The heavens declare the glory of God;
the skies proclaim the work of His hands.
Day after day they pour forth speech;
night after night they reveal knowledge.
They have no speech, they use no words;
no sound is heard from them.
Yet their voice goes out into all the earth,
their words to the ends of the world.
—Psalms 19:1–2

Exciting things were happening in the year 2000. Caleb received an opportunity with his Zimbabwean friend Saul to start a hunting company in Tanzania that would allow Caleb to be the professional hunter for his clients. This had always been Caleb's dream (not just to sell trips from the U.S.), and this new company would lease hunting grounds, build camps, and hire professional hunters and a full staff to run the camps with trucks, tents, and all the trimmings to make a complete luxury camp. So Caleb and I planned a two-month trip to Tanzania and Zimbabwe for that June and July to prepare for his new company. This was the perfect opportunity for my parents to join us for a portion of our trip. Caleb and I had talked with them for years about them coming with us to Tanzania to experience the amazing adventures we had described.

My daddy was born with an adventurous spirit, and had wanted to visit Africa for years. My mom, however, didn't have an adventurous bone in her body. She had always been perfectly happy to stay home, and her idea of adventure, was to read a good book in bed. Mom had been raised with a silver spoon, and she was concerned about visiting a third-world country and about our accommodations there. Especially since she'd heard all the stories of the rugged places where Caleb and I'd stayed, and some of the squirrelly situations we had gotten ourselves into. We promised her we would only stay in five-star resorts, and not do anything too wild. So my mom, who was a great sport, agreed to take a leap of faith. We were all a little surprised she said yes to travel to Africa, including her.

In July, my parents arrived at the airport in Arusha for their three-week safari. They looked like stereotypical American tourists, all decked out in their safari outfits my mom had ordered online through Orvis. My daddy was rocking his safari hat. Caleb and I'd been in Africa for over two weeks already, and had come to pick my parents up from the airport, quietly agreeing when we saw them that they were adorable.

The next morning, we headed out of Arusha in our Land Cruiser for our big adventure to the Ngorongoro

Crater, Lake Manyara, Maswa Game Reserve, Serengeti, Tarangire, and finally, to Zanzibar. We stayed in lovely resorts for three to four nights at a time, some with thick fabric tents for lodging, some with thatched-roofed cement huts, but all with modern-day luxuries. Caleb wanted my parents to see the Big Five—lion, leopard, rhinoceros, buffalo, and elephant—and we did. In fact, we saw all kinds of animals—zebras, wildebeest, monkeys, crocodiles, and gazelles—and it was glorious. We even stayed at the fancy Ngorongoro Crater Lodge overlooking the Ngorongoro Crater, where Caleb and I'd gone to enjoy Cokes on previous trips, and where I'd wanted to stay years earlier and Caleb hadn't let me. And yes! It was even better than I imagined it would be, staying at this lodge. Each room had a private rock porch overlooking the crater's magnificent rim. Caleb and I drank hot Tanzanian chai (which is the Swahili word for tea, and is a delicious locally grown black tea mixed with half milk, half water, and lots of sugar and other yummy spices) out on our porch in the morning, as the sun came up and burned the fog off the rim of the crater. In the evening, after a long day of safari, we watched the sunset from our porch as the giraffes quietly came close, lingering by our high-up room to eat the leaves and twigs from the treetops. It was fantastic.

In this conservation area, we spent our days driving down into the crater to observe the various animals. As we would start our descent each morning down the road into the bottom of the crater, my eyes took in the magnificent sight of thousands of flamingos, which caused Lake Magadi—the soda lake inside the crater—to glow pink as the morning sun beamed down. We sat for hours watching large prides of lions with their adorable cubs playing mischievously, we watched the hippopotamuses with their calves splashing in the lakes, and we sat among the enormous elephants, which blocked the roads occasionally so we had to wait to continue our game drive. We also spotted the elusive rhinoceros. Two in fact, which is a major score on any safari. My parents were amazed, and Caleb, who loved my parents like his own, was proud to get to show them his beautiful Africa.

The Massai were the local tribe who lived in that area. As I watched them walk down the roads in their bright red garments, I remembered Caleb and I had been camping two years earlier in the hunting grounds where he grew up. The deep beat of steady drums had started beating in the distance at about three in the darkness of the morning, and woke us up. As we listened from our tent, drums eerily responded from three sides of where we had been camping, back and forth went the drums, a call from the south and then responses from the north and east. Caleb told me it was a warning—the tribe's quick communication announcing danger, and everyone needed to be on the watch. He wondered out loud if another tribe was attacking, or if cattle had been stolen. We had stayed awake, alert and listening for hours to see if we could hear any danger coming close to our tent. The next morning, we found out the Maasai had stolen some prized cattle from Caleb's tribe. Caleb's tribe was scared of the Maasai, so they let the cattle go without fighting that night. Over the years, Caleb had told us many times he was afraid of the Maasai.

One foggy day, we were driving on the dirt road on top of Ngorongoro Crater, in the mountains fronting the Rift Valley. We saw three Maasai warriors on the side of the road. My daddy, who never met a stranger, saw these three Maasai warriors and said, "Caleb, pull the car over so we can talk to them."

My mom immediately replied, "Dugg, no! Caleb says they are dangerous."

But Caleb stopped the car and spoke to them because my daddy had asked him to, and Caleb respected my daddy.

"Caleb, I want you to translate for me everything I want to say," said Daddy, knowing Caleb spoke fluent Swahili. Before we knew it, Daddy and the Maasai warriors were in conversation. Then, much to our surprise, my daddy decided to get out of the Land Cruiser to continue their conversation. The rest of us weren't sure what to do, so we followed him out, and Daddy, who grew up on a dairy farm in East Tennessee, asked Caleb to ask the warriors all about their cows. "How much does a cow cost?" Daddy wanted to know. "What type of currency is a cow? How many cows would it take to buy a good wife? Do you have to defend your cattle from wild animals with your spears?" And a wide variety of other questions. (It was customary to pay for your wife in Tanzania.) He even explained, putting his arm around my shoulders, "Now, this is my daughter. How many cows should he," he pointed to Caleb, "have to pay for her?" Then he laughed hard, throwing his head back. The warriors laughed with him and were obviously enjoying the conversation. It was live entertainment.

Caleb was respectful of the Maasai as he spoke to them. He did not want to upset them in any way or offend them because they had the reputation of killing people with their spears if you made them mad. And yes, they were carrying their spears, and carrying them proudly. As my daddy spoke and Caleb translated, a friendship was formed. The Maasai warriors enjoyed the conversation with Daddy about their prized cows so much that they invited us to come see them. The next thing you know we were driving down a walking path off the main road to their nearby family compound on the side of the mountain. Dense fog smothered the air as we got out of the Land Cruiser. The Maasai wives, who held their babies wrapped around their backs with kangas, stopped working over their outside fire and came over with the children and the elderly family members to see their foreign white guests. There were about twenty family members in all. Mom and I started playing with the children while the men showed my daddy and Caleb their cows.

After a few minutes, my daddy and Caleb called in excitement for my mom and me to come to them. We quickly rushed over and the warriors showed us one of their cows with a wooden plug in its neck. They explained to Caleb, who translated to us why the wooden plug was there: to cap the blood the Maasai would drink. We had heard rumors that the Maasai drink cow's blood, and now we were witnessing the truth of it, right before our very eyes. The Maasai then demonstrated the process: one man pulled out the plug and then stuck a wooden bowl to the cow's neck as blood squirted into the bowl with each heartbeat. Then he stuck the plug back in the cow's neck, stopping the flow of blood. "The cow does not have to be killed or hurt at all for us to collect its blood," the other man explained. Surprisingly, the cow stood there oblivious. Then the warrior added fresh cow's milk to the bowl from another cow's udders, and mixed it in with the cow's blood. One of them put the bowl to his mouth and took a sip to show us it was a warm and delightful drink, and then he offered it to us.

Shaking our heads and smiling, my parents and I said timidly, "No, thank you."

I was thinking, *Oh my, what is going to happen now?* Caleb laughed nervously because he didn't want to offend these men. He said, "Our white tribe does not enjoy the same drinks the Maasai enjoys. Our stomachs are weak, not strong like the Maasai."

Finding this very funny, the warriors threw back their heads and laughed. Then one said something to Caleb, and Caleb translated to my parents and me: "They're inviting us into their hut."

My parents and I looked with uncertainty at each other. Then I looked at Caleb; he was nervous about the situation, I could tell. All the ethnic groups in the area respected and were fearful of the Maasai, so my heart skipped a beat when my daddy replied, "Yes, we would love to! Tell them thank you, Caleb."

Yikes.

The extremely foggy day combined with literally just witnessing these warriors drink cow's blood mixed with milk made it especially unsettling as my parents, Caleb, and I made our way toward the thatched-roofed huts made of dry grass and mud. *I can't believe my mom is doing this*, I thought as we walked, purposely not making eye contact with her, afraid she might pass out cold. I'm still not sure how her feet continued to move forward toward that hut. My daddy on the other hand seemed curious, like an excited boy on a great adventure. I was always eager for an adventure myself—that side of me almost always won. *Well, here we go,* I thought as we were about to step inside.

The hut was very dark. Caleb stepped in first behind the Maasai warriors, then stuck his hand out for me to hold. Taking Caleb's hand, I stepped into the darkness behind him, then reached out my other hand for my mom. My daddy stepped in last and took hold of my mom's free hand. We held hands like this as our eyes adjusted to the deep darkness and as the warriors led us through a series of small corridors. We wound through until we finally reached a large room where a fire was burning. My eyes came into focus then, and in the dim firelight I saw some beds on the side of the room and some elderly family members sitting by the fire. My eyes burned as the elders spoke to the warrior who led us in. Caleb greeted them in Swahili and then introduced himself and us. Still holding my hand, he pulled me protectively close to his body, and I pressed myself into his arm. Then my parents and I murmured the one greeting in Swahili we knew: "Jambo."

The room stunk. It smelled like human feces being burned, and something made my eyes burn. Never in all my life had I smelled such a horrible odor, and I prayed silently, *Oh God, please don't let us get killed. I know I always seem to be in these situations.* Then I turned to look toward my mom, and I could not believe she was enduring this dangerous and stinky situation. Especially considering her fearful nature. Even I felt uneasy and was trying to simmer the disturbing thoughts sizzling through my mind. I could barely see her in the darkness, but she seemed to retain a calm demeanor and was keeping with us step for step.

When we were finally escorted back out into daylight,

I sucked the fresh air into my burning lungs. My eyes felt relief too, as they adjusted back to fresh air and daylight. Then the warriors who had shown us their homes began to chant a song in their native tongue and jump for Caleb, my parents, and me. The Maasai are known for their jumping. It was beautiful to watch these warriors, who were very tall and thin, shoot straight up like arrows into the foggy air, with their spears in their hands and their long knives strapped around their waists. The Maasai family members gathered around as the warriors jumped, and with all of us together like this, it felt like we were a part of their tribe.

When the men stopped jumping my daddy said, "Caleb, ask if any of these warriors would be willing to sell me his personal knife around his waist." Caleb, who got a big kick out of both of my parents, laughed. Then he translated and immediately all the men started pulling their knives and spears out to bargain with my daddy, which thrilled him and tickled my mom. The two of them examined the unique artistry of each carved handle and leather sheath as they decided on which one to get. Once they chose their favorite knife, Caleb negotiated the price with the warrior it belonged to, and my daddy paid. As the warrior handed the knife over to my daddy and he looked at his new purchase, I saw in his eyes the look of a young boy's excitement over such a special prize.

Daddy talked about this prize for years: "I bought a knife straight off a Maasai warrior in Tanzania, and let me tell you, they are fierce! No one messes with the Maasai," he'd say with a twinkle in his eye. "All the other tribes respect them."

I still have the knife to this day.

Before leaving the Maasai homestead, we took pictures with our new friends, then loaded back into the Land Cruiser, all of us reeking like the large dark room we'd stood inside. As we rolled down the dirt path back toward the main road, my mom spoke through her laughter, "Well, they ended up being so nice after all the warnings and stories of how dangerous they could be. I *knew* they were getting ready to kill us when we all filed into their dark hut. No one would have ever known where we disappeared to in this fog." She said what we had all been thinking. All at once we roared with laughter, then all admitted how we had been afraid and had wondered if those were going to be the last moments of our lives. Caleb also thought this, he admitted, laughing as we drove off. Until this day he had always kept a respectable distance from the Maasai. Certainly he'd never stepped inside one of their huts before, so he was a little shocked that our adventure played out the way it did. If not for my daddy's childlike enthusiasm to go on this adventure, none of us would have participated in it. Sometimes it takes an outsider's perspective to show you a treasure that's right before your eyes.

Clean and refreshed, we continued on our expedition the next day, and everywhere we went on safari my parents told any traveler or local who would listen: "Caleb, our son-in-law, speaks fluent Swahili like a native. He was born and raised right here in Tanzania on the shores of Lake Victoria." Then they would turn to Caleb and say, "Say something in Swahili so they can hear you speak."

Caleb would blush and laugh quietly with embarrassment. At the same time, he enjoyed the praise from my parents, because he loved them and wanted to please them. So he would do anything they told him to. "What do you want me to say?"

Each day of our safari, Caleb acted like a young boy who was excited to show us his heart and the country that he loved. We made a special stop at his childhood home on Lake Victoria—a place Caleb wanted to show my parents as badly as they wanted to see it—then we stayed at a wonderful, tented camp called Kirawira Serena Camp. Here the luxury tents had the traditional zipper entrance, but sat on wooden decks with private porches overlooking the great Serengeti. In the morning the staff would wake us by bringing our chai in a silver tea set on a silver tray to our private porch. Caleb and I would sit in our pajamas drinking hot chai while watching the wildebeest, zebra, and Grant's gazelle—a miraculous sight. One of the mornings we joined my parents on their porch and enjoyed our chai and coffee together. It's something magnificent to witness God's amazing creation and see the vast amount of animals He created perfectly. The fact He provides each animal with everything they need each and every day is even more outstanding, and it is extremely comforting to know God is in complete control.

At night, hot water bottles were placed in our king-size bed that was enclosed with a mosquito net hanging from the top of the tent and tucked into our mattress. The throaty growls of lions could be heard off in the distance, and it was romantic listening to these powerful animals in our cozy cocoon. Here Caleb poured his heart out to me and told me his vision for his new company and what the hunting camps he was preparing to build over the next year would look like. It was during these talks that I accepted Caleb was really going to build a hunting camp. I accepted that this was his dream, despite what I declared before we got married about not wanting to live in Africa and not wanting Caleb to be a professional hunter who would be gone for long periods of time. *I love him, and it's worth it to have a good marriage,* I told myself. *I might as well help him plan the nicest and best camp possible since it looks like I'll be living here several months out of the year.*

So I did. From then on Caleb and I dreamed about and planned together for his new hunting company, taking notes about what we loved and appreciated as guests at this tented camp, which could not have been a more desirable place to be on a safari. During our days here, we saw the Great Migration of wildebeest, zebra, Grant's gazelle, Thompson's gazelle, eland, and impala. My parents had been hoping to see the Great Migration of over 1.5 million wildebeest and 200,000 zebras since we'd planned our trip, so Caleb had picked our travel dates to give them the best chance. The fact that we did see this mass migration of animals through the plains was a spectacular gift straight from God, and the purest evidence of His supernatural timing.

During these three weeks with my parents, we not only encountered animals but met the people who make Africa so beautiful. The workers at every resort adored my parents because my parents were genuinely interested in them. My mom would ask all about their lives, their families, and where they were from. It didn't matter whether it was the resort manager or the person who cleaned the rooms, my parents thought everyone working did such a fantastic job and that the resort couldn't run without them. And they would tell these people and everyone else so.

My mom never complained once. Not once. I was wondering how she would do, knowing she was not a fan of traveling. Her beautiful attitude touched me, and I have thought of it many times when I've wanted to complain, hoping I could resemble her amazing grace. When the trip was over, she laughed. "Well, I made it, and I'm alive. I've been praying for months, a nervous wreck about this trip, and the Lord took care of me. I did it. I did it afraid, but I did it!"

"We're proud of you, Mom," Caleb and I told her.

Caleb adored my parents and was proud to finally show them his home country he had vividly described to them over the last thirteen years. It was a trip of a lifetime. Caleb had never stayed at any of the fancy resorts before, so it was as exciting for him as it was for us. He was protective of me and took amazing care of my parents and me, packing up the Land Cruiser with our luggage after each stop, making sure we had anything we might want or need for the day like drinks, snacks, and lunch. When there was a flat tire, he fixed it quickly. The whole trip he was attentive toward me, holding my hand often, and pulling me in close, proud to let people know I was his girl.

When it came time for my parents to leave Africa, Caleb and I stayed to continue our travels. As we said our goodbyes, I knew the last three weeks had been a gift of wild and precious adventures, moments I would treasure for a lifetime.

And I do.

CHAPTER 14
CLARITY

For God has not given us the spirit of fear, but of power and of love and of a sound mind.

—*2 Timothy 1:7*

Once Caleb and I returned home from our fabulous two-month trip to Tanzania and Zimbabwe, we went right back to work. We continued to spend all of our free time together, and we also spent a lot of time with my family. We ate dinner at my parents' house usually once or twice a week, in addition to Sunday lunch with my whole family, and most weekends we got together with one of my sibling's families. Caleb never missed a family event, church, or any social outing with me. His new work hours were Monday through Friday from 8:00 a.m. to 5:00 p.m., and after his workday he'd follow me around the house as I put away clothes or as we cooked dinner, telling me all about his clients and outfitters he was working with and his ideas for trips he wanted us to embark on. He knew I loved our travels and adventures, and he'd ask for my opinion on his ideas. At night he'd share his hopes and dreams with me for our future. He continued to ask me for children, and my mom even began to ask when I'd be ready. Regarding this though, I still had concerns because of the confusion I faced about Caleb's mind games and lies. I was also deeply concerned that the other side of him was getting bigger and stronger. His other side that had a cold heart. I was at a loss for what to do.

Continuing to pray to God to give me clarity, that fall I bought a Christian book called *His Needs, Her Needs.* I asked Caleb if we could read it together and if he would read it to me while I listened. One night when we were in bed, he started reading the book aloud. He didn't get very far when he simply closed the book, pretty hard, and said matter-of-factly, "I am not reading this."

I asked, "Why?"

"Because you and I both know that you are meeting my needs, and I am not meeting yours...and I don't want to meet your needs."

I was hurt. I asked, "Why would you not want to meet my needs so we can have the best marriage possible?"

Instead of answering my question he said, "You're not going to change me, and I'm not going to talk about this anymore."

I was a sinking ship. Sinking, and Caleb seemed happy with the situation. He knew I was sinking. I felt like he knew he was driving me insane, and now he was telling me clearly that he was not going to stop, nor did he care. My life felt out of control.

Feeling desperate, I called my brother Bill the next day

while running errands. I remember exactly where I was while driving down the interstate in my BMW while I was talking to him. My brother and I were very close, and Caleb was one of his best friends.

I was at the end of my rope as I confessed, "I feel like I might be having a nervous breakdown. I think I am losing it. Sometimes, I feel like Caleb is driving me insane."

Bill said very quietly, "I am not surprised."

I was surprised at his response, "What do you mean?" I asked.

"Caleb is selfish. He neglects you, and you do all the work in the marriage to try to make it good. He gives you a little attention only when it is convenient for him." We had never spoken about my marriage before. Again, it was soothing to my soul to hear the truth from someone, anyone. And just as it had been when I confided in the young couple in Africa and in Phil and Sheri', it comforted me to hear someone else tell me I wasn't crazy for feeling the way I did. Bill knew both of us and loved both of us, and I knew he was telling me the truth. I loved Caleb and I was loyal to him. I did not want someone talking bad about him, I wanted truthfulness. That is what Bill gave me. When I got off the phone with him, I felt I had gained a touch of the clarity I was praying for.

But nothing changed in my marriage.

CHAPTER 15
A DISCOVERY

Ask and it will be given to you; seek and you will find;
knock and the door will be opened to you.

—Matthew 7:7

The following year, in 2001, Caleb was busy preparing for the upcoming summer of safaris with his new company. He had gone to Africa one time, the fall of the year before, without me, and I had gone to Mexico, out of rebellion, so I didn't have to stay home alone. When we both came home, I was distant. Once again, Caleb pursued me with his all. He came to pick me up at the airport with roses and a beautiful sapphire and diamond ring he had purchased in Africa, declaring his love for me. I was the focus of all his attention as he devoted himself to cooking us dinners and romancing me like I was the most beautiful woman in the world. This was the typical pattern we seemed to live by for the past nine years. He would try to drive me insane with mind games by controlling me, or by completely ignoring me. Then when I would pull back and get some distance and try to get clarity, or have a scare, like the man at the end of my bed, or someone confronting me like the couple in Tanzania about how badly he treated me, he would flip back to the man I fell in love with. Swooping in like a prince charming with flowers and proclamations of his love and how he wanted to lead our family toward Christ. He would say God had blessed him, and he had not appreciated me the way he should have; the dance went on, just like it had for years. Yes, pursuing me with everything in him, the chase would be back on, and our marriage would be really good and back on track for months. I was becoming numb to the two extremes of my marriage.

This year he said he wanted to go to Africa and prepare the hunting camp for his new company before I came. The property was rough: no water, no electricity, and no tents or bathrooms. His plan was to oversee the building of the luxury camp. He thought I should stay on Signal Mountain for June and July, working, and then come to Tanzania and spend the rest of the summer with him leading hunting safari trips.

I was not happy with him leaving for so long again, and I told him I wanted to go with him. But after I voiced my opinion, I knew he would do exactly what he wanted to do. He was going to do what he wanted, and it would not help to fight. It never had, and believe me we had fought hard about these issues. We could both hold our own in the battles, as strong willed and stubborn as we both were.

On the night before he left for Africa, we were on our way to my parents' house and Caleb said, "I never want to go away from you for this long again." I stayed quiet. This would be the second time in our nine years of being married to be away from each other for over two weeks.

"Why are you not saying anything?" Caleb asked.

"Because we have had this same type of conversation before, Caleb. You say things will change, I get happy and hopeful, and it never changes. I will just wait this time and see if you really do what you say you will do. I am tired of playing this game." He shook his head, and I could tell he was mad that this was my response.

Instead of fighting, we stopped talking about it.

The next morning, Wednesday, June 6, as Caleb packed up the last few things for his trip, he started going on and on again about how much he was going to miss me and how he didn't want us to be apart for this long ever again. I smiled through the hurt, hoping he was telling me the truth and that he really would change. It seemed a part of him wanted to, but it never lasted.

We got into the car, and I rode with him for the two hours to the Atlanta airport. On the way, we talked about his plans for building out his new camp, and about what I would get done before joining him in Africa. Caleb and I had a great friendship. We confided in each other and discussed business and decisions we would be making. We were both extremely confident and enjoyed hard work; we understood each other in that aspect. But Caleb had played mind games with me for so long. I was struggling. I had poured all I had into making our marriage a good one. I told myself that no one else could perceive what I was feeling. I would never look weak, that was not my personality. I could handle it all and have a good attitude, even if I was withering away inside. And I was determined to do just that. Caleb made sure he was always in control of me, saying very little. He knew I did not want him to leave me for so long, but he didn't care. He would give me a little attention and hope for our marriage just when I thought I could not continue.

We got to the airport, and I walked him to his gate. We hugged to say goodbye, then Caleb started crying, which was out of character for him. He told me I was everything to him, he loved me so much, and he never wanted to be apart again for such a long time. He confessed he knew it was not a good decision to leave me for this long, and he was not going to do this again. I had great compassion for him as tears flowed from his eyes. I thought, *Wow. He is serious this time. He really is convicted.* I told him I was finally ready to start the family he had been begging me to start for the last five years. We had been talking the last several months about when to start a family. I had just turned twenty-nine years old, and we had already decided to go off birth control when he left for Africa. So I reminded him that I would come to Tanzania ready to start trying to have a baby. "I'm ready," said Caleb, smiling through his tears. He'd been waiting for a baby for a long time, I knew. As we stood at the gate waiting for him to board his plane, his open sincerity to change was now bringing me peace about having a baby too. After all, I wanted several children and knew I needed to start trying in case it took a while to conceive.

Then he wept, and not just a tear or two. He was not in control of his emotions, and I was surprised as I tried to comfort him as we were saying goodbye. Caleb's flight was called to board, and we kissed our final goodbye. As I made my way back to the car, I thought about how sincere he was in our conversation. He called me from the plane once he was seated and told me how much he loved me and again told me he would not know what to do without me. Caleb confessed he wanted to be the husband he knew he needed to be. I told him how much I loved him, that I was so happy we would not be apart again for so long, how he seemed sincere, and how that meant so much to me. Caleb sent me an email as soon as he landed in Africa. He would write me love notes throughout our marriage and in his email, he confessed how much he loved me and told me of all his future dreams with me. He wrote that he would look at my picture every day and would call and email me and would be looking forward to seeing me in Tanzania before long. He was thankful I was finally ready to start a family and have a baby with him. God had blessed us, and he was so thankful for me. I was the best wife and his best friend. I was appreciative at his outpouring of affection and his promises to not be apart anymore.

I felt incredibly loved.

However, while Caleb was away, I was lonely. During the next month we wrote emails, and he would call me often. He went to Zimbabwe first to acquire all the supplies he needed. He stayed with his partner Saul for two weeks and then drove to Tanzania with hunting trucks and supplies to build a new camp in the Selous. On the phone and in emails he was loving. However, as June turned into July, Caleb's emails and phone calls became less frequent. *He's in the middle of nowhere. I'm expecting too much*, I thought. So I tried not to be hurt by his dwindling communication. I just told him I was lonely and that I missed him when he called.

My night terrors continued. I never knew when they

would come, so when he was gone, I did not want to sleep. I would stay awake until around three or four in the morning, and then finally, I would need sleep so badly that I would crash. I never knew when my night terrors would torment me. I begged and asked, "God please take these from me. Please help me. Cover me with your protection."

I was suffering. Suffering in sleep, and suffering in being manipulated and controlled. Caleb had for years tried to convince me he treated me with respect, even though deep down I knew he was driving me insane. He'd become an expert at not being direct with me, but saying things or acting a certain way to manipulate me into doing what he wanted me to do. It was a game. I was trying to make him happy because he was not content. It was like trying to fill an empty void. No matter what I did, it made no difference, but I kept trying. It wore me down, this invisible battle I was fighting alone. I did not understand what was happening. I was pouring myself out, and he was taking all of me without much reciprocation in return. I would get discouraged and pull away to get distance from him to try to get some sanity, then he would decide he needed me and would pursue me hard. If we were apart, I would feel like I was getting some innate strength back, but then he would chase and woo me with gifts and attention and I would fall back into his control. Because I loved him and wanted my marriage to be successful, I felt like it was my responsibility to fix my marriage. It was actually sick the way our relationship had developed.

He was drawn to my strength from the beginning—and it was the one thing he wanted to take away from me the most.

In July I prepared to go to Fripp Island, South Carolina,

with my whole family; about sixty of us in all. We had gone
every year since I was a little girl, so I told Caleb I would
join him in Tanzania after my family vacation. At the beach
I felt unrest and a heaviness in my spirit about my marriage.
So, as soon as we got home, I called the travel agent we
used and asked her to start looking at flights to Africa. She
mentioned that Caleb's next hunters had just booked their
flights. She revealed that it was two ladies and a man. I was
stunned—but kept my composure. Caleb had told me before he left for Africa that it was a single man by himself and
that no one else would be on the hunt. He told me it would
be best to come to Tanzania after that hunt, since it was
a one-on-one. I asked if they had just decided to join the
hunt. "No," the travel agent said. "It's been the three hunters since the original booking over a year ago." My stomach dropped. *Why was Caleb lying to me—again? Everything
was lies...*I was exhausted from his deceit, and also furious.
Caleb was across the world and was having two women he
hadn't told me about come on a hunting trip with him. The
trip would be two women and two men including Caleb.
Does Caleb intend to have an affair? My mind spun. He had
never been late coming home when he worked for the police, and he spent almost all of his free time with me so,
truthfully, I didn't think an affair was ever possible before.

However, I knew something was wrong. Very wrong. My
spirit was on high alert. I wanted to speak to Caleb immediately but would have to wait for him to call me because
he was using a satellite phone that he only turned on when
he needed to make a call. Then he'd turn it back off. As I
waited, I stewed. I emailed him to call me.

I was ready to know the truth.

CHAPTER 16

LIES

There are six things the Lord hates, seven that are detestable to Him: haughty eyes, a lying tongue, hands that shed innocent blood, a heart that devises wicked schemes, feet that are quick to rush into evil, a false witness who pours out lies and a person who stirs up conflict in the community.
—Proverbs 6:16–19

"Why did you lie to me?" I asked Caleb when he called me. It was the day after I emailed him. I was at home.

"What are you talking about?" he asked.

"Your upcoming hunt," I shot back. "You said it was only going to be one man for the eighteen days, but I found out two women are going also."

Caleb waited a moment before speaking. "You're overreacting," he said. "The women booked late, and I don't even actually know if they're coming or not."

I literally couldn't believe he was saying this. "I spoke

to the travel agent, Caleb, and she confirmed that the two women booked their hunting trip over a year ago." I was furious, and my voice was shaking.

"No. You misunderstood her. And why does it matter if they booked early or late? Do you really not trust me enough to not cheat on you? We've been married nine years. Why would I lie to you or cheat on you now after being faithful all this time? I can't believe you, Anne G., for accusing me of something like that. I've tried to be a good husband to you, and I came to set up camp for you so it would be nice when you arrived."

Why would he try to keep something like that from me? I had been apart from him for two months, and I knew he was setting me up. I knew he had lied again, and I was mad.

I said, "I am coming to Africa—*now*." He got furious at me.

He said, "If you can't trust me, I think we need some time apart. I am not sure if I am happy being married to someone who can't trust me after all these years." I was stunned. Completely stunned. Not much else was said. He was determined to get his way. He silenced me quickly to be on the defense—again. I could not believe the implication of divorce had come into play. I got off the phone knowing my marriage was on the rocks. *How could this man who proclaimed his love for me all the time tell me he did not know if he was happy being married, and it was because I did not trust him?*

I was spinning. I wondered, *Lord, what should I do?*

The next moment things became clear. I immediately called the travel agent and booked a flight to Africa. I packed my bags and took off. On August 3, I arrived in Dar es Salaam, Tanzania. Caleb's assistant Richard told Caleb that I was already on my way to Tanzania the next time they spoke on the phone. Richard had also arranged for Caleb's coworker and friend Abdul to pick me up at the airport. In addition to meeting guests upon their arrival, Abdul's job was to run errands in town while Caleb was at camp, and schedule flights for the private plane you had to take to get in and out of camp. When Abdul picked me up, I wanted to get on the private plane right away, but it was expensive. I was reluctant to wait, but Abdul convinced me to wait less than thirty-six hours until the clients (the man and two women) arrived so I could fly with them into camp, and therefore not waste money on an extra trip.

While waiting for the private charter, I went to stay at the house we rented during the hunting season. A professional hunter named Ryan, who Caleb and I'd been friends with for years, was staying there also. He was between hunting trips and was waiting to meet our new clients in town, and then he would fly into camp with us. That afternoon, Ryan and I went to the Sea Cliff Hotel, where our clients usually stayed, and where we could socialize with other hunters and outfitters. The luxurious hotel, perched beautifully overlooking the Indian Ocean, had a new manager named Liesel who was around my age. She was from England, and when we met we hit it off and immediately became good friends. She was absolutely lovely. I spent the afternoon, evening, and all of the next day with Liesel and Ryan. I was feeling heavy about my marriage, but I keep this tucked away in my heart.

When the hunters arrived, I learned they were from Texas and that the man, Dan, was in his fifties, and the women, Grace and Charlotte, were in their mid thirties. The women were cute and vivacious. When we met at our house for lunch, I casually asked if they'd ever met Caleb, and they said no. However, they did say they couldn't believe this was really happening, that they'd been planning this trip with Dan for over a year, and that they were so excited. My heart sank hearing this truth, even though I already knew the truth, regardless of what Caleb had said. His truth versus the real truth never seemed to line up in our marriage. I was deflated in my own heart. *Why was there such a thread of deceit in my marriage? Why can I not fight it out, manipulate it out, be kind to it, rage against it, be absolutely perfect, be indifferent?* I had tried it all over the last nine years, and nothing worked. I was exhausted from trying to make my marriage successful. It was as if I was rowing the boat of our marriage, and Caleb never used his oar except every once in a while, when I was about to give up. I was rowing in circles and becoming more and more confused, the more I pulled both my and Caleb's weight. I could *not* figure out why he refused to try at all.

Later that afternoon on August 5, Ryan, the three clients, and I flew into camp. Despite everything going on, I was excited to see Caleb. We had been apart for so long, and I missed him. When I got off the plane, Caleb was sitting in a Land Cruiser truck with the doors removed and his feet propped up on the dash. He did not get out of his seat to greet me. I was disappointed he was being so rude. He was respectful to me most of the time, so this was hurtful. He had the trackers load my suitcase in the truck. Then he said in a very cold voice, "Hello." I went over to give him a hug, and he stood up and barely touched me.

The ride to camp was quiet. We were alone in our own truck; the clients had loaded up in a different truck with another driver. I said, "I missed you—I'm so glad to see you."

When he finally spoke, there was rage in his voice.

"I want a divorce," he said, furious and unable to hide it.

Why is he so angry? I wondered. *I guess he is mad I came without him knowing I was on my way.* He rarely had a temper with me, only in very heated arguments. That was not his style. *Why had he confessed before he left that I was his life and that he would not travel away from me for a long time ever again?*

I asked, "What happened since you left me, when you were crying at the airport telling me you wanted to not be apart anymore, and you wanted to have a baby?"

He was hard hearted toward me, that is the best way to describe it. I had glimpses of his hard-heartedness toward me before in the last nine years of marriage, but never to this degree. This was a completely different person. Riding beside him now to camp, I felt like a stranger was talking to me—I did not recognize him at all. In fact, he had a completely different personality.

I thought, *He'll calm down. He just didn't like that I surprised him by coming early. He'll get over it.*

I couldn't have been more wrong.

CHAPTER 17
STRONGHOLD

The Lord is my rock, my fortress and my deliverer; my God is my rock, in whom I take refuge, my shield and the horn of my salvation, my stronghold.

—Psalms 18:2

Praise Him, sun and moon; praise Him all you shining stars. Praise Him, you highest heavens and you waters above the skies. Let them praise the name of the Lord, for at His command they were created, and He established them for ever and ever—

—Psalms 148:3–6

The only two books I took with me to Africa were my Bible, and *The Power of a Praying Wife*. I had prayed over my marriage from the time I was a young girl. I knew God could do anything and I was hopeful, but I was confused. Caleb had told me half truths for so long. I think he loved me as much as he was capable of. As far as I could tell, he loved me more than anyone else in his life, including his immediate family. So, I prayed. At camp, I tried to act normal—loving and respectful toward him, while he was hateful to me. When he looked at me, I saw another person looking back at me, and I was afraid of him for the first time in my marriage. This was a totally different man, nothing about him was familiar. We stayed with the clients and Ryan, the professional hunter, and Caleb certainly tried to stay away from me. He treated me horribly in front of the clients, and even worse in our tent.

The first night I arrived, he made love to me. I assumed it would make everything better, but it was as if he was a stranger. As we were going to sleep, I asked if he would pray with me.

"No," he replied, "I am not going to pray with you anymore, so don't ask me again."

I was overwhelmed and heartbroken at his declaration. We had always prayed together every night for the last nine years, not to mention the five years spent dating. He was like a machine with no love. Nothing was familiar about him.

The next morning, my first morning in camp, Caleb took the clients out hunting and he left me at camp. Through all the hunting trips I had been on, I had never stayed at camp. I never had the desire to kill anything myself, but I was always on the truck enjoying the outdoors, enjoying the clients, and most of all, enjoying the adventure. I was *not* a stay-at-camp girl. Like, it never happened. I couldn't believe he left me. This was a first.

I spent the day praying over my marriage, and devouring the Bible and *The Power of a Praying Wife*. On my knees, I cried out, asking God to heal my marriage, and I prayed the prayers out loud from *The Power of a Praying Wife*. I didn't understand why Caleb had switched so suddenly from wanting to start a family to wanting a divorce. *Why such an extreme?*

When he returned to camp later that afternoon I asked, "How was your day?"

He barely answered.

That evening, I had dinner with the clients in the beautiful thatched building beside the river running through our camp. As the clients, Ryan, Caleb, and I sat around the big dining table, we watched the hippos in the river and listened to them grunting in communication. It was lovely, but Caleb didn't address me or communicate with me much at all, which was degrading, especially in front of the clients.

So later that night, I went out alone on the big rock down by the river to try to gain some perspective on things. There was a campfire going on the rock with some chairs beside it. I took a seat next to the flames, feeling the heat on my legs as the hippos nearby grunted deeply, splashing in the water. I gazed up at God's magnificent creation of stars, who were praising and worshiping Him along with me. And I was asking my God to help me. I stared at the cluster of stars known as the Southern Cross, that seemed to have been perfectly placed in the Tanzanian sky for just me at that moment, as my heart desperately cried out to Jesus. I was afraid for the first time in my marriage, and it was sobering why I was so afraid. Caleb scared me the way he looked at me with such hatred. I felt like he wanted me dead. *That's a crazy thought*, I told myself. *Lord, why do I keep thinking that?* I wondered. *Am I losing it? Is it all in my mind?*

A few minutes later, Charlotte came down to the fire. "May I join you?" she asked.

"Of course," I said, happy to have some company.

She asked how I was doing. By now everyone at camp knew things were bad between Caleb and me, so there was no reason to pretend.

"Not so good," I said. "I'm praying. Asking God to heal my marriage."

She asked what I believed, and I told her I was a Christian. With excitement she said she was a Christian too. We began talking about the Lord, and we connected over our simple conversation of faith in Jesus Christ. It was amazing the Lord had sent me someone to connect with in the middle of the bush in Tanzania. I told her, God had sent her to be with me on this trip, I had no doubt. I asked her to please remember to pray for me, I really needed it. Charlotte said she would. It was refreshing to have a normal conversation with someone, and to worship the Lord and see all his amazing creations in the depths of Africa.

After I spent time with Charlotte, I went to tell Caleb I needed to make a call from the satellite phone to let my parents know I had arrived in camp safely. He set up the phone off to the far side of camp in the dark of the night. It was always set up away from camp so no one could hear others' conversations. I called my parents. My daddy answered the phone, and I told him I had arrived. He was happy to hear from me and his voice was jolly. He asked how everything was in Tanzania.

I said, "I don't know what is wrong, Daddy, Caleb is being really mean to me, I do not even recognize him. It's like he's a completely different person. He looks at me like he hates me, and he told me he wanted a divorce as soon as I got off the plane." My daddy asked me some questions, and I answered everything as truthfully as I could. This was the first time I had ever mentioned any problems in my marriage. Remember I mentioned my pride and my loyalty? He asked if it had been going on for long, and I answered, "He has been cold toward me before, but this is very different. I am not sure what is happening. He wanted to have a baby with me when he left the United States." Then I confessed, "I do not know who he is. When I look into his eyes, it's like he's a complete stranger, and I'm really afraid of him."

My daddy could hear the concern and the fear in my voice. And he knew that it was not typical of my personality to be fearful of anything. He took a moment to respond. Then, solemnly, he said, "Anne G., I am worried he is going to try to hurt you, he knows that area and no one would be able to find you if he did something to you. I do not trust Caleb. I want you to get a plane out of there and come home now."

When my daddy told me he was afraid Caleb was going to hurt me, everything in me agreed with what he was saying. I believe the Holy Spirit in my daddy and in me was confirming what my own thoughts had been. But I had prayed, and believed for years that God could heal my marriage. I didn't want to walk away from it without knowing I had given it my all. So I told my daddy, "I want to try to make my marriage work, and I can't get out of camp now because we're on an eighteen-day safari, and this is day two."

My father had never spoken about anyone hurting or killing anyone to me; we did not generally talk like that in my family. It was bizarre he was speaking what I had been thinking. So much was going on in my mind, I was trying to process it all, and I felt so alone on the other side of the world. My daddy loved Caleb like a son, so I did not expect him to confirm my own fears in my heart. He told me he loved me and to come home as soon as I could. I told him I loved him too. At that moment I realized how far away I was from home. Out in the middle of nowhere. And it was a sinking feeling knowing that no one knew how to get to me. I didn't even know exactly where I was on a map. I got off the phone and pondered for the next week what he had said. I kept thinking over and over that Caleb might kill me, and I was surprised my daddy was thinking the same thing. I was still praying constantly for God to do a mighty work and make all this go away.

Over the next few days, Caleb remained hateful. I quietly told him one night in our tent that he was scaring me, and that when he spoke it did not sound anything like his voice. He sounded and acted like a completely different person. He did not respond and when he looked at me, there was absolutely nothing in his eyes, like he had no soul. I had never experienced anything like this in my marriage. There was a complete division between us, a coldness, and there was a presence of something evil, I could feel it. Each time we interacted, whatever it was, it was as if he was a different person from my husband, and there was no warmth and no love.

I was afraid.

During that first week on safari, I went on a few of the hunts, but mostly stayed at camp to read my Bible and pray. I did not want to share my fears of Caleb with the other people in camp. I thought I would look cuckoo for cocoa puffs for sure. I continued to pretend to be in a good mood when everyone came in from their day of hunting. Each evening I enjoyed dinner with the clients. A week passed. Caleb continued to treat me disrespectfully in front of everyone.

In the middle of the second week of the hunt, I told Caleb I needed to call home when he set up the satellite phone to make phone calls himself. After dinner, in the dark area of the camp where he set up the phone, Caleb made his own calls, and then he called me over to come make my phone call. He was alone. As I walked up, I said gently to him in the darkness, "Caleb, you are very unhappy—I think you're depressed, and you have been for a long time." It was a raw moment, because we had not been talking much, but it was a pure moment of truth where we were speaking honestly; no blame, just the facts.

He looked at me and said, "What do you think would make me happy?"

"I don't know, I have been trying to make you happy for years, and I can't do it, no one can. Only you can do it, with the Lord's help."

"Why do you think I am unhappy?" he asked sincerely.

"I don't know. It is like a black hole, and no matter what I do, it is never enough." We stood there, close but not touching. Speaking as honest people who cared about each other. Both knowing it was an ultimate problem of his life and our marriage.

"I am not happy," he confessed, "and I don't know what to do to make myself happy."

"I know." I said somberly. And I did know. It had been the battle I had fought alone, trying to fix anything I could, desperately trying to make Caleb happy, and I was weary.

It was a sad moment of us sharing the truth of our hearts.

Caleb walked off, and I waited to hear him talking with someone back near the tents.

I called my brother Bill. I needed wisdom from someone who was thinking clearly to speak the truth to me. Bill loved me and he, like my daddy, also loved Caleb. He answered the phone. He asked how everything was with Caleb. "Not good," I said.

I told him Caleb wanted a divorce and had been mean to me since I got to Tanzania. "I'm afraid of him," I told Bill. "And I've never been afraid of Caleb since we have been together."

Bill told me how Daddy had come down to Bill's house the week before, after my phone call, to tell him how worried he was for me.

"I agree with Dad," said my brother. "I'm really worried about you."

"I know." I confided.

Bill said, "Caleb is cold blooded." He paused for a minute. "Dad and I are scared Caleb will try to kill you."

I said soberly, "I know, I am too." I was surprised that I was admitting my thoughts out loud, but at the same time I was thankful Bill was speaking the truth to me. I also was thankful these thoughts of mine were also my family's same thoughts. It confirmed I was not losing my mind, which was like drinking the living water of truth.

He asked me to come home right then, I told him it would be almost impossible to get a charter out, and it would also be very expensive. There was only a week left of the trip and I would fly out with the clients. He said I should try to get a plane out, but he could tell I was not ready to leave Caleb. I told him I was praying for God to heal my marriage. He told me he loved me and to call him when I got to Dar es Salaam.

Then we hung up.

I realized again how far I was away from home and the people who loved me.

CHAPTER 18
THE VISION

She gave this name to the Lord who spoke to her: "You are the God who sees me," for she said, "I have now seen the One who sees me."

—Genesis 16:13

Several days had gone by since my phone call with my brother. There were only two days left of the hunt. Caleb came in from hunting with his client, and I went to the skinning shed to meet them and see how their day went. I walked up and Caleb actually spoke to me. I was so happy I started thanking God in my heart. We were standing a few feet away from everyone else. Caleb looked at me, then said in a kind voice, "I'm getting ready to go sight in my gun. You want to go with me? Just the two of us?"

My heart leaped with excitement. *He's back*, I thought. *Here is my husband, finally. And he wants to be with me.* I started praying, *Thank You, Lord!* My heart was flooding with joy. I opened my mouth to say, "Yes!" But before I could say a word, I had a vision. All I can say is everything in me knew it to be real. It was as if it actually happened at that moment. I can still see clearly in my mind what happened to this day.

I could see exactly where we were on the river, as I had been there before. It was just the two of us, Caleb and me. I was standing on a large rock overlooking the river. I was full of joy, smiling big. As I looked out over the beautiful river with wild hippos dotting the water, I turned around to look back at my husband. Caleb was standing on the driver's side of the Land Cruiser truck with his rifle pointed at me, and he shot me. My vision ended.

I had never had a vision before, and what I saw almost took me to my knees. I closed my mouth and thought I was going to fall over from my body going weak. It was very real, like I had experienced it in real life. I was shaking badly and quickly went back to my tent, overwhelmed. I got there and was shaking uncontrollably, and I started praying, *Oh God, please save my life.* I curled up on the bed, rattled, soberly realizing—I was in big trouble.

A few minutes later Caleb came into the tent. "Are you ready?" he said.

I was still shaking but didn't want him to know it was because I was terrified, so I pretended to be sick. "No, I'm not feeling well," I said softly.

"You sure?" he asked casually, his voice pleasant as if this were a normal day at home on Signal Mountain, and as if he hadn't been hateful to me for the last two and a half weeks.

"Yes. I'm sure," I said.

"Okay. Suit yourself." Then he left the tent.

Lying in bed, my entire world was spinning. I was so

certain now of what Caleb's intentions were, that nothing and no one could change my mind. My father, my brother, and now I had had a vision I knew was from God, all warning me. *Oh, God, please have mercy on me and get me out of here. Cover me in the shelter of Your mighty wings. Please get me home safely and don't let Caleb kill me*, I begged.

For the next two days, I stayed away from Caleb as much as I could before we flew out of the Selous. Every fiber in my being knew he wanted me dead. On the last day of the hunt, I called my parents to let them know I would be flying out of the Selous and heading back to Dar es Salaam the next day. They told me to come home as soon as I could.

Caleb and I spoke in our tent the night before we left the Selous hunting camp. He said he was going on a hunt in another part of Tanzania out of Arusha in two days. His plan was to fly to Arusha after the clients left to go back to the United States. He said I needed to go home, and he would divorce me when hunting season was over. I was not speaking back much. I was overwhelmed wondering what was happening. When he asked if I was going home, I simply responded, "I don't want our marriage to end."

The next morning we flew out of the hunting camp. Caleb, Ryan, and I got settled at the house we had rented in town while the clients went to the Sea Cliff Hotel, the plan being that Caleb, Ryan, and I would meet the clients for dinner at the Sea Cliff. As we were getting ready, I noticed there was a perfume bottle in our bedroom that was not there the day I left eighteen days earlier. I thought that was unusual. I picked it up and asked Caleb what woman would be staying in our room when we were not there. He said it was probably another professional hunter's wife, and he had no idea. But it piqued my interest, and it stayed on my mind. So I asked Ryan in the next room whose bottle it could be, but he said he had no idea whose it could have been.

We got ready and went to the Sea Cliff to have dinner. We had a large outdoor table overlooking the sea, seated for six. There was live entertainment and Liesel, my good friend who was the hotel manager, came to visit with me at the outside bar. I introduced her to the clients, and we chatted. She could tell I was not myself and asked if I was all right. I told her things were not good between Caleb and me. So Liesel stuck close to me and introduced me to the entertainer for the night, who was a singer with a lovely voice. We spoke and enjoyed visiting.

When it was time to sit down, Caleb sat at one end of the table, and I sat at the other, which had never happened before. We had always sat next to each other, for the nine years we were married and the many years we had dated. It felt as if we were so divided, and I was broken. I remember thinking, *It is over. My marriage is over. I have no control of anything in my life.* Caleb acted as if I did not exist. As we sat and ate, the man sang beautiful music. My soul was hopeless. Then the singer said he had a special song he wanted to dedicate to a beautiful lady and special friend who was here tonight. "Angie" by The Rolling Stones. As he started singing the haunting song, it felt like God was telling me, "Your life is falling apart, you are alone on the other side of the world from where you are from, but I see you, I love you, and you are beautiful to me. I am the God who sees you." A single tear ran down my face as I listened to the music and thought about my life that was so out of control.

A small, kind gesture from a stranger who had no idea what I had been living out for the last nine years was exactly what I needed; I needed a simple, kind gesture like I needed breath in my lungs. It was God speaking to me. "I am here, you are not alone. I am making a way for you in the desert. You are mine." *Oh Lord Jesus, Father God, what am I going to do?* As much as I was afraid of Caleb, this other part of me wanted to believe he would never really hurt me, and maybe our marriage could be healed.

After dinner, Caleb went and started playing blackjack in one of the back rooms. I visited with the clients, some other hunters from other hunting companies, and Liesel. I tried to put on a brave face, pretending everything was okay. Then someone privately came to me and asked me how things were going with Caleb; they acted like they understood how bad it was. I am not sure why, but I confessed to them that I could not figure out why he was acting so mean to me and that he told me he wanted a divorce when I arrived in Tanzania. This person asked me if there was any way he could be cheating on me.

"No," I said, "I do not think so." They looked at me with a sad face. "What?" I said, "If you know something, please tell me. I have been praying for God to show me, so if you know anything, I need to know now. I am supposed to go on another hunt with him tomorrow to Arusha, or go home to the United States, and I am trying to decide what to do."

They quietly told me most of the people there that night, except me, knew Caleb had his very young Zimbabwean mistress in camp before I came. He had to pay to charter her out the same day I arrived because I came early and surprised him. That is why he had been so angry at me since I had arrived. As I was hearing these words, it is sad to admit I was stunned. I never thought he would actually have an affair. I was spinning in my thoughts. I thanked them for being honest with me, and promised I would never tell anyone who it was that told me.

I remember trying to act like my world had not suddenly crashed down on me as everyone mingled in the open air of the night. The next hour was a blur. I was pretending like I was present in the conversations going on around me, but all I heard was noise. When it was late and almost time to leave, I walked to where Caleb was playing blackjack in another part of the hotel. It was the first time I had seen him since I knew the truth.

When I looked at him sitting and playing at a table across the room, something strange happened. I always felt love when I looked at Caleb. For the first time, I just saw a person. He was not my husband anymore. I think the Lord knew He had to do something to cover my heart, and that is what He did. It felt as if a cover slid over my heart the moment I laid eyes on Caleb, and my feelings for him switched off as quickly as a light switch. I saw it happen in my mind's eye, and it surprised me. For nine years of marriage, I had loved this person for better or worse. Suddenly, when I saw him, it was as if he were a stranger, an outer shell of someone I did not know. My heart was not Caleb's anymore from that moment on, and it would never be again. No longer did I think he was handsome and wonderful.

When I saw him, I saw a stranger.

When we got back to the house, I did not want to touch Caleb in bed, even with my foot. He was a complete stranger to me now, and it was weird being in bed with him. *How could I have been married to this man I did not know?* He had a whole different life I was completely unaware of. *What else does he hold in secret?* Caleb fell asleep, and I waited for hours before I snuck out of the house with the satellite phone. I went into the yard in the deadness of the night. There were dogs barking, and I could hear people talking and laughing from a local bar—city life. We had a brick wall with broken glass cemented along the top and it wrapped around our house. It was the customary style of wall in East African cities used to keep people from climbing over, but I was still afraid. I called my brother. I told him what I had found out. He said he was not surprised Caleb had a girl-friend, and he told me there was no reason to stay and join Caleb in Arusha for the next hunt. He said that he did not trust Caleb and told me that whatever I did, I should not tell Caleb I knew anything about his girlfriend.

I agreed and thought there might be a chance I could hold my tongue.

CHAPTER 19
AN ANGEL APPEARS

Where can I go from Your Spirit?
Where can I flee from Your presence?
If I go up to the heavens, You are there;
if I make my bed in the depths, You are there.
If I rise on the wings of the dawn,
if I settle on the far side of the sea,
even there Your hand will guide me,
Your right hand will hold me fast.
If I say, "Surely the darkness will hide me
and the light become night around me,"
even the darkness will not be dark to You
the night will shine like the day,
for darkness is as light to You.
*   —Psalms 138:7–12*

From the moment I heard Caleb was cheating on me, it is like God Almighty filled my spirit. I cannot explain it. I slept maybe an hour or two that night, and I woke up early and took a driver from our house to the airport of the private charter company without telling a soul where I was going. I walked into the airport and told the lady who was working that I needed a list of all the flights our safari company had completed in the last two months. She told me she could not get that information for me because it was private. I told her my name and that I owned the company, and said we would not be using them for their services anymore unless I received the information I was asking for—immediately. The woman left to speak to someone else, then returned. She said she could let me look through their logbook, but she would not be able to go through it herself, as it would take a long time. I told her I would be happy to do that. So, I took the binder to a table by myself and started looking for the dates around the time I came to Tanzania, because I knew Caleb had to fly his girlfriend out of camp for me to fly into camp. First, I found where he flew her into camp; she was the only person on the plane. It was a day that I was with my family at the beach. Caleb knew I would not be coming on that day; I had never missed that trip. The paperwork had her name as identified on her passport, her passport number, and the country she was from—Zimbabwe—and her birthday. She was twenty years old. I was twenty-nine and he was thirty-three. She was thirteen years younger than him. Next I found the flight she flew out of our camp on, which was the same day I arrived. I asked if I could get two copies of the log information showing our safari company; Caleb paid for the charter, and she was the only person on the plane in and out of the camp. I hit the jackpot. I knew he had cheated on me, and I had proof in writing of the girl he flew in who was not a client nor a hunter on the calendar. I had her complete name and her passport number.

Israel, the Lord who created you says, "Do not be afraid—I will save you. I have called you by name—you are mine. When you pass through the deep waters, I will be with you; your troubles will not overwhelm you. When you pass through fire, you will not be burned, the hard trials that have come will not hurt you.

—Isaiah 43:1–5

Next I asked where I could go to book an international flight back to the United States. The lady behind the desk told me to go to the Sheraton Hotel in town, a fancy place downtown in Dar es Salam. I'd stayed there the year before with Caleb and my parents when they traveled with us. It was where the president of Tanzania and the diplomats from other countries stayed if they were in town.

In the basement there was a travel agency and airline office where I could book a flight home. With this information I zipped to the outside of the airport where my driver was waiting for me.

"Could you please take me to the Sheraton Hotel and wait for me there?" I asked as I hopped into the car. Pulling up at the front door of the Sheraton Hotel, the Tanzania flag was proudly hung, and the hotel gleamed of prominence. I hurried down to the basement, found the office, then got in line. When I stepped up to the desk I asked when the earliest flight was out of Dar es Salam to Chattanooga, Tennessee, United States. She said there was a flight that night, which was great news, except I learned the only ticket available was for business class, so it was more expensive. Also, this flight was set to land at Gatwick Airport in London, but my connecting flight was out of Heathrow Airport, which was a little less than an hour away from Gatwick by car.

I told the lady I would buy the ticket; what other choice did I have? I was ready to get home and away from Caleb. The travel agent told me to give her a few minutes so she could get my seat confirmed, and I could go to the waiting area.

Walking to the waiting area I silently prayed, *Holy Spirit, I don't know if I'm doing the right thing. I need You to guide me. How in the world will I get from Gatwick to Heathrow? Please help me.*

The waiting area was a small space, with only a few chairs. There was an attractive, well-dressed man who looked to be in his mid-thirties waiting also. When I walked in, he stood up to offer me his seat. His accent revealed he was American.

"No, I'm okay," I said. Then he insisted I sit in his seat, and I thanked him. He sat down in the chair near mine. He looked at me. It was only the two of us in that small area.

He said, "Are you all right?" The way he asked me was as if he was in tune that something was wrong. As our eyes met, something strange happened. I was completely raw and brutally honest, and it all came tumbling out.

"No," I said, "I am not all right. I just found out my husband of nine years is cheating on me with a twenty-year-old Zimbabwean girl, and I am here buying a ticket back to the United States. He has no idea I know about his mistress or that I am buying a plane ticket home. On top of that, I am getting a ticket from Dar es Salam to Gatwick Airport and then I have to figure out how to get to Heathrow to make my connecting flight and I have no idea how I am going to do that."

"What is your name?" the man asked.

"Anne G.," I said.

"Miss Anne G., are you on the British Airways plane leaving tonight?"

"Yes."

"Well, I'm leaving on that plane also," said the man. "All you need to worry about is getting on that plane tonight. When you arrive at Gatwick, I'll have a private chauffeur waiting to drive you to Heathrow Airport. I will take care of everything, all right?" Then he introduced himself as Mark Gamble and said he was in Tanzania for business.

"Oh, you don't have to do that," I said, referring to the chauffeur.

But he insisted, "I know I don't. I want to."

Normally, I would never accept such a grand gesture from a handsome stranger, or any stranger for that matter, but I needed all the help I could get.

"Thank you so much," I said, completely relieved. Then Mark continued looking me straight in the eyes and said, "It's going to be all right."

Those were the simple words of truth I needed to hear most at that moment. It was as if God Almighty had spoken them through Mark straight to my heart, and it was powerful.

I said, "I don't know if you are a Christian or not, but God put you right here, right now, just for me. You are like an angel for me right now."

Mark smiled then asked if I needed help getting my luggage and getting to the plane.

"No, but thank you," I said. "I need to take care of some business with my husband first before going to the airport."

"Are you sure?"

"Yes," I said with determination.

Mark smiled at me again, truly seeing me, and said, "Then I will see you tonight on the plane."

"Yes," I said. "Thank you."

CHAPTER 20
PARTING THE RED SEA

*I am sending you out like sheep among wolves. Therefore be
as shrewd as snakes and as innocent as doves.*
—Matthew 10:16

When I left the travel agency, I felt like I was in a
dream. It was like God was parting the Red Sea for
me with each step I took. *Thank you Lord,* I prayed. I had
been praying nonstop for what seemed like forever, and I
felt so alone. Now I was seeing God was working on my be-
half, placing people in my path to give me exactly what I
needed each moment that I needed it. *God really is directing
my steps,* I thought. I called my parents from the Sheraton
Hotel and told them I had a ticket to come home. They told
me not to go back to the house or see Caleb. I told them
Caleb did not know I knew about his mistress or that I had
purchased a plane ticket home, and I had to go back to the
house to get my suitcase and all my belongings. They told
me to be very careful and emphasized whatever I did—I

should *not* tell Caleb I knew about his girlfriend. Both my parents and my brother knew my mouth was an issue, and it was obvious they were all worried about me keeping it under control. Then they told me to get to the airport as soon as I could and get home.

When I took the car back to our house, I walked in confidently. I appeared much more confident than I felt. I am a prideful person, and I would never beg, especially once I had all the information confirmed that Caleb had a mistress. It was game on. I knew it was important how I handled myself, and I was ready. I walked in and Caleb came straight to me like a doting husband asking where I had gone. He said "I've been waiting for you all morning. I woke up and you were gone, and I have been worried about you." I walked upstairs to our bedroom and he followed me. In the privacy of our room, I told him I had gone to get an airline ticket back to the United States.

"There was only a business-class ticket left, and since you want to divorce me," I said, "I bought it with your credit card. You can pay for me to go home. I'm leaving tonight."

Caleb acted really sad and even started to tear up. "Just like that? You're leaving?" he asked, as if this were out of the blue.

"Really?" I quickly responded. "You've been mean and hateful to me since I arrived in Tanzania, telling me you want me to go home and that you want to get a divorce, treating me horribly in front of the clients and everyone else. Now that I *am* leaving you want to pretend like you are upset?" My attitude had completely turned in a different direction since I knew about his girlfriend. I had been loving to him and praying for weeks for a miracle. I was done. I got my suitcase out and put it on the bed. I put a few things in it and Caleb sat on the bed and started to cry. He was wiping the tears in his eyes, and it honestly made me furious. "You have *not* acted like a husband to me since I got here," I said. "I haven't even recognized who you are. It's time for me to take care of myself, because you are obviously not taking care of me."

As he continued to act upset sitting beside my suitcase on the bed, I looked at him with clear eyes and said, "God is so amazing to me. You are not going to believe what just happened."

I told him about my issue with the ticket and how I prayed asking the Lord to help me because I didn't know what to do. I told him how the handsome businessman who was a stranger about our age started talking to me and asked me if I was all right, and I told him that I told the businessman my dilemma and that he told me he would have a private chauffeur waiting for me at Gatwick to drive me to Heathrow. And I told Caleb that I didn't know if the businessman was a Christian or not, but that God had put him there at that moment just for me. "Can you believe how God always takes care of me?"

Caleb looked straight into my eyes, with tears cradling his eyes. He nodded soberly, "Yes. God always does take care of you, Anne G." He said it in complete honesty. It was a raw moment of truth between us. The truth. For the fourteen years Caleb and I'd known each other, God had always been providing, had always been blessing, and had always been caring for me in supernatural ways, and we both knew it.

Oh, Holy Spirit, help me now, I prayed in my heart. *Please, Jesus, help.*

I then went into the bathroom and started running my bath. Caleb followed me into the bathroom and sat down to watch me take my bath. I looked at him and said, "What are you doing?"

"I always talk to you while you take a bath," he said.

"No," I said. "You are not my husband anymore, you need to get out." Caleb was surprised at my words, and so was I. But I felt as if I was speaking to someone I didn't know. Everything in me felt as if our marriage had been over from the moment I saw him playing blackjack and God covered my heart. I had a renewed strength that I believe was the Holy Spirit giving me His power to walk in confidence. I was all business. I walked over to the bathroom door and stood there waiting for Caleb to leave. Caleb got up, walked out, and I locked the door.

When I finished my bath and was finishing up packing, Caleb was pouting around the bedroom like he had just lost his best friend. Then the house cook called up to him, and he went down to the kitchen for a few minutes. *This is my chance*, I thought. I quickly stole his laptop out of his briefcase and placed it in the middle of my carry-on suitcase to keep it safe. I made sure to leave the briefcase exactly how I had found it. I wanted to make sure I had any evidence I needed on his infidelity once I got back to the United States. If he had a mistress, I was sure they were emailing each other. He came back into the room, and my heart was hammering. His eyes were red, and he asked if I would let him take me to lunch before I flew out. There was a special place he wanted to take me that I had never been to that he thought I would enjoy. It was already after lunchtime, and I did not need to be at the airport for hours. I agreed to go, so Caleb loaded my luggage into one of our driver's cars, then opened the door for me to get in the back. Then he slid in beside me and had the driver take us to the restaurant he had in mind. However, it was closed, so Caleb had the driver take us to the Sea Cliff Hotel instead. I was numb and had thousands of thoughts swirling through my mind; I didn't care where we went. I didn't care.

I sat in the back seat looking at this man and had no idea who he really was.

CHAPTER 21
LAYLA

But no human being can tame the tongue. It is a restless
evil, full of deadly poison.

—James 3:8

At the Sea Cliff Hotel, we went to the restaurant on the open deck overlooking the Indian Ocean. Because it was after lunch time there was no one there except us. We sat down and ordered two Coca-Cola's. The waiter brought our drinks, and we sat sipping them, looking out on the vast, blue sea. Caleb tried to talk to me sweetly, but our roles had reversed now that I knew about his mistress. He asked me if I ever thought I would come back to Africa.

"I don't know. Probably, but not anytime soon." I said, "I might bring my husband and children one day." He asked a few more questions, trying to make small talk. I was not very talkative since I had all this information bubbling up inside me, and I wanted to erupt. Caleb was all of a sudden being extra attentive for the first time since I had arrived in Africa, opening the doors for me and all of his attention was on me; he was fawning all over me. It fueled the fire inside me. I played along, trying to remember my brother and my parents' request for me to keep my mouth shut.

Then Caleb looked at me and said, "Anne G., you're my best friend. I will always love you. I love you more than anyone. Just because we get divorced doesn't mean I don't want to come visit you on Signal Mountain all the time. We'll talk on the phone, and I want to still date you. I just don't want to be married. I want to focus on my business right now, and that's all. But it's so good between us, I still love you, that will never change."

That ticked me off. Fire raged now from deep down in my spirit.

His words reminded me of all his lies he'd spun around me like a spiderweb for years, and of the confusion I lived tangled within them.

"Really?" I asked, revealing the rage bubbling up out of me. "Best friends? You want to still date me and come see me all the time at home? Really? Nothing will change between us?" I paused. "Well, what about Layla?"

I could see the surprise on his face, but he hid it well, "I don't know a Layla," he replied.

"Oh really? You don't know Layla?" I spewed out the sass.

"No," he said.

"Don't lie to me, Caleb." I sat there staring at him, and waited. A few minutes went by of him denying his affair before he finally confessed.

"I had a relationship with a girl named Layla on the internet," he said. "It was online only. I've never seen her in person, I swear to you."

"Don't lie to me, Caleb. We're getting divorced, so just be honest with me. Who is Layla Mwanza?"

There was shock on his face when I mentioned her last name. "Okay," he said. "When I was in Zimbabwe, before coming to Tanzania last month, Saul introduced me to a girl named Layla Mwanza, but nothing ever happened between us. She came into his office, and we met each other. I never saw her again after that, that's it. Why? Who told you about her?"

I was furious and I reached into my purse and pulled out one of the copies I had obtained from the charter company that morning. I threw it down on the table. Caleb picked it up and studied it as I said, "There's her full name, her birthday, passport number, and the flight number for the plane you paid to charter her into *our* hunting camp on July 26, when I was at Fripp Island with my family. You flew her in by herself when you knew for sure I wouldn't be coming. A twenty-year-old girl. Really, Caleb? Is she worth it? Is she worth our marriage and our dreams and the life we've built? Is she worth all of it?"

The look on Caleb's face was sheer terror. I had never seen Caleb look completely terrified the way he looked at that moment. He was a caught rat. I had documentation that was undeniable. Paid in full only by him. It stated where the plane had flown into and the company who had hired the plane.

I picked up my Coca-Cola and threw it in his face. "You bastard," I said. "You can have your little whore, but I get everything else. You better not try to take anything that's mine."

I got up from the table, grabbed my purse, and walked off the outside deck into the hotel.

Inside the hotel, I vanished into the women's bathroom. I was thinking, *Oh no! I did exactly what I promised I would not do; I could not keep my mouth shut and now I am in a real mess.* I was shaking with rage and needed a minute to think. I was afraid of Caleb, and it was not a good situation before, and I had just put gasoline on a burning fire. *What's going to happen now?*

A minute later Liesel came into the bathroom. "I've been looking all over for you," she said. "I saw what happened while I was exercising in the gym that looks out on the deck. I saw you throw the drink in Caleb's face."

I nodded. "I found out he has a twenty-year-old Zimbabwean girlfriend he has been cheating on me with."

She gasped. "Oh no. I'm so sorry."

"What did he do when I left?" I asked.

"He stood up, wiped his face, brushed the Coke off his shirt, then paid the bill," Liesel said. "Then he ran his hand through his hair and pulled out a pack of cigarettes. He put one to his mouth, lit it, took a big drag, then slowly blew it out while leaning back his head."

Surprised, I said, "Caleb doesn't smoke."

"Oh, yes, he does," Liesel confirmed. "He is definitely a smoker. I think there might be a lot you don't know about your husband."

I had no idea at that moment how right she was.

CHAPTER 22
ALERT

Be alert and of sober mind. Your enemy the devil prowls around like a roaring lion looking for someone to devour. Resist him, standing firm in the faith, because you know that the family of believers throughout the world is undergoing the same kind of sufferings.

—1 Peter 5:8–9

For I am the Lord your God, the Holy One of Israel, your Savior; I give Egypt for your ransom, Cush and Saba in your stead. Since you are precious and honored in my sight, and because I love you, I will give people in exchange for you, nations in exchange for your life. Do not be afraid, for I am with you...

—Isaiah 43:3–5

In the bathroom I told Liesel I had bought a plane ticket and was catching a flight out of Africa that night to head back to the United States. I told her that I was afraid of

Caleb, that my dad and my brother both separately told me they were also worried, and they never talked like that. I told her I promised them I would not tell Caleb I knew about his girlfriend until I was home, and I just blew it. The good part was, I did have my passport and my airline ticket in my purse, I knew not to be without my passport. I asked Liesel to go look and see if she saw Caleb anywhere in the hotel. She went and looked and then she asked her staff who confirmed he had left the hotel in a car. *Oh, no,* I thought. *Did he drive off with my luggage? If he finds out I stole his laptop, he is going to be furious.*

"Goodbye, Liesel. You're amazing," I said, now on a mission to try to get my luggage back before my flight. "I'm so glad I have you as a friend."

I knew it was just me and the Lord. I needed His strength more than ever. I had this odd businesslike, calm attitude. I had a very clear and distinct thought I believe was the Holy Spirit: *Okay. I am in a mess. Be smart and be watchful, Anne G. This is your life you're dealing with here. Caleb is dangerous, and he is fearful that you know everything now. Your life is in great danger.*

All of my senses were on high alert.

Outside the hotel I looked for a driver. Abdul, Caleb's good friend and business partner, owned several Land Cruiser taxis, and I recognized one of the drivers. The driver had driven us around town several times before, and we knew each other.

The thing about being in Tanzania is, I always needed to be smart. I never got into a car in which I did not know the driver since I was a woman by myself. So, I wanted someone who knew who I was, which would be safer. I also needed someone who spoke some English since I did not speak Swahili. I walked up to his truck and greeted him with a big smile. "I need you to drive me somewhere, please." I said with great confidence.

"Yes, of course, madam," he said. "Get in."

When we left the hotel, the driver told me he needed to call Abdul to get some gas because he was on empty.

"Oh," I said. "I have money here, I'll tell Abdul I filled you up."

"Thank you, madam," the driver said.

As he was getting gas, I started thinking I needed my suitcase with the laptop in it. I was hoping it would be in the car Caleb and I took to the Sea Cliff, and hoped maybe the car was parked at our house, since I looked and it was not at the hotel anymore. I hoped I could grab my suitcase out of the trunk and then head to the airport. I asked the driver to take me by our house so I could get something. He knew where it was, and he drove me there. My heart was beating a million miles a minute. I prayed the whole way from the gas station, *Oh, Father, please help me. I'm in a real mess. I need the laptop for proof of infidelity if Caleb tries to fight me in court. Please get me out of this safely.*

We arrived at the house and the car we had taken to lunch was not in the driveway, no cars were. I quickly ran into the house. The man who cooked and cleaned was there, and I greeted him kindly, then ran upstairs; our bedroom door was locked. It wasn't locked when we'd left to go to lunch, and it had never been locked before. I called for the house-keeper to come upstairs and asked him to unlock the door. "I am sorry, madam," he said. "But Mr. Caleb told me not to unlock the door." I could tell he was uncomfortable telling me no, but he was obeying Caleb's wishes. So I dashed back out to my driver and jumped inside the truck.

"Please take me back to the Sea Cliff," I said, thinking *Caleb was just here and left, maybe he's heading back to the Sea Cliff with my luggage.* My heart was beating wildly. However my mind was very calm and alert. My focus was on the driver and where we were going, aware of the fact that he could have information from Abdul and could take me somewhere else. I kept praying silently, *Father God, please keep me under your mighty hedge of protection and under your mighty wings so I am safe from all harm. Protect me Father, I am yours. In Jesus name, Amen.*

Back at the Sea Cliff I didn't see Caleb, but I ran into Charlotte. I told her I had discovered Caleb was cheating on me and that I had documentation from the charter flight with all the information on his Zimbabwean girlfriend and that we had just gotten in a big fight and that I told Caleb I knew all about his girlfriend. "If anything bad happens to me and I end up dead," I said, "I want you to know that Caleb did it. If something happens, please tell my family about our argument." She looked straight at me and saw I was serious.

She said, "Okay, be careful."

What had been in my heart for several weeks was finally being spoken out of pure terror. I knew I was in big trouble, and I asked Charlotte to please pray for me as I walked away. I had no time to make a phone call to my parents. There was no one except me. If he killed me, at least my family would know we fought and that I told him I knew about the affair. Then I begged God Almighty to save my life. *Please Lord God, keep my enemies far from me. Deliver me from evil in the name of Jesus, Amen.*

I returned to where my driver was waiting for me outside the Sea Cliff, and I got in the passenger's seat. Using the driver's phone, I called Abdul and told him I would be at the hotel until four thirty, then would go to the airport. "Please tell Caleb he needs to meet me at the airport with my luggage." When I got off the phone, instead of staying at the hotel, I immediately told the driver to take me to the airport, which was a good thirty-five minutes away.

About fifteen minutes into the drive, the phone rang. The driver looked at the phone and smiled at me, "It is Abdul."

"Oh, thank you. I need to speak to him," I said, placing my hand out for the driver to hand me the phone. "Hello?"

Abdul was surprised I answered. "Oh, Anne G. Where are you?" He asked.

"I am at the Sea Cliff Hotel," I lied.

He said, "Are you alone or with clients?"

"I am with the clients," I said coolly.

"Where at the Sea Cliff? We have been looking for you."

"I am just waiting here at the hotel," I lied again.

Abdul said, "Okay." Then we hung up. I took the phone and put it between my legs in the front seat of the Land Cruiser. I trembled with fear, thinking and praying. *I need to stay calm. Jesus, help me, I need You.*

A few minutes later, the phone rang again. It was between my legs. I know it was the Holy Spirit giving me wisdom to place the phone between my legs after the first phone call. I answered the phone, and it was Abdul. He said, "Anne G. I need to speak to my driver, I need to get him some gas."

"I just got him gas." I said.

"Where are you? We have been looking all over and we cannot find you."

I did not answer.

"Anne G.," said Abdul, "Caleb is very upset. He says you two got in a fight, and he wants to speak to you. You need to meet with Caleb before you go to the airport."

Fear prickled my whole body. "Is Caleb with you?" I asked.

"No. He is not with me," said Abdul. "He wants to meet you, and we want to know where you are so we can come get you. Caleb is crying and upset about your fight, and you need to work this out. You do not need to leave for the United States fighting with each other like this."

Then I heard Caleb speaking in Swahili in the background, and I knew that Abdul had lied to me. He and Caleb were together. I knew Caleb's voice, and he was telling Abdul what to say in Swahili. I heard him speak Swahili all the time, although I understood very little of the language.

"Let me speak to the driver," Abdul said again.

My heart raced. I was petrified with fear.

When I didn't give the driver the phone Abdul said, "Anne G., I need you to come to my house so we can talk about this situation. I will tell the driver to bring you here now. Let me speak to him."

I had a calm, clear thought in my head of me going to Abdul's house and Caleb tying me up, and putting me in the trunk of a car. I knew beyond a shadow of a doubt what Caleb had in mind. I do not know if Abdul knew it or not, but I did. I was calm and my spirit was on high alert.

I quietly said, "No. I will see Caleb at the airport. He can bring my luggage to me. Goodbye."

I kept thinking and praying. *Lord. Please get me to the airport. I can get my luggage from Caleb once I am at the gate.* I kept the driver's phone between my legs the rest of the drive. The drive seemed to take forever, but we finally pulled up to the international flights. I thanked the driver and handed him his phone and got out of the car.

I started walking toward the gate, which was about sixty feet away, where I could see a policeman standing on the sidewalk. As I continued walking toward the gate, a car pulled up and to my surprise, Caleb got out of the car. He quietly started walking beside me. All my senses went into overdrive. I immediately thought, *Caleb is dangerous. I need to make sure he cannot force me into that car with him.* Although Caleb had never been physical with me in the past, my spirit inside me told me he was desperate. He said, "Why did you leave the hotel?" I said nothing. My eyes were fixed on the gate I needed to get to. I kept walking and did not stop walking until I was close to the policeman and the gate, so if I called out for help, he would be right there. Then I turned to look at Caleb. His eyes were bloodshot red, I had never seen eyes that red before. They almost looked like pure blood. He was shaken and was trying to act like he was in control. But I sensed with every fiber in my being his complete desperation. He was a master deceiver, but I was finally seeing him clearly now.

"I have been looking all over for you," he said quietly, so he did not draw attention to us fighting.

I was watching the policeman, and I was watching Caleb. My body and everything in me were super aware of my surroundings at that moment. In my spirit, it felt like I was an animal being hunted, and I knew instinctively with everything inside me—my life was in danger. I still wanted to make sure he could not force me into his car with his driver, which was now parked right next to where we were talking. He spoke softly. "I don't want to fight with you."

I did not say a word. I just wanted that laptop before he found out that I had stolen it from him. He said, "Come on, Anne G., and get into the car with me, let's go somewhere where we can talk. Your plane doesn't leave for hours," he coaxed sweetly.

"No," I said. "I am not going anywhere with you."

Tears welling in his eyes, he said, "I just want to talk; we can sit here in the car so no one can hear us. You don't want to leave Africa like this, do you? With us fighting?"

I got out my documents, ready to show my ticket and show my passport, and my hands were shaky. I wanted Caleb to know I had everything I needed to get on that plane. I looked at Caleb and I was strangely calm even though I was terrified from the tip of my head to the tips of my toes. I knew at that moment it had to be God himself in me.

"I need you to get me my suitcase and my carry-on," I said quietly but with great confidence. He had the driver get my luggage, and when the driver handed me my bags, it felt as if a huge weight had been lifted off my chest. I could tell the laptop was still in my carry-on by its weight, and I breathed deeply.

Caleb looked at me; he was crying and could not stop; he had no control over his emotions. I think he was crying because he was fearful and angry that he was not in control—not because I was leaving. For the first time since we married, I was completely aware of the game he was playing, the web of confusion he was spinning, and I was not going to participate in it.

"Please don't do this," he begged as I inched closer to my gate. "We can do this without fighting, please don't leave now."

I could have quietly gone through the gate without saying a word, but I didn't. I had to say something. Now I had his laptop in my carry-on and I knew the policeman was close. I could walk through the gate, and he could not force me into the car with him.

I looked at him and raised my head up with a fire in my gut. Fire poured out of my mouth. It was like a Holy Cleansing. Burning away the webs of lies and deceit I had been tangled up in for the last nine years. It was all coming to a head at that moment.

I said in a calm voice, "Caleb, you are getting what you want. You can have your little whore—and I get everything else. I will take you for everything you have, and if you try to fight me or try to touch any of the assets I brought to this marriage, I will see you in court, and you know I will win."

I hit a nerve. I could see it in his eyes. Those bloodshot eyes looked at me with hatred. "If that is what you want," he said, "I will see you in court."

It was as if I saw him for the first time, and I hated everything he stood for. When I looked at him, I did not see anything that resembled the man I fell in love with, or the man I thought I had married. I saw a disgusting stranger who was a liar who had deceived me for the last time. I turned from him and started walking to the gate with my passport, my luggage and ticket in my hand.

As I took those steps walking toward my plane out of

Africa, I started being honest with myself. I finally started to realize the truth. It was washing over me as I walked away from Caleb and toward my plane. Back home, Caleb and I had a lot of equity in our house, but besides the house and the belongings in the house, he had his two businesses, his trophy animals, and his 4Runner SUV. I owned half the house with him. Independently, I had an inheritance that was in a stock portfolio that was in my name only, several pieces of real estate, and an interest in the shopping center on Signal Mountain that I had inherited with my fifteen cousins. If he killed me, it was all his. *I'm worth a whole lot to him dead,* I thought. *I am worth much more to Caleb dead than divorced. That is why he wants me dead.* I had not wanted to consider all the reasons he would want me dead until that moment. I had been praying so hard for so many years for God to heal my marriage, and I had been pushing the thoughts away for the last few weeks until I was safe. It all came rushing down like a cleansing rain. It was sobering. It was as if I could only deal with one problem at a time. And now that the gate separated Caleb and me, I could finally see clearly why I was in danger.

It felt like God was speaking loud and clear.

Caleb had always loved my family. He told me he was closer to my family than he was his own. He wanted to keep my family, he just did not want to keep me. I was through the security checkpoint, almost in a daze from the events of the last few weeks. Running over all that had happened in my mind, I was still praying, *Oh Jesus, help me. Guide me, Holy Spirit. I am so afraid.* I walked into the waiting area of the airport with restaurants for international flights. I saw a clean-cut Arabic businessman who was on his cell phone.

He hung up from his phone call and I said to him, "Excuse me, Sir, do you know where there is a pay phone I could use? I need to make a phone call to the United States." I assume he could see the dazed state of my being.

He handed me his phone and said, "Here is my phone, you can call anyone you wish, and you can speak as long as you would like." Then he motioned for me to go away from him. I thanked him and walked over to a table as far away from anyone else as I could get.

My hands were shaking as I dialed my parents' home phone, and they answered. I could not say a word. I started crying. Just the sound of their voices brought so many fears of losing my marriage, my life, and my family—fears that I had been stuffing down within myself—to light. And now I cried. It was a hard but good release—my first cry since everything in Africa had occurred.

My mom answered and my daddy picked up the other phone line.

"Anne G., are you in the airport?" My mom asked.

"Yes," I barely got the word out.

"Is Caleb with you?"

"No," I sobbed.

"Are you checked in and at your gate?"

"Yes." I started weeping. It was all crashing down on me, what all had happened in the last few weeks. I was shaken to my core. It felt like a nightmare that I was walking out of in real life. My mom spoke to me, encouraging me that I was doing the right thing, that I needed to come home and we could figure out what we needed to do from there. They asked if I was all right. "No," I said, "I am not all right."

Everything became a blur—literally and figuratively. I

was exhausted and afraid, but one thing I was not: I was not defeated. Battered and broken though I was, I was still taking one step at a time. That was all I could do. In faith, one step at a time. I stayed on the phone for a while, needing to feel their support. They told me to call when I arrived in England for my layover. "We won't stop praying for you, baby," Mom said, followed by the words that filled me with hope: "We'll be at the Chattanooga Airport to pick you up when you land at home. We love you."

CHAPTER 23
SUSTAINED

*Listen to me, you descendants of Jacob, all the remnant of
the people of Israel, you whom I have upheld since your
birth, and have carried you since you were born. Even to
your old age and gray hairs I am He, I am He who will
sustain you. I have made you and I will carry you; I will
sustain you and I will rescue you.*

—Isaiah 46:3–4

A couple of hours later I boarded the plane, happy that
Caleb had at least paid for me to have this good seat
to fly home. I had a lot of legroom and a big chair, and I
sat thinking over what all had happened, and wondering
what was coming next. I ate the dinner that was served, flying bulkhead as I'd become savvy at traveling internation-
ally. After dinner I took out my carry-on and placed it so
that I could prop my feet up onto it. I'd only had one-to-
two hours of sleep the night before, and soon fell into a
deep sleep. I awoke over seven hours later when the captain

notified over the speaker that we'd be landing soon. Sitting up and getting some things together, I felt someone touch my shoulder. It was the handsome stranger Mark from the hotel travel agency.

"Hello, Miss Anne G.," he said, smiling kindly as he stood beside me in the aisle. "Did you get some sleep?"

"Yes." I smiled back, feeling groggy. "I did. And it was much needed."

"I came to check on you earlier," he said, "but you were sleeping. I'm glad you got some rest on this long flight. If it's all right with you, I was planning to meet you in baggage claim to help you with your luggage, and then escort you to your chauffeur."

"That sounds wonderful," I said, still waking up, wondering if I'd been drooling—or worse—snoring, when he came over earlier and found me asleep. "Thank you so much."

Mark smiled, tipped his head, then said, "My pleasure."

Wow, I thought as he walked back to his seat. *He's a real person. This is really happening. Thank you, Lord, for taking such good care of me.*

Once off the plane, I headed to baggage claim where Mark stood waiting for me with a baggage cart. A gentleman, he loaded up my bags, then, knowing his way around, walked me out to the parking garage to a black Saab. The driver popped out of his seat to greet us then asked, "How was your flight, Mr. Mark?"

Mark replied that it was good, then asked the driver how he was, calling him by name. They conversed for a minute, making it apparent they knew each other well. Then Mark introduced the driver to me and said, "Miss Anne G. will be riding to Heathrow Airport with you. Here is her luggage."

"Hello, Miss Anne G.," the driver said kindly. "It's nice to meet you."

He loaded my luggage into the trunk and as he did, Mark stepped over to me and said, "If you're comfortable, I'd like the driver to drop me off at my house, which is on the way to Heathrow Airport. But if you're not comfortable, I'm happy to get another ride."

"Of course," I said. "I'd love the company. Thank you for being so generous."

And dashing, I thought. *Mark is like a knight in shining armor. Is this really happening?*

He opened the back door for me, then stepped around to the other side and slipped into the backseat beside me. He asked the driver to take him to his house first, and then the driver would drive me to Heathrow Airport for my connecting flight to the United States. The driver obviously knew Mark well, and knew where Mark lived without directions. He said, "Yes sir," and off we went.

Almost immediately, Mark and I started talking, and the driver seemed to fade away. Everything faded away just like the road behind us. It was only the two of us and our conversation. He asked me about what had happened, and I gave him a quick description of my life, my marriage, and what had taken place the last few weeks with the unraveling of my marriage. Because I had never seen him before and would probably never see him again, I was brutally honest about every detail of my marriage and my life. It was out of character for me to open up like this to a stranger; I was being much more transparent than I would even be with a good friend.

He told me he was an international lawyer, and he was

in Tanzania for work and traveled frequently to East Africa for his job. He asked me about our financial situation, and I told him everything, which was also unusual for me. He asked about my finances, and asked if we had ever put money into a joint account. "No. I always knew to keep my stocks in my name alone," I said. He asked if he could give me some advice on going forward. "Yes. Please," I said.

He told me Caleb would be feeling guilty for cheating on me for a short window, and after that short amount of time, he would probably try to fight me for a better settlement. Mark wanted me to quickly get a lawyer, have a settlement written up, and ask for everything I brought to the marriage, along with whatever else I wanted to ask for. "If you two work things out or decide to change the settlement later, fine. But get his signatures now while he's feeling guilty."

All the advice Mark gave me made good sense to me, and I thanked him for all his help. Our conversation then turned to focus on Mark. He opened up to me about his life, revealing some very personal details you wouldn't normally reveal to someone you've just met. From Virginia, Mark had moved to England for his job, and he had never been married and was not currently dating anyone. He worked long hours and traveled to East Africa frequently. He'd worked hard and obviously was very successful at his job, and had a plan for early retirement within less than five years. His family, with whom he was close, lived in the United States, and Mark owned some real estate in Washington, DC. "I travel back to the U.S. several times a year," he said.

During our drive it was easy to deduce that Mark was extremely driven, but humble; a strong yet gentle man who carried himself with a quiet power. I felt safe in the back seat of his driver's car; he and I were both vulnerable and keenly present, resulting in a conversation that was purely divine. I have never in my life had such an open-hearted conversation with another person I had just met. We both spoke truths about our lives, sharing intimate details we normally wouldn't have spoken out loud to anyone, and it was powerful. Soberly I thought, *God is literally directing my steps, and this conversation is divine.*

A few minutes later, when we were getting close to Mark's house, he handed me a business card and asked if I had one too. He looked at my real estate business card and said, "Signal Mountain, Tennessee?"

"Yes?" I smiled.

"Do you happen to know the Boehm family?"

I could not believe my ears. "What?" I said.

"I went to college at Georgetown University in Washington DC with a guy named Erik Boehm from Signal Mountain."

I stared at him. "You are kidding me? Erik is my best friend's brother; Denise Boehm and I have been best friends since we were three years old. The Boehms are like my second family. Denise and I went to Georgetown University and stayed with Erik to do a 'college tour' our junior year of high school, although we really just toured around DC," I laughed.

Mark and I sat in disbelief over this shared connection. He and Erik hadn't stayed in touch since graduation, but Mark was glad to hear that Erik was doing well.

When we arrived in front of Mark's home, the driver left the car running in park and, before getting out, Mark asked, "Would you mind if I called you in a couple days to make sure you got home okay?"

I nodded. "I would love that. Thank you."

"And if you're not opposed, I could also be in touch with your lawyer to go over paperwork to make sure you're being well-represented," he volunteered.

"That sounds wonderful, Mark. I would appreciate that."

Then Mark exchanged a few words with the driver and said goodbye to me.

I wonder if I'll ever see him again, I thought as Mark got out of the car.

The driver unloaded Mark's luggage, then took me to catch my flight.

CHAPTER 24

JUST WALK

Then Moses stretched out his hand over the sea, and all that night the Lord drove the sea back with a strong east wind and turned it into dry land. The waters were divided, and the Israelites went through the sea on dry ground, with a wall of water on their right and on their left.

—Exodus 14:21–22

"What an amazing man," I said to the driver as he got back into the car, and we started to pull out of Mark's driveway.

"Oh, yes," the driver said. "Mr. Mark is a wonderful person. He is always very kind."

It had been about forty-five minutes since we'd left Gatwick Airport, and now that I wasn't in deep conversation with Mark, I took a good look out the window. "Wow. What a nice area of town," I said, staring at Mark's stunning house and the new Audi sports car in his driveway.

"This is the second nicest area in London. Mick Jagger lives right around the corner there," said the driver, pointing.

Staring out the window at all the beautiful, immaculate homes, I thought, *Dang, Lord. You are always so good to me. An international lawyer with great wisdom and a private chauffeur? You amaze me.* I knew with everything in my being God was parting the Red Sea for me. I could sense the walls of water on each side of me with each step that I took.

When we arrived at Heathrow Airport, the driver got out to open my door and help me with my luggage. I quickly pulled out some tip money as he set my luggage on a cart. When I thanked him and handed him the money, he shook his head. "Mr. Mark told me to tell you he took care of the tip, and that he hopes you have a nice flight."

"Oh, thank you," I said, warmed by yet another act of kindness from Mark. "Please thank him for me."

"Have a safe trip home, Miss Anne G. It was very nice to meet you."

I got a little choked up, but held it together. Mark had been so kind to me. Beyond kind. It was as if God was giving me a hug through Mark, saying to me, "I have you, Anne. G. Trust Me. We will take one step at a time. I am parting the sea for you. Just walk."

Inside the airport, after checking in for my flight, then going to the business class lounge to wait for my plane to the U.S., I started to second-guess myself. *I think I made a bad decision leaving Caleb. I should have tried harder to make my marriage work. What am I doing? I should go back to Africa. I love him. I've been married to him for nine years.*

I was being bombarded with doubts until I started to cry. Feeling alone in England, I was afraid. I was at war within myself. A few hours earlier, while I was talking to Mark, I had been confident that I needed to move forward. I finally called my mom and voiced my vicious doubts, and she gently told me to come home, and that I was making the best decision. I boarded the plane with swollen red eyes.

I remember thinking, *Lord, am I really making the right decision?* I prayed as I inched down the aisle to my seat. *Should I get off this plane right now and go back to Africa? Lord, help me.* Just then, as I reached my seat and sat down, the information sheet sticking out of the compartment on the back of the seat in front of me caught my eye. It read, "Boeing 777." I felt peace and I knew the Lord was saying to my heart, "This is the plane I lined up for you with My holy numbers 777 to take you safely home. Trust me. I love you. Sit back and relax. I am in control, and you are safe under My wings and the hedge of My protection."

When I arrived at the small Chattanooga Airport the next day, Saturday, August 25, I'd been out of the country for twenty-two days and welcomed the hot afternoon, as well as my parents who were there waiting for me. I was relieved to see them, and glad to get home, mentally exhausted from everything I had been through. When we arrived at my house, all my siblings, Happy, Frank, Bill, and Mary Lee all came to my house to support me, along with most of their spouses and children. My sister, Mary Lee, who is also one of my best friends, stayed with me at my house for the first night. It meant very much to me that she, as well as Happy and his family who also lived out of town, had traveled back to Signal Mountain to offer me encouragement. Mary Lee was heartbroken for me and grieved with me. She couldn't stay long, needing to get back to her small children, but after she left Signal Mountain, she called me every day to check on me and to talk through what was happening, which was healing.

Happy owned a company he needed to get back to, but he remained an encouragement to me, calling to check on me often and to tell me he loved me. As the oldest of our crew, Happy had always been very protective of me, which I loved. I had always felt very close to him too, even though we were fourteen years apart. Mary Lee and Happy both had flowers delivered to my house shortly after they left to remind me that my family loved me. I placed them on my kitchen counter. They glowed as warm as the sun, and my home felt less empty. My siblings and their families provided a safe sanctuary for me of love and support. I loved and still love them very much.

My son, keep your father's command and do not forsake your mother's teaching. Bind them always on your heart; fasten them around your neck. When you walk, they will guide you; when you sleep, they will watch over you; when you awake, they will speak to you. For this command is a lamp, this teaching is a light...

—Proverbs 6:20–23

The next morning, Sunday, I went to my parents' house to visit with them. We were alone and I told my mom and daddy everything that had happened in Africa. I also confessed that I could not understand it, but I felt a demonic evilness around me the entire time I was in Tanzania. And even now that I was home, I still felt it. I could feel this darkness around me, and I knew in my spirit. I was in trouble, and I did not know what to do. I had been praying, but it was heavy around me.

I shared my entire heart with my parents and told them I didn't recognize Caleb in Tanzania. My parents believed the Bible was completely true and that we are in a spiritual battle as it says in Ephesians 6. Our family talked about the devil and his evil plots, but none of us had experienced anything like what I was experiencing. What I appreciate so much is how both of my parents were completely on board with me. They never said, "that seems crazy." Instead, my mom looked at me sincerely and said she was going to do everything in her power to help me. She had Holy Spirit discernment, a God-given gift the Lord had used in her in powerful ways to minister to people. Now I was one of those people. My mother was chairman of the board of the Chattanooga Bible Institute, and she said, "I've never had any experience with anything like this, but I know someone who does. He's on the board with me at the Bible Institute, and he deals with these kinds of issues."

So, she made a phone call to her friend Reid Henson, and she told him what was happening in my life, and that I sensed a demonic evilness was all around me. He agreed to meet me at my grandmother's house on our family property. Granny also had an apartment downtown and did not stay at her house much during the week, so we would be alone. When my mom got off the phone with Reid, my parents and I prayed together and asked God to direct our steps and give us wisdom. We had no idea what we needed to do, but God did.

CHAPTER 25
THE ARMOR OF GOD

What, then, shall we say in response to these things? If God is for us, who can be against us?

—Romans 8:31

Later that same day, my phone rang. It was Mark. He was calling to make sure I arrived home safely and to check on me. "Thanks for calling. I'm trying to get settled in," I said, then told him my plan to go speak with my pastor at our church on Monday before going to speak to a lawyer. I hadn't told Mark, or anyone except my parents and Bill, that I was worried Caleb was going to try to kill me, so our conversation was pleasant. We chatted about my trip home and about Mark's life, which was a good diversion for me. He told me more about his work. He was a protector, which I appreciated.

Early the next morning, I met Reid at my grandmother's house. In his early sixties, Reid was a prominent businessman in Chattanooga who lived on the mountain. He attended Signal Mountain Presbyterian Church, and was on the board at the Chattanooga Bible Institute with my mom. That was all I knew about him. Sitting in my grandmother's living room, he asked me a few questions, and I gave him a quick description of what had happened over the last several weeks.

"May I pray over you and anoint you?" he asked.

"Yes. Please."

We got down on our knees in front of my granny's couch, and Reid began to pray. He prayed powerfully over me, proclaiming that the blood of Jesus be washed over me. Then he pulled out a little glass bottle of oil from his shirt pocket and anointed me, telling me the oil he'd smeared in the sign of the cross on my forehead and wrists represented the blood of Jesus Christ. "I command in the mighty name of Jesus any evil spirits, dark powers, or curses be broken and must come off of Anne G.," he prayed after my anointing. "I command that no venereal diseases or any other sexually transmitted disease can be attached to her. And I command that no infirmities of any kind can be attached to her. She is separated from all darkness that could have come from her husband or anyone else, in the name of Jesus Christ."

My ears were listening, and what he said all made sense to my spirit, although I had never heard anyone pray like that before. After we finished praying, he told me he wanted me to go down and meet with a friend of his that was a Baptist preacher who had the gift of discerning spirits. He thought I needed the "big guns", because he sensed this was more than he was used to dealing with. I agreed. I knew in my spirit God Almighty was directing my steps even though

I had no idea what to do. So Reid set up a time for me to meet with his friend.

My appointment with my pastor, Jim Suddath, took place after my time with Reid. Jim pastored at First Presbyterian Church, which was the church I'd grown up going to, the church out of which Caleb's parents were missionaries, and the church where my great-grandparents, grandparents, and my parents had attended for generations. I came into the meeting feeling so ashamed of my life. With my upbringing, I never thought I'd be sitting in front of my pastor like this, confiding in him that my husband did not want me anymore. It was humiliating to the maximum degree.

During the meeting I summarized getting to Africa, Caleb telling me he wanted a divorce, finding out about his girlfriend, and coming home. Again, I didn't say a word about the spiritual warfare I was enduring or my fear that Caleb wanted to kill me. I didn't want my pastor to think I was mentally unstable. However, even without revealing these things, it was a hard conversation to have. As I sat before Jim, I wept as reality hit. I was twenty-nine and realizing I was not going to have a husband anymore. Caleb and I'd been married nine years and attended church and Sunday school every week if we weren't traveling. *How could this nightmare be taking place?* Through tears, I answered each one of Jim's questions, waiting for him to tell me that divorce was wrong. Although I would not have said it was wrong for anyone else in my circumstance, my pride was telling me it was wrong for me.

Pride is blinding.

Then Jim counseled, "You're vulnerable right now. You're hurt and not thinking clearly. Now is not the time to talk to or confide in any man who is not a family member or counselor."

I paused, thinking of Mark. "Well, there is this guy I met in Tanzania who set up the chauffeur for me in England…"

Jim pondered on this a moment. "How about no communication at all with any man except family members or counselors until after Christmas? The New Year can be your fresh start. At that time, you can talk to any man again as a friend, and if you're ready, you can start dating again too."

That seemed wise and fair. *Although,* I thought vehemently, *I will not be wanting to date.*

Jim explained I needed to go ahead and start the divorce process with a lawyer. I asked if I should wait on Caleb to do that. I wondered if it was wrong for me to file.

He read scripture to me about divorce. "Biblically, he cheated on you, and you have biblical grounds for divorce. He wants to be divorced, and you do not need to stay married to this guy. He is not being a husband to you."

It was heartbreaking, but I needed to hear the truth. I agreed.

After meeting with Jim, I called one of my friends. I was sitting in my car in the church parking lot downtown and told her I couldn't talk to Mark for a while. I was disappointed. When Mark and I'd spoken on Sunday, he told me he was planning to come to the U.S. in four weeks to visit his family. He said he wanted to come visit me in Tennessee and meet my family, which I was looking forward to. Now his visit would have to wait. "I'm sad I can't talk to him until after Christmas," I told her. Then I asked her about lawyers. She recommended her Uncle Walter, who was a divorce attorney. I called him next, and set up a meeting for Tuesday morning.

My brother Frank went with me to see Walter McGuire the next morning at his downtown office. A financial adviser, Frank made a list for the divorce paperwork of my family assets I brought to my marriage. I was very thankful my older brother went with me to offer me support and to make sure I didn't forget to include anything. Which could have easily happened if I'd gone alone with how overwhelmed I was. It felt like I was living in a heavy fog. I'd left Caleb in Tanzania Friday, and now it was Tuesday. Three days hadn't been enough time at all to adjust to what was taking place.

"Will Caleb agree to all of this?" Walter asked after reading the list.

"I'll call him today to settle everything, and then get in touch with you so you can write up what we agreed upon." I didn't want to fight with Caleb over the settlement and hoped he didn't want to either. I was running out of steam. Besides, it would cost a fortune if we fought.

Walter wrote down the information Frank gave him then asked, "When can Caleb come to sign the paperwork? He has to be here in person."

"Could you have it all ready on Friday?" I asked.

"Yes," Walter said.

"Okay. Then I'll find out what time Caleb can get here and let you know."

"Sounds good," Walter said.

Just then Mark's advice to get everything signed quickly popped inside my head. *Things couldn't be going quicker than this*, I thought. Wrapping things up, Walter informed me that our divorce would take about thirty days to process since there were no children and since we wouldn't be going to court—as long as we agreed on all terms.

"Okay, thank you," I said in a daze.

Then Frank and I left.

After lunch I went to see Reid's friend, the Baptist preacher Dr. Robert Sanders. Heavyset with salt-and-pepper hair and wearing glasses, Dr. Sanders was a different type of person. I could tell this right away after entering his office, introducing myself, and sitting down in one of the two chairs before his desk. He sat behind his desk, looking all around me as if he were seeing something. Then he made eye contact with me and got straight to business.

"Reid called and told me you needed to meet with me as soon as possible. He told me he'd seen a spiritual black cloud over you when you two met."

Reid hadn't mentioned this black cloud to me. But I truthfully was not surprised. I felt it—I could feel it now in my spirit. I knew it was there. I just couldn't see it.

Dr. Sanders said, "The Lord led you to the right place." He said he had a gift from the Lord and that he could see in the spirit. I was not really sure what he meant, but I was willing to do anything at this point. I knew I was in trouble, I could feel it. And I knew the Holy Spirit had guided me here. He told me we would pray, and asked the Holy Spirit to show us what we needed to do to get the darkness around me gone. When he said, "Amen," I did too. Then I did not know what to say, so I did not say anything.

Dr. Sanders didn't ask me any questions except if Jesus Christ was Lord of my life.

"Yes," I said with confidence.

"Okay," said Dr. Sanders "Good." He asked me for my full name. Then he stepped over to where I sat and anointed my forehead and wrists with oil, saying it represented the blood of Jesus. He returned to his chair behind his desk, then prayed over me next, asking God the Father to help him by filling him with the Holy Spirit, and to give him wisdom in the name of Jesus. "Anything that has a claim over Anne Gillespie Powell Sharp's life," he prayed, "in the name of Jesus they must be obedient and show themselves now." He paused and looked all around, which was strange for me. Then in his office of Bibles and books, it was as if he started to see something appear. *He is seeing spirits*, I thought, although I was not seeing anything out of the norm. By his expressions it seemed he was watching one spirit appear after another in the room. He observed these spirits for a while before he finally looked at me and said, "Do you know your husband wants to kill you?"

My heart stopped. I had not told him anything about myself or my relationship with Caleb. Tears started streaming down my face. I nodded my head yes. I had no words, just tears. All my fears of what I thought, my vision, and what my daddy and my brother thought were bubbling up. Just like that, right off the bat, he called it out. One by one, Dr. Sanders started listing off the curses and assignments that had been spoken over me and, in Jesus' name, commanded that they be broken, dissolved, and hold no power over me anymore. He prayed all kinds of amazing prayers, and I could feel the words of God Himself being wrapped around me powerfully. It felt like armor, and it was a supernatural experience since he had never met me and did not know my family. What came out of his mouth could have only been from God. I knew it. Tears streamed down my face as I prayed along with him silently. Then he listed off all generational demonic spirits from my family, which resonated with my spirit as I recognized this man knew things he could not know, and he commanded them to leave in Jesus' name. He finished and looked at me.

"It is going to be all right," he tried to comfort me. "It says in the Bible we have God on our side. 'If God is for us, who can be against us?' Romans 8:31." I was not as confident as he was. I was shaken to the core.

Then, he stopped abruptly and looked behind me and to my side, and he asked, "Do you see that?"

When he asked, suddenly I could see in my mind's eye an image. I saw something much taller than any human I had ever seen, with widespread wings, standing behind me. He was all white, like light. He drew a sword out and it flashed behind me, and it was flashing all around me, fast as lighting.

Dr. Sanders said, "Did you see that?" I nodded my head yes through the tears that were still being shed from how upset I was. "That is your guardian angel, did you hear what he said?" I listened, but I could not hear anything.

"No." I said.

"He said his name is Heroled. He has been with you since you were born, and he will never leave you. God has a hedge of protection around you."

In awe, I thought of Psalm 91:4: "He will cover you with His feathers, and under His wings you will find refuge; His faithfulness will be your shield and rampart." This psalm is about our Lord, but the description fit the angel I'd seen exactly. All of a sudden I went from feeling broken to feeling a calm empowerment after witnessing the power and beauty of God's protection over me. After feeling so alone in Tanzania, and even here at home, even though my wonderful family surrounded me, now I had a peace that surpassed all understanding.

Shortly after Heroled's appearance, Dr. Sanders wrapped up our meeting. I was still in a daze over seeing my guardian angel and hearing the things he knew about me and my life that were not learned from me. "You are going to be all right." He said again as I stood to leave. "Call me if you need to meet again." His tone was nonchalant, as if this were just another day in the office for him.

"Okay, thank you," I said, not totally sure what had just taken place. As I left his office, my mind felt heavy and saturated. Everything I'd just experienced wasn't typical for my Christian upbringing. I was in a new realm of faith, a realm I knew in my heart was real because I'd experienced it. But a realm my mind was taking longer to absorb.

Wow, God. Did all that really just happen? I thought as I reached my car.

CHAPTER 26
MIRACLE

The Lord will grant that the enemies who rise up against you will be defeated before you. They will come at you from one direction but flee from you in seven.

—*Deuteronomy 28:7*

Later that day, I told my parents and siblings about Dr. Sanders and that I saw my guardian angel, which encouraged us all. I also told them about the generational spirits he commanded to leave me, which we all found very interesting. I was staying at my house at night but would go to my parents' during the day, and it was healing to be able to talk to them and my siblings there.

After speaking with my family, I dropped Caleb's laptop off with my Uncle Windy. I knew when I was stealing the laptop in Tanzania that I would bring it to my uncle who lived next door. Uncle Windy was a retired urologist whose hobby was to program computers. "I need any information about Caleb's mistress you can find," I told him while handing over the stolen goods. He found and printed the emails between Caleb and Layla before the day's end. Caleb had deleted them all, but Uncle Windy was able to recover them.

When I returned the next morning to pick up the laptop and printed emails, Uncle Windy said, "Caleb refers to you as his 'headache' in his emails to his girlfriend."

I waited until I was back home to read the emails. They'd started at the end of June. Layla's were about going out partying and getting drunk. Caleb wrote back saying things like he wanted to take a bath in a big jacuzzi with her. His comments sounded familiar from within our own marriage. In almost all of his emails, he wrote that he needed to "get rid of his headache"—which I soon realized, like Uncle Windy had said, was me—and then they could be together. He wrote that he'd been in a loveless, sexless marriage for years and that it was great to be in love and have great sex. Everything he wrote about me was a lie. It made me wonder if I ever knew him at all. *I don't recognize the person writing these emails*, I thought. He even cussed and spoke crudely—my husband who never cussed around me. It was heartbreaking. I had loved someone I truly didn't know.

Later that day, I went to the Chattanooga Health Department to get an HIV test and to be tested for any other venereal diseases. As humiliating as it was, I'd told my mom I needed to do this, and she'd agreed I needed to get this off my mind. At my appointment, first they tested me for pregnancy, which was thankfully negative. Then I explained to the nurse that I just came home from Tanzania where I'd learned my husband was having an affair with a Zimbabwean girl. The nurse looked at me with complete fear in her eyes, which didn't help my disturbing thoughts at all. I was afraid and felt very alone.

"It's going to take over a week to get your test results back for HIV," the nurse told me before I left. It was a long, mind-battling wait. When the health department finally called a week later, I became weak-kneed when the nurse told me I had no venereal diseases and that I was negative for HIV.

Oh, Lord God Almighty. You are my stronghold. I worship You, I praise You, Jesus. I immediately went down and prayed on my knees in the living room of my house. I felt profoundly thankful for Reid's prayer of protection over me, and I thought, *God has just performed another major miracle in my life, thank you God for Reid and Dr. Sanders.*

CHAPTER 27
TAKING CARE
OF BUSINESS

But those who hope in the Lord will renew their strength.
They will soar on wings like eagles; they will run and not
grow weary, they will walk and not be faint.

—Isaiah 40:31

S hortly after I got tested at the health department, Mark
called. I was at my house, excited to hear from him since
he was a refreshing diversion from what was going on. He
was an encouragement and strength to me, asking if I was
getting all the paperwork done at the lawyer's office, being
specific about what should be included.

"Yes, I'm doing things quickly like you encouraged," I
said, thankful for the wisdom Mark was giving me about
my divorce paperwork. We spoke for a little while about
what was going on in our lives—where Mark was traveling,
how I was doing. Then he mentioned coming to see me,

so I finally said, "Mark, my pastor has counseled me to not talk to any man who is not a family member until after Christmas because I could become emotionally dependent on them and that is not healthy for me. I need to rely on the Lord and heal. He said that I could make some bad decisions if I become emotionally dependent on someone. I am weak and vulnerable right now, and you have been my knight in shining armor. I think my pastor is right and I want to be wise." I was so raw. I had no filter. I said exactly what I thought. Mark was always gracious, and told me he understood. He told me he respected what my pastor said, and he would check on me after Christmas. It was very hard for me to say goodbye to Mark. I thanked him and told him with a little glitch in my throat and tears in my voice that I was going to really miss him. I confessed he was my security blanket and my pastor was right, I was leaning on him too much and it was not healthy for me. We hung up and I cried, just like I had when I left Caleb in Africa. Again, I was losing someone I loved. I had only been in Mark's company for less than two hours total, but he was my forever friend.

So I looked forward to after Christmas.

Things continued to move quickly. I obtained the satellite phone records via email to see who Caleb had called over the last few months. It turned out, he had called the same Zimbabwean cell phone four to five times a week, whereas he'd only called me once or twice a week during the two months we were apart. His calls to the Zimbabwean number ranged from fifteen minutes to fifty-five minutes long. I called the number from home, and a young woman with a Zimbabwean accent answered. I hung up. Heart racing, I called again, still trying to prove to myself that Caleb really was a liar. This time Caleb answered. I was still lining up all the lies to prove to myself that he was a liar. As sad as it sounds, a part of me still wanted to believe he would never cheat on me.

Shortly after my call to Caleb's girlfriend, Caleb's parents called from Tanzania. I answered and his mother spoke while his father listened beside her. She told me Caleb had called them to tell them he was divorcing me. But he would not explain why.

I'd always loved Caleb's mother and told her how Caleb had been so mean and hateful to me when I came to Tanzania. "He told me he wanted a divorce as soon as I got off the plane." Then I told her about Caleb's twenty year old Zimbabwean girlfriend that he had to fly out of camp because I surprised him by coming early.

"I'm so surprised," Caleb's mother said. "I've seen the way Caleb looks at you. He loves you, Anne G. This doesn't make any sense to me. I'm sorry this has happened to you. Do you think you could try to talk him into going to speak to one of the pastors at church and convince him to stay married?"

Feeling defeated, I said, "Caleb has been very clear he wants a divorce. I did everything I could do to try to save our marriage."

Caleb's father had very little to say. Caleb's mother didn't say much more. Caleb's parents usually did whatever he told them to do, and he made most of the decisions in their family. It seemed clear to me from our short conversation that his parents would not be speaking to Caleb about our marriage situation anymore. Especially since they had to get the reason for the divorce from me. I answered all his mother's questions, and then we hung up.

I never heard from his parents again.

At this time Caleb was supposed to be in Arusha, Tanzania, leading a hunt for his clients. I knew he was with his girlfriend because he had answered her cell phone. I just didn't know where they were. Caleb called his assistant Richard, who worked out of our house, shortly after my phone call with his parents. The telephone operator asked Richard if he would accept a collect call from Caleb from the Kingdom Hotel in Victoria Falls, Zimbabwe. Richard said, "Yes, I accept."

When the operator connected the call, Caleb lied and told Richard he was on a hunt with clients in Tanzania. They talked about business. Then Caleb told Richard, "I'm worried Anne G.'s going to drain my bank account. Could you call the bank and have them freeze the account so she can't get any money out?"

Richard said, "Yes," then asked, "How's the weather in Tanzania?" He was trying to see if Caleb would admit the truth that he was really in Zimbabwe. But Caleb continued to lie about where he was, telling Richard about the weather and even telling a few made-up stories about what was happening on the hunt. Richard came downstairs after the call to tell me about it. "I'm surprised at how effortlessly he lied to me," he said.

I wasn't surprised at all.

I was trying to piece together what had happened before I had arrived in Tanzania. How had Caleb changed his mind so quickly about our marriage? He'd done one hunt before the hunt with the clients I'd joined, with a husband

and wife who were in their sixties. I had met the wife previously and had called her Tuesday to ask her how the hunt went. She said it was wonderful and they missed having me on the hunt. When I asked if there was anyone else on the hunt, she said no. It was only the three of them and the staff. I told her that when I arrived in Tanzania about a week after their hunt, Caleb told me he wanted a divorce.

She told me that very much surprised her, because she had spoken to Caleb about our marriage on the safari, and he told her how much he loved me and was missing me. She went on to say he actually said, "Anne G. is my life." She said, "Those are strong words for someone to say, I am shocked he wants to divorce you. He acted like he completely adored you." I sat there on the phone confused. I told her there was a young girl from Zimbabwe he was having an affair with. The client said, "Oh goodness. I met her. The day we were leaving, Caleb took us to the airport, and she was with him. I did not speak to her much. She is *very* young."

I said, "Yes. She just turned twenty this month."

She said, "Caleb told us she was the daughter of a friend of his from Zimbabwe, and that he was taking care of her while she was in Tanzania."

My heart sank. More lies. I thanked the client and hung up.

So. After reading the emails, calling and hearing Caleb answer Layla's phone in Zimbabwe when he was supposed to be in Tanzania, and learning that he told his parents we were getting divorced, I was mad. I decided it was time for Caleb to come home and divorce me. I called Saul on his cell phone and said, "Caleb told Richard he was in Tanzania on a hunt with clients, although he just made a collect phone call from The Kingdom Hotel in Zimbabwe. You tell Caleb he needs to call me. We need to discuss our divorce. He needs to get home and sign divorce papers—now."

"Yes," Saul confirmed, "Caleb is in Zimbabwe. I am shocked he has run off with a girl like Layla. Caleb met her for the first time when he got to Zimbabwe in June. He has not been acting like himself. I have no idea what he is thinking. As soon as you left Tanzania, he flew to Zimbabwe to be with his girlfriend and has been staying at the Kingdom Hotel." (Which was an expensive tourist hotel next to Victoria Falls.) "Layla does not seem like Caleb's type. She is a very young girl, from a low-income family. And she has a bad reputation with men."

This just made me more irritated. I really didn't care what Saul thought. I was done with Caleb humiliating me. I told Saul, "You tell Caleb if he does not call me by the end of the day, I will take everything he has and be happy to fight him in court. Who knows Saul, I might be your new business partner."

Lo and behold, within the hour, Caleb called.

I told him I had been to the lawyer, and we could either fight and pay lawyer and court fees, or agree and get divorced in thirty days. Caleb told me he did not want to fight, he wanted me to get all the paperwork ready, he would be home at the end of November to sign, and we could get divorced. It was Wednesday, August 29.

He lit a fire in me. I said, "I don't think so. That is not going to work. You are disrespecting me, traveling all over Africa with your whore while you are married to me. You need to fly home now, get your clothes out of my closet, get your toothbrush out of my bathroom, get all your stuff out of my house, and get out of my life. If you don't come home now and divorce me, I will take your company and everything else you own."

There was silence on the phone. He could tell I was serious.

He said, "I can't come home, I have hunts booked and I need the money."

I said, "Well, you blew the last hunt in Tanzania off to run around with your girlfriend in Zimbabwe and stay at the Kingdom Hotel, so it looks like money is not a problem."

He did not have anything to say to that.

"I'll get everything written up with the lawyer and we can sign it all this Friday," I said. "That's in two days. I want the house, all the furniture, and all my assets I brought to the marriage, including all my stocks, which would be mine if we went to court anyway. I also want my BMW. You can have your business and your 4Runner."

A long pause. Then Caleb said, "I want both safari companies along with all their assets, my 4Runner, all my animal mounts, all my guns, all my hunting equipment, the office furniture, and the computers in my office."

"Okay," I said. "I get everything else."

Caleb said, "Okay. I'll make plans to be there Friday."

"All right," I said. "Goodbye."

Next I called my pastor Jim and updated him that Caleb would be coming home in two days so we could sign divorce papers. Jim told me he wanted me to pack up Caleb's clothes as neatly as possible, better than if I packed my own things, and pack up his entire office and animal mounts, and rent a storage unit to put it all in. He wanted me to change the locks to my house and give Caleb the storage key when he came to town. I told him I could not pack up the office because Richard was still coming to work every day. I didn't want to ruin him financially; he had clients actively on hunts. But I could do almost everything else. So, my cousins Meg and Tatia volunteered to come help me pack Caleb's personal stuff from our bedroom and around the house. It was a big job. We packed everything neatly and labeled the boxes. We stacked them in my garage. I didn't want to touch any of the safari business stuff because I didn't want to mess up any computer stuff or client's information. I was furious at Caleb, but I would never put his business at risk or damage it in any way, especially since we'd worked hard to make it as good as possible. I did, however, have the locksmith come that afternoon to change the locks to my house. He made new keys, and I threw the old ones away. I also took the garage door opener out of Caleb's 4Runner.

My stomach was in knots over all of this. I kept thinking back to my appointment with Dr. Sanders. During it he showed me a prayer out of Ephesians 6 to pray over myself every day. He said I didn't need to be afraid, but I needed to be wise. I needed to cover myself with the blood of Jesus, especially when Caleb returned home. I knew speaking scripture over myself was powerful, so as I stood in the garage surrounded by the boxes of Caleb's things, I prayed:

> Therefore put on the full armor of God, so that when the day of evil comes, you may be able to stand your ground, and after you have done everything, to stand. Stand firm then, with the belt of truth buckled around your waist, with the breastplate of

righteousness in place, and with your feet fitted with the readiness that comes from the gospel of peace. In addition to all this, take up the shield of faith, with which you can extinguish all the flaming arrows of the evil one. Take the helmet of salvation and the sword of the Spirit, which is the Word of God (Ephesians 6:10-18).

I knew God heard me and was with me. I could feel my relationship with Him was growing in leaps and bounds. The Lord was speaking to me in ways He had never done before, words were leaping off the pages of my Bible when I read it in the morning and at night, penetrating my soul and spirit. It was very real, and I was desperate. With His help I was able to get everything done swiftly for Caleb to come home and sign the divorce papers. I was doing it all with a brave face, but I was rattled to the core. Now that reality was sinking in that Caleb would be home in two days, I was scared.

Because down deep inside, I knew that I was not safe.

CHAPTER 28
THE VALLEY

Even though I walk through the valley of the shadow of death, I will fear no evil. For You are with me: Your rod and Your staff, they comfort me. You prepare a table before me in the presence of my enemies. You anoint my head with oil. My cup overflows. Surely goodness and mercy will follow me all the days of my life and I will dwell in the house of the Lord forever.

—Psalms 23:4–6

Thursday morning, as I was finishing packing up Caleb's things, Richard called me from upstairs: "Anne G., Abdul is on the phone calling from Tanzania saying he'd like to speak to you."

A chill ran down my spine. Abdul was Caleb's good friend who'd tried to get me to come to his house to meet with Caleb the day I left Africa. *Why is he calling me? Is he trying to trick me the way it seemed he was trying to trick me in Tanzania?*

"Okay," I answered Richard, then walked upstairs, thinking, *Relax. This is a phone call. Caleb and Abdul are in Africa and can't hurt me from there.* Then the thought flashed through my mind that maybe I was overreacting—maybe those convictions about Caleb wanting to harm me were all in my head.

Upstairs I told Richard I'd take the call on the extra office phone in the spare bedroom. Richard put Abdul on hold. I went to the bedroom, shut the door, and picked up the phone.

"Hello?"

"Anne G. It's Abdul. How are you?" He sounded genuinely sincere.

"Not so good," I said, wondering what this was about.

"Yes, I have heard what is going on. I am very sorry."

"Thank you," I said. "It's a mess."

"Anne G., I just now spoke to Caleb on the phone. He is not acting like himself and he has me worried."

I didn't say anything, just listened.

"He says he is getting a flight home to the United States, and I wanted to let you know he is on his way there now."

Why is he calling to tell me this? I wondered. "Yes," I said. "I know. We're meeting at the lawyer's office tomorrow to sign divorce papers."

"Okay. So you know he is on his way home."

"Yes," I replied, wondering what Abdul was getting at.

"I am worried Caleb is going to try to harm you," Abdul said, and there it was. "He said some things to me when I spoke to him last. He is not acting like himself. Do you understand what I am saying?"

His words hit my ears in slow motion. All the intense fear I had experienced in Tanzania came flooding back. I'd tried not to think about what had happened in Africa days earlier, had tried to pretend that I was safe, that everything I'd endured in Tanzania was in the past. But from what Abdul was calling to tell me from across the world—I was not safe. Not safe at all, confirming my innermost feelings. My heart started racing. My thoughts started spinning with the speed and power of a tornado.

"Anne G.," Abdul said. "I wanted to call to tell you this because you are my friend too, and I am worried for your safety."

"Thank you, Abdul," I said solemnly. "I hear what you're saying, and I'll be careful."

Although, I didn't know how to be. I was completely paralyzed in fear.

Looking back on this conversation, I wish I had asked Abdul several questions. *What did Caleb tell you?* for instance, and: *What was his plan of attack?* But I was too overwhelmed at the moment to think straight.

"I do not want Caleb to know I called you, Anne G. Okay?"

"Okay, Abdul. Okay…"

He said something else, but by this point all I could hear was the loud static of fear inside my head.

"Thank you for calling," I said in complete shock.

"Be careful, Anne G. Goodbye."

Oh, God, help me, I prayed out loud when I got off the phone. *Please, Lord God. What am I supposed to do?* Evil swarmed around me, and I felt like I was walking through "the valley of the shadow of death." I cried out for my God, the One who had delivered me out of Africa, the One who was my stronghold and my protector: *Oh, Jesus, help me. I need You. I have nothing but You, Lord God. Please cover me with the hedge of Your protection,* I pleaded out loud.

How can this be happening? I thought as I prayed. My heart pounded against my chest so hard I felt like I couldn't breathe.

I went straight over to my parents' house and sat down on their living room couch. They sat down next to me, seeing that I was upset. I was terrified from the top of my head to the tips of my toes. I was absolutely done. I had nothing left, nothing. I needed my parents to prop me up. I told them Abdul had called me and told me he was worried Caleb was going to try to harm me. The words came out of my mouth like a foreign language. I wasn't sure I even understood what I was repeating. I told them everything Abdul had said. My parents grew concerned. I felt like I was living inside a never-ending nightmare. The looks on my parents' faces revealed they felt the same way. My parents listened, but we all knew it was not good news. My parents and I knew God was speaking loud and clear, especially now that one of Caleb's closest friends was confirming the visions my daddy, my brother, Dr. Sanders, and I had had about Caleb's will to end my life. There was no doubt now what Caleb's intent was. My parents and I spoke briefly about the different ways he might try to kill me. It was a disturbing conversation. Maybe Caleb would hire a hitman, we hypothesized. Or maybe he would take matters into his own hands. We didn't know, but we did know he obviously shared his thoughts and possibly plans with Abdul.

After our discussion, my parents and I simply sat together. I started to cry. My parents tried to comfort me, but there wasn't much they could do or say. They did suggest that I move in with them until all of this was over and Caleb was gone. I agreed. My parents were both very independent people, and they allowed their children to be independent. So I looked at them through my tears: "Caleb wants me dead. I'm going to call my lawyer, Walter, to ask him to write me a will. I'm going to leave everything I own to my siblings, split evenly between the four of them. I hope nothing happens to me, but if it does, I don't want Caleb getting anything of mine. I'll also tell him when he gets home that I have a will written and signed."

My mom, who normally had plenty to say, stayed quiet. She looked at me with fear in her eyes. "I think that's a good idea."

"Yes," said Daddy softly. "I think so too."

It was a solemn and scary time. I was thankful my parents were walking through it with me. One decision at a time, we were putting our trust in God to guide us.

I left their house and called Walter about writing up my will. I told him to do it as soon as possible, then explained my phone call with Abdul. I wasn't dramatic, I simply told him the facts. To be honest, I was kind of embarrassed about it.

"I'll get the will ready," Walter said. "You can sign it and the divorce paperwork when you and Caleb come in tomorrow."

"Make it as ironclad as legally possible," I told him. "In case I end up dead."

"Okay," Walter said with a hint of disbelief.

I thanked him, still feeling embarrassed by my request. I kept thinking, *I am just a normal Signal Mountain Southern girl. I cannot believe this is really my life. This feels like a movie that I'm living out in real life.*

Generally in life, I preferred to pretend that everything was going to be okay, but now I had to be completely honest in order to protect myself. *Who cares if Walter thinks I'm over-reacting*, I thought. *I know the truth. I need a will, and he needs to know it's a priority.*

I need to be ready for Caleb when he comes home.

CHAPTER 29
AUTHORITY

Do not go on only drinking water, but have a little wine for the sake of your stomach and your frequent ailments.

—1 Timothy 5:23

You are of God, little children, and have overcome them, because He who is in you is greater than he who is in the world.

—1 John 4:4

I am a fixer, so I had been busy since my conversation with Abdul, getting ready for Caleb to come into town. I stayed busy so I did not have to think about the weight of our conversation. After taking care of all the things I needed to do before Caleb got home, I was finally finished. Caleb would be flying in the next morning to Atlanta, Georgia, and we were to meet at the lawyer's office in Chattanooga later that morning. It was late afternoon as I walked inside my parents' house, and only my dad was there. I went and sat down on the couch in the living room, next to his chair. Everything came crashing down as I absorbed my reality. I typically try to not think about my big problems; I would rather just go do something fun and adventurous instead. I try to spin it in my mind the best way possible and tell my-self, *It is all going to work out, it will be okay.*

Now I confessed, "Daddy, I am afraid," and tears started streaming down my face. My parents rarely drank wine, but they did occasionally. My dad was sitting in his chair next to me and he got up and went into the kitchen and poured us both a glass of wine and brought it to me. My dad had never encouraged me to drink anything, and I was surprised when he handed me a glass of wine and had one of his own. He sat down next to me and said, "The Bible says a little wine is good for the stomach, let's have a glass together and settle our stomachs." I rarely drank, but I figured if the Bible said it was okay in moderation, and it's good for the stomach, and my Daddy of all people was handing it to me, I would be happy to try it. We sat and both had some wine in the living room together. I had never had a drink with my daddy before. It made me feel like I was a real adult. Daddy let me have a good cry as I sipped my wine.

After letting me cry for a little while, my daddy looked at me and said the words I will never forget.

He said, "Anne G., I do not want you to ever forget, He that lives within you is greater than he that lives within this world. You do not have to be afraid; God is with you."

Those words wrapped around me in a powerful way in that moment. His simple Christlike faith gave me hope. I listened as he told me God was in control and we had to trust Him through this. My daddy told me he, my mom, and my family would be with me, and we would pray and continue to trust the Lord and be wise. I would stay with my family and not be alone with Caleb or alone at my house. God's hedge of protection had been around us from generation to generation, and he held us in the palm of His hand. My daddy told me we would not be controlled by fear, because fear was from Satan. My daddy's words were powerful. I knew what he spoke was truth; I was weak and needed him to speak truth over and around me like I needed air to breathe.

After a little time, I noticed the wine did work. It took off the edge and calmed my stomach down. I think it calmed my daddy down too. He was not saying much, which was unusual. He was a jolly man. He was very quiet that day. I was quiet too.

It was quiet before the storm.

I had moved some clothes over to my parents' (when Abdul called), and I was spending the night there again. I had my Bible and was reading the pages off of it. Taking in everything I could get. Praying for God to protect me. My parents refused to live in fear, and I was trying to follow suit, but it was a struggle. I had so many things floating through my thoughts: Dr. Sanders' prayers and my guardian angel I saw when I was with him, Abdul's phone calls both in Africa and since I got home, my pastor Jim's advice, so many things. I remember praying before I went to bed. *Lord, I am so afraid. I know You got me safely out of Africa when my life was in great danger. You can blind the enemy so he has no idea where I am under the shelter of Your mighty wings. Please keep me safe. He that lives within me is greater than he that lives within this world.* I fell asleep after reading my Bible and woke up around midnight with one of my night terrors. I had a bad feeling something was trying to kill me. I reached over and turned on the light and opened my Bible. I did not know what verse would be on the page, I was sleepy and in great distress. This is what I read from Luke 10:16–20:

> Whoever listens to you listens to Me; whoever rejects you rejects Me; but whoever rejects Me rejects him who sent Me.
> The seventy-two returned with joy and said, "Lord, even the demons submit to us in Your name."
> He replied, "I saw Satan fall like lightning from heaven. I have given you authority to trample on snakes and scorpions and to overcome all the power of the enemy; nothing will harm you. However, do not rejoice that the spirits submit to you, but rejoice that your names are written in heaven."

The word washed over me and popped off the page and filled my fear with truth. Truth of the Word of God, which gives us freedom and healing.

> *"I have given you authority to trample on snakes and scorpions, and to overcome all the power of the enemy; nothing will harm you. However, do not rejoice that the spirits submit to you, but rejoice that your name is written in heaven."*

I felt like God was saying, "You have the authority. Now you have to use My Word to defend yourself. Stop allowing Satan to torment you." I was not sure what it meant for my life, but I knew it was powerful. I was ready to stand in faith, even if my legs were trembling. I had been tormented for over five years, and the demons had to submit to me by the authority of Jesus. Dr. Sanders had told me that, and now God Almighty was speaking to me through His Word. I was washed with peace at that moment. It was like a hug from God as He told me, *I am here with you. Do not fear. You are mine.*

Caleb was coming home the next morning, ready or not.

I fell back asleep and woke up the next morning. I opened my Bible back to the verse I read at midnight and let the words wash over me. They were powerful, and I could feel the words penetrating my spirit. It is something amazing and full of power when the Holy Spirit gives you a verse that you know beyond anything, and that you understand fully, is for you directly. I felt like God Almighty through the power of Jesus Christ and the blood He shed for me was equipping me for a spiritual battle. I felt like God was showing me the torment I had lived under for five years through night terrors, and that I had authority over them. They had to submit to me in the mighty name of Jesus. I prayed for my day, armored myself as Ephesian 6 says to do, and read this verse out loud, proclaiming even the demons have to submit to me in the name of Jesus. I have authority over them. The six days I had been home from Africa until Caleb arrived were like a boot camp of learning to pray in a whole new way.

God was teaching me through His people and His Word how I could have freedom.

CHAPTER 30
TO HAVE HER BACK

The Lord your God in your midst, The Mighty One, will save; He will rejoice over you with gladness; He will quiet you with His love, He will rejoice over you with singing.
—*Zephaniah 3:17*

The next morning was Friday, August 31. Caleb arrived at eight thirty in the morning at the Atlanta International Airport, where Richard picked him up. I'd set up our appointment at the lawyer's office for eleven that morning, not wanting Caleb to have time to go to our house first before signing the divorce papers. I knew he would be mad that I changed the locks, and I also didn't want him to go home and remember all that we owned before he signed. I got dressed and went to meet Walter McGuire and Caleb down at Walter's office. I was thankful I felt very calm and in control of my emotions; I had been praying I would be calm and would not cry in front of Caleb. I was determined to not look weak, and although I felt weak at times, God covered me with His grace and gave me a peace that had to be from Him.

I arrived right at eleven o'clock and Caleb was sitting in a chair in the waiting area. It was awkward for both of us. I went to the reception desk and told the secretary I was there to see Walter. I sat down and waited. Caleb nodded his head at me and said very stiffly, "How's it?" Which was something that was said in Zimbabwe when you greeted someone.

I said, "Hi." He seemed like a completely different person. It was strange to not have any loving feelings for him at all. I had loved him for literally half the years of my life.

Walter came to the waiting room and called me back alone. I was surprised he called me alone. We went to the conference room, and he went over the final details of the paperwork. Then he called Caleb to come join us. Once we were both seated, Walter went over with Caleb and me the entire divorce decree and answered questions about our agreement. He casually mentioned that I was going to keep the name Sharp, unless I wanted to go back to Powell, which was my maiden name. Something sparked in me. "Wait," I said, "I can do that? I can go back to Powell?" I asked with a surprised face and a big smile.

"Yes," Walter said, "It is very simple, I can write in this paperwork you will revert your last name back to Powell, it is a simple change of one line."

"Yes!" I said immediately. "I would love that. I definitely want to go back to Powell. I love being a Powell."

Walter said, "Okay, that is easy to do."

Caleb, who had been very distant since we got there, almost robotlike, turned and looked at me. His face got red and he shook his head side to side in disgust. He was extremely

A Light Shining in the Dark

angry and was not able to hide it, master at hiding his feelings though he was. "You always were a Powell," he said.

"Yes," I smiled. "I was—and I always will be." I was surprised he was so upset about that of all things.

Walter told us he would be back, he needed to make the few adjustments we discussed and the change to the divorce decree to change my legal name to revert to Anne Gillespie Powell. I said, "Thank you so much, Walter, that makes my day. I did not realize it would be so easy to do that." Walter nodded, then left the room.

As soon as the door closed, Caleb looked at me; he was still mad over my name change.

Anger was burning in his eyes. *Why would my name change of all things upset him so much?* I wondered.

He said, "Why did he call you back here first? What were you talking about?"

I said, "Not much. He just wanted to go over paperwork with me."

Caleb said, "I don't know what you two are up to, but I know you two are trying to trick me and I am going to figure it out."

I kind of laughed, "Caleb. You know me better than anyone, I am not trying to trick you. You are being silly." I could see he was paranoid. I thought it was odd because he rarely questioned my truthfulness. Now it made sense why he always suspected people of lying and being dishonest. I never realized he was the deceptive one and that was why he suspected everyone else of being deceptive too. Just then Walter called me out of the conference room to come to his office. He had a question for me about the spelling of my name. He also had me sign my will.

After addressing these things, Walter asked, "Is Caleb all right?"

"What do you mean?"

"He seems a little out of it, don't you think?"

"I don't think so," I said, puzzled. "He seems normal to me."

Walter sat silent in his chair a moment, then said, "Does he do drugs?"

"No," I quickly said. "Caleb would never do drugs." Then I remembered the cigarettes in Tanzania. "At least, I don't think he would."

"Okay," Walter said, "I just wanted to make sure that was normal behavior for him."

I shrugged my shoulders. "He just arrived in town from Africa and came straight from the airport. He probably hasn't been to bed in twenty-four hours or more."

"Okay," Walter said. "Just checking."

I went back to the conference room and sat down. Caleb told me he should not sign the papers since he had never been unfaithful to me, and I was filing for infidelity. I just rolled my eyes, and said, "Oh yeah, right Caleb."

"That was really smart of you to steal my laptop," he said. "There was nothing on it except my business stuff."

"Well, now I have all the emails you and your girlfriend sent each other. Uncle Windy printed out all the emails you deleted between the two of you from your hard drive. In case you wanted to fight, I wanted to be sure to have all the evidence I needed."

"Don't pretend like you are innocent. I know you have slow danced with other men," he said.

"Yes, I have. You are right." I admitted. He was trying to

argue, but I was not going to. If he had said something like that to me when we were married, I would have jumped to explain and defend any of my actions that he even thought were off base. He knew that. He was trying to take the spotlight off himself.

He told me he was going to move to Texas and do his safari company from there because there was big money down there. I did not say anything. We were not fighting, just speaking calmly to each other. It was strange.

A minute later, Walter came back into the room. He had Caleb and me sign the divorce decree, then told us he would go file the paperwork at the courthouse. I needed to come to the courthouse on the day of hearing, but Caleb did not need to come since I was divorcing him for being unfaithful to me. The last thing Walter did before our appointment was over was hand me a stack of paperwork. "Here's a copy of your new will, Anne G.," he said. "And here are copies of what we signed today for both of you. Caleb, good to meet you. Anne G., I will be talking to you soon."

We both thanked Walter. I got up and walked to my car. I was not in a hurry to get home. Caleb got into his Toyota 4Runner and took off like it was a race, so I got into my BMW and made sure to not be in a hurry.

As I was driving up the mountain from the city, I was thankful to have the thirty-minute drive to digest the fact I had just signed divorce papers. I called my parents to let them know the appointment was over and I was heading to my house to meet Caleb. *He's not going to be happy when he realizes I changed the house locks,* I thought.

I was right. When I pulled up to the house, Caleb was standing by the garage, mad.

"My key doesn't work," he said when I got out of my car. "Why did you lock me out?"

"I changed the locks," I said, then hit the garage door and it opened in front of him." He stepped inside. The door inside the garage was unlocked and he went into the house. I waited outside until my daddy showed up a few minutes later. He wanted to be with me while I was at the house with Caleb. I entered the kitchen while my daddy waited in the garage.

Caleb met me in the kitchen and said, "Why are all my clothes gone out of the closet, what did you do with them?"

"All your personal things have been packed neatly and are in boxes labeled and in the garage," I said, then followed Caleb out there. My daddy was there. He and Caleb had always been close, and they loved each other. Caleb, surprised to see my daddy, greeted him stiffly.

My daddy said with a jolly voice, "Hey, Caleb," and stuck his hand out to shake his hand. Caleb shook his hand, because my daddy did not give him a choice.

"Well, I hear you're giving our daughter back to us," my daddy said with confidence, looking Caleb straight in the eye.

"Yes, I am," said Caleb. I could hear the nervousness in Caleb's voice.

"Well, we're happy to have her back!"

"Well, good," said Caleb. Completely out of his comfort zone.

It was as if the handshake was some kind of agreement my dad wanted to make clear. I was no longer Caleb's. My daddy was taking me back, under his protection. I was not expecting my daddy to say that. But it was endearing he was standing up and declaring I was his again. I gave a small smile at my daddy while Caleb was walking back inside.

I followed Caleb into the kitchen. I told him I was leaving to go to my parents', and that I would be sleeping at their house while he was in town. I placed my will on the kitchen counter along with some other paperwork. I said, "Oh, also, I wanted you to know I had a new will written by Walter. He has a copy of it filed at his office, and my parents have one too. If anything happens to me before our divorce is finalized, all my assets, my stocks, and properties, go directly to my four siblings, split evenly." I said it nonchalantly, like I was saying I had done some chores around the house, just details. All our interactions since he had been in town had been nonemotional, just business. Strangely, I was in an almost quietly pleasant mood. I think it was all the Holy Spirit giving me His mighty peace. Then I casually went on to tell Caleb a few other details and ask some questions about some things we needed to discuss. I said, "Okay, see you later." He almost seemed surprised I was leaving. Like there were some things he wanted to say. But I left. I knew Richard would be at the house working the next few days, and I could talk to Caleb later if we needed to say anything to each other. I did not want to be at the house alone with him, but I was okay with someone else there. My daddy left in his truck right behind me.

In the summer on Sundays, my family and I attended the Little Brown Church in our neighborhood that only holds service from Memorial Day to Labor Day. My great-grandmother was one of the women who spearheaded building this church in the early 1900s when the residents of Summertown drove horse and buggies, and it would take all day to get to and from church downtown. The church was a simple wooden structure with no air conditioning and an outhouse out back. Tucked within the old-growth forest, it was built for simply worshiping God the Father, God the Son, and God the Holy Spirit. It was nondenominational, Bible believing, and Bible teaching. The founders believed the Word of God was completely true, and that is what was taught. All denominations worshipped together for the summer, Baptist, Catholic, Methodist, Presbyterian, Episcopalian, it did not matter, we all came together for the summer to worship God and read from His word.

After the service, most of my family—my parents, grandmother, aunts, uncles, siblings, cousins, and their spouses and children—would gather for Sunday lunch. It was at my Uncle Windy's pool house this particular day. After eating, we sat at the large tables in the shade of the Tennessee summer heat, and my cousins asked me to tell them what had happened and the details about leaving Africa. I told them about how Caleb had asked for a divorce as soon as I got off the plane in Tanzania in the hunting camp, and about finding out about his Zimbabwean mistress, meeting Mark at the hotel, the private chauffeur in England, and finally coming home. I never mentioned being afraid of Caleb; I was pondering all those things in my heart. As I told my story I cried, and my family cried with me. It was comforting to have my family love me. Even in the midst of my worst moments, they loved me. I was so ashamed since I was one of the youngest of my grandmother's fifteen grandchildren, and the *only* grandchild who was going to be divorced, and I felt like I wore the scarlet letter on my chest, for everyone to see, only my letter was a "D" for divorce. I cried as much for the shame I carried as I did for all the other shattered dreams.

It was a sad time as I shared my brokenness.

CHAPTER 31
BROKEN

The Lord is close to the brokenhearted and saves those who are crushed in spirit.

—Psalms 34:18

The next day, I called Richard on his cell phone to ask if he was working at our house. I told him I was coming over, and I wanted to make sure he did not leave the house while I was there, and to be listening to make sure everything was okay from upstairs. I had some paperwork Caleb needed to sign off on, and some family business stuff for two companies I had an interest in. I went to the house and stepped into the master bedroom first to get some things I needed. I noticed Caleb hadn't been sleeping there, which was unusual. He came downstairs and said, "Hi."

I smiled, "Hi."

He said, "What have you been doing?"

"Oh, nothing. Just getting some stuff I need."

Not knowing what would happen, I went into the kitchen

and Caleb followed me. I asked him to sign the paperwork I'd brought over, and after he did he said, "You want to sit down and talk?"

"Sure." I said.

We went and sat in our living room. I sat in a formal chair on one side of the room, and he sat in a club chair on the other side. We usually sat touching each other on our couch, which was in the middle of the room. It was almost as if there was a line drawn down the middle of the room. He started telling me he was moving to Texas and would live with his travel agent who offered for him to come live with her and her husband until he found a place of his own. He said the movers would be coming in a few days. We talked about what he planned to do once he arrived in Texas.

After talking for a while, Caleb asked, "What do you plan on doing with the house?"

"I'm going to try to keep it," I said. I was not sure if I could afford it or not, that was a big concern in my heart.

He let out a small laugh. "You'll never be able to afford to keep this place."

His words felt like a challenge, and I thrived on a good challenge.

In my heart I said, *Lord, I am going to do everything it takes to keep this house.*

It was as if someone lit a fire of determination under me. I pledged to my Savior that I was going to battle. I shrugged my shoulders and said nonchalantly, "I guess we will see." But inside, I knew I would work long hours in real estate to make sure I never had to sell my house. Now more than ever. I never used any of my inheritance to live on, and I was very frugal about what I spent. In fact, Caleb had tried to talk me into cashing in some of my inheritance and investing it in a safari business in Africa. Oh, how thankful I was, as we sat there, that I had refused to touch any of my savings. It would all be gone, just like he was getting ready to be.

We talked some more about Caleb's next steps before I looked at him with clear eyes and boldly asked, "Will you be honest with me and answer one question for me? We will never be seeing each other after our divorce so there is no reason to lie to me."

"What?" he asked. "What do you want to know?"

"How many other women have there been?" I asked.

He gave a surprised laugh, "What, you want a number?"

"Yes," I said seriously. "I do. I think you can tell me the truth. Now that all the papers have been signed, there is no reason not to be honest. Just tell me the truth."

He sat there looking at me for a long time. I could tell he had a lot going on in his mind, he was weighing out what his words would be or if there would be any words. I waited for a while, then I pushed gently, "It doesn't matter now. We're never going to see each other again."

Finally, and without saying a word, he held up one finger.

"One?" I said. "One woman? Only Layla?"

He nodded yes slowly. I said, "Okay, I don't believe you. I was hoping you would tell me the truth for once," I said, then dropped the subject.

Caleb went on to tell me his plans to go back to Africa for a few hunts after he got settled in Texas. Even though I felt like he'd lied to me about how many women he'd been with, it was strangely comforting to talk to him. Comforting for both of us it seemed. So much had happened over the past few weeks, and there had been almost no communication between us about it. I could tell he wanted to talk to me as much as I wanted to talk to him, especially since he'd always loved telling me about what he was doing and thinking. So, we continued to sit there in the daylight just talking.

He asked if I was ready to start dating.

I shook my head no and said, "I am not the one who wanted out of our marriage."

He said, "I know, but you will have lots of men trying to date and marry you. Anne G., don't get married too fast. Be careful, you are really naïve and there are lots of bad people who don't have good intentions."

I said honestly but casually with a small laugh, "Well, I dated you for five years, and that didn't help me out."

Caleb looked at me. He got very quiet, then, after a long pause he said, "You are my best friend." I just looked at him. I knew he was speaking from his heart, and that he did love me.

It kind of broke a new piece of my heart, a part I did not expect. He had betrayed me in our marriage and that was one brokenness, but this was a different part of my heart. I had grown up with Caleb. We had been best friends for almost half of our lives. We were always together. We went hunting and traveling all over the world together, we went four wheeling through the mountains together, and we enjoyed being together just watching television and working around the house and the yard. He had been my first almost everything. My first steady boyfriend, and the first person I fell in love with. I went out of the country with him for the first time to Africa. He was the first person I made love to on our honeymoon night. We went and explored so many new places for the first time together. We encouraged each other in our dreams. I might not have been a realtor, and he might not have started his business selling safaris if it wasn't for each other being best friends and believing in each other. I was losing my husband, but I was also losing my best friend. It was a truthful and raw moment between two people who had been in a relationship for fourteen years of their lives.

I wanted to say, "You are my best friend too." He looked at me as all these thoughts were running through my head. I guess he saw the weakness in my eyes.

He said, "I want to continue to come visit you and call you. I want to date you."

I sat there. He was completely being honest. He had no idea he was breaking my soul open. More in that moment than any other moment. I did not want to lose my best friend, but I had no choice, he happened to be the same man who had cheated on me and lied to me, deceived me and treated me with disrespect. I was so broken in that single moment. I did not shed a tear and Caleb probably never knew any of my deepest feelings. From the outside I was just listening as a friend. He knew how much I loved him, that was never a question. But he thought because I had always loved him and had always sacrificed for him, that I always would. He knew I was always his cheerleader, I am loyal to a fault, and that is not always a healthy characteristic. He knew it. He knew me. But I knew in my broken soul that I could not put him before myself anymore. He was no longer my husband.

I said solemnly, "Best friends don't do what you have done to me. I can't see you anymore."

He said, "Are you saying you don't want to see me after I leave?" He was really surprised. Which surprised me. He said, "We are best friends. I need you in my life, and you need me. I still love you, and I know you love me."

"No. When you leave here I do not want any contact with you at all. No phone calls, no emails, nothing," I said.

He laughed and said, "You don't mean that. You will want to date me; it is too good between us and you know it. You are just upset, but you will change your mind. We'll see," he said, confidently.

My pastor, Jim, had counseled me to have no contact at all with Caleb once he left. None. I had been struggling with that deep down, praying about it, legitimately wondering if I could do it. Now Caleb's words had sealed the deal. I vowed to myself at that moment that I would let him completely go.

"I'm serious, Caleb," I said softly and full of sadness. "When you leave, I want no contact with you ever again. This is your choice to leave our marriage, not mine." I rose from my chair. "I need to go now. I'll see you later." Caleb sat there smirking in total disbelief of what I had just proclaimed.

I left my house feeling sad but thankful we could talk as friends and not be hateful to each other. Our marriage had not been bitter. Yes, we had major fights, when we did fight. But we did not fight often. I loved being married; I was mourning the loss. I left my house a little more broken than I had already been. I went back to my parents' house and got into the bed and pulled the covers over my head and cried. No—wept. Because I was losing my husband, but I was also losing my best friend. And now that I was alone with the Lord, I could let it all out.

"Oh, God. I am so broken," I mourned. "Have mercy on me. Please. God, have mercy."

CHAPTER 32
BLOOD OF JESUS

We know that God's children do not make a practice of sinning, for God's Son holds them securely, and the evil one cannot touch them.

—1 John 5:18

That afternoon, I went to see Dr. Sanders. Caleb was leaving the next day, Tuesday, and I wanted to ask Dr. Sanders to pray for me and pray for Caleb. Dr. Sanders told me I needed to get out of the way so the Lord could deal with Caleb, and I needed to let him go. My pastor Jim had told me the same thing. I needed wise counsel. I was in an almost dreamlike state of mind. It felt like my life had been turned upside down and inside out and all the weight started coming down on me. I felt like I could help Caleb. He was miserably unhappy and had confessed that to me in Tanzania. I asked Dr. Sanders if he ever met with people who were demon possessed?

He said, "Yes." He was not startled at my question, just

spoke as if it were a completely normal topic. I confessed to Dr. Sanders that while I was in Tanzania in the hunting ground the month before, one night I told Caleb he was scaring me. I did not recognize his voice or his eyes, it was like he had a demon or something in him. I asked Dr. Sanders if he would meet with Caleb and have some kind of intervention. He said only Caleb could ask for that, the person has to want to change. I was surprised at my own words confessing out loud what I was wrestling with in my heart.

"I think he does have a demon inside of him." I sat there surprised that that is what actually came out of my mouth. Then, to my surprise, I got a fire in me and the truth came pouring out. I said, "I know he does. He told me stories about when he was growing up in East Africa. I don't know when it came into him, maybe when he was a boy. There was a large black panther that he told me followed him around the hunting grounds for years when he was young. There are no large black cats in Africa, and he thought it was a dark spirit. Or, it might have come into him when he was a little older and shot a poacher," I said. "I don't know when, but I know it's in him. I *know* it." Then I remembered: "About five years ago, I felt him change in bed, there was a coldness. He told me I was his good side. He said he had a dark side, but that I didn't have to worry about that side because I would never see it, he would protect me from it."

Revealing these things, all the pieces of this puzzle in my mind were coming together. I was not sure myself if it was true, it was as if I was working out the pieces of my life that never added up right there in that meeting. I wondered how Dr. Sanders would respond. I was telling my most intimate thoughts that I would never share with anyone.

Dr. Sanders listened and said in a calm normal voice, "You might be right. And if he ever decides he wants help, you can bring him to me. But once he leaves, you need to let all of this go. I'm sensing it is the demon of death that dwells inside him," Dr. Sanders said. "He'll have to decide for himself what he wants. It is his choice. Only God can help him now."

I left Dr. Sanders' thinking, *How could I have actually been married to someone I think had a demon?* It was upsetting to me. I kept having the same thought over and over, *I do think he has a demon, I really do.* I was kind of wrestling with this thought. When Dr. Sanders said he sensed it was the demon of death, it resonated in my spirit just like when my daddy and brother told me they were worried Caleb was going to try to kill me. Everything in me agreed with what I had revealed to Dr. Sanders: that Caleb had a demon in him. I kind of believed myself, kind of didn't. It made sense, but it was hard for me. I was born and raised in Southeast Tennessee in a Christian home where we didn't have anything like this happen. I was working through all this with the Lord. The verse God had given me a few nights before was a key verse in my prayer and worship time. I kept meditating on this verse thinking more and more that God was speaking.

> *And they overcame him by the blood of the Lamb and by the word of their testimony.*
> —*Revelation 12:11*

So now here I was, working through all of this with the Lord. Battling it out in my mind and in my heart. Clinging to the Word of God as a lamp to my feet and a light to my path—to show me the truth.

I spent the afternoon thinking about what all had happened. It was a lot, a whole lot. Especially for someone like me who did not like to deal with unpleasant feelings or thoughts.

I'm the enthusiast on the enneagram personality test. You know, the person who wants to go do something adventurous and spontaneous instead of facing any problems or pain of any kind—emotional or physical. There was no good mind space happening, none. I had been a runner from any problems my entire life. Now there was nowhere to run. I had to deal with it; Caleb's potential demon. I had so many things swarming through my head. Dr. Sanders had told me to pray the blood of Jesus over me every day, but especially if I was going to be around Caleb. I looked up all the verses about the blood of Jesus and prayed them over myself. *I have been bought and paid for with the price of Jesus' blood.* I was fearful, but there was this strong urge inside me. I was finally coming to see a picture I had not been able to figure out for years. I wanted to know if I was right. I wanted to confront Caleb with the evidence of this demon. I knew he would leave, and I would never be able to talk to him again. It was eating away at me. As much as I wrestled with not wanting to know, the larger urge was to find out. This was my last chance. Caleb was leaving the next day. I waited all afternoon, thinking and praying about what I would say and do.

In the evening, at dusk, I asked my cousin, Tatia, to go with me to my house because I was afraid to be there alone with Caleb. I walked in the front door and Caleb called out from the upstairs, "Who's there?" I said it was me. He told me to come on up to his office. I had Tatia wait in the living room, which opened to the balcony beneath Caleb's office, which meant she could hear me easily if I called out for help. I walked upstairs to his office at the top of the stairs and told him Tatia was here with me, and she was waiting downstairs. I wanted him to know we were not alone.

He greeted me, "Hey." He was sitting at his desk.

I walked fully into the room and said, "You have everything ready?"

"Yeah, I think so. The movers will be here at 8:00 a.m."

"Okay." I said, "I'll come over in the morning."

I wanted to be present to make sure the movers did not take anything that we had not agreed on him taking. We talked for a few minutes. It seemed like a long time, with what was on my mind, but it was only a few minutes of small talk.

"Caleb," I finally said, my voice shifting into a more serious tone. "I was wondering if you would go with me to see a Baptist pastor who I went to see today. He has a gift from the Lord; he can see spirits." I felt weird saying it out loud. I was not sure how he was going to respond.

He looked at me. "Why?" he said, looking me in the eyes.

I kind of gave a small laugh nervously. I prayed the blood of Jesus over myself right there silently.

Thank you, God that I am covered in the blood of Jesus, nothing can harm me or come against me, the enemy has to surrender to me in the mighty name of Jesus.

Then I composed myself and said, "I think you need help." I said, locking my eyes onto his, "You are miserably unhappy, and I think you are in spiritual warfare." He kind of looked at me and his relaxed demeanor got hard to read, so I kept going. I walked closer to him, and I was now standing right in front of his desk. He was looking straight at me. We were about four feet apart.

"I think you are depressed, and I also think you have a demon inside you. You will never be happy living like that."

After the words came out of my mouth I thought, *I cannot believe I just said that out loud.*

Caleb looked at me, he laughed kind of blowing it off and said, "You think I have a demon inside me?" I stood firmly in my place, determined to not be waivered.

"Yes." I said quietly confident, "I do."

He looked at me, with a little smirk on his face. He paused as if thinking about what he would say. I wondered which way this was going to go.

"When we dated, you told me about the large black panther that followed you around the hunting grounds for years, stalking you when you were young. Then you told me in bed the morning I saw the man at the end of my bed that you had a dark side, and that I would never see that side of you, because I was your good side. But I felt you change that morning in bed. I felt a presence come in between us and divide us. I know you, Caleb, looking back over the last nine years of being married to you it is all coming together. I saw you change when we were in the Selous hunting camp, I did not recognize your voice or your eyes. I *know* you have a demon inside of you. It can't hide from me anymore, and you know it."

Then I paused, even for myself to realize all the evidence was undeniable. I stood there for what seemed like eternity. Waiting for Caleb to respond. I was nervous, but determined.

He leaned back in his chair and picked up a hunting knife that was on his desk and started looking at it. From handle to tip, the knife was about eight inches long, with a razor sharp blade designed for cutting open dead animals. Caleb looked at the knife, still saying nothing.

I continued, "I can help you. The man I want to take you to can cast demons out of people." I stood there, firmly planted before him giving the evidence from the years of our marriage.

He still had his hunting knife in his hand, he was turning it side to side, and then looking at me, he changed in front of me. There was a presence that took Caleb's place, this time I actually saw it happen with my eyes and not just with my spirit. He became cold hearted and distant, and I felt a division of something come between us, the same way it felt days before in the hunting camp and that morning in bed, years earlier when he admitted he had a dark side. It looked like Caleb's body, but it felt nothing like his spirit.

He kept moving the knife side to side, looking at it, then he looked at me with pure hatred in his eyes. I knew at that moment with every part of my being, he wanted to kill me. I saw it in his eyes.

It scared me, really scared me.

I didn't care how it looked, I got a fire in my belly deep down. I looked straight at Caleb and opened my mouth and the Holy Spirit of God filled my mouth like a mighty wind, delivering me the words to speak, "I am covered in the blood of Jesus Christ, you cannot touch me, and you know it. I am a child of the most high God and He lives and breathes inside me. You have to submit to me in the name of Jesus, it says so in God's word." Then I waited.

His voice was not Caleb's voice, and he gave a small type of laugh, and said, "Demon...that is such a bad word."

Then he paused, "It sounds so bad when you say I have a demon."

I stood there, kind of paralyzed knowing this was what I had been waiting on, I was not talking to Caleb, I was talking to the demon inside of him. Every goose bump on my body was standing up. This thing speaking to me was nothing like my husband, his voice was completely different. The first time I heard it speak, days before in Tanzania, I knew it, but later, I had questioned myself in doubt.

I was seeing it with my own eyes and ears. However, this time I knew what I had experienced before, so I was almost waiting to see if it was really true.

I looked at the knife, and I pretended that I did not notice the demon was talking to me. Then I said quietly, but with confidence, "Caleb, give me that knife, you are bothering me playing with it."

The evil thing inside Caleb looked at me with more hatred than I had ever seen from anyone before. "Why?" it said. "Are you scared of me?"

"No," I said confidently, pretending I was speaking to Caleb and not the demon. "But I'm trying to have a serious conversation with you, give it to me."

For several seconds Caleb looked at the knife. Then he did it. He set the knife down slowly on his desk. In the blink of an eye I reached over and grabbed it.

"Thank you," I said, a little surprised by my audacity, because inside I knew I was dealing with two different personalities, but in a very strange way, I did know that Caleb loved me as much as he could love anyone, so I was addressing him.

I was still standing in front of him, not saying a word. It seemed like a long time. I waited.

Finally, he looked straight at me and said, "You and your parents did not believe me when I told you stories about the dark spirits in Africa." He paused. "You finally believe me now, don't you?"

At that moment we were looking into each other's souls.

Caleb had returned. It was in the way he said it, and in the way he looked at me now. Exposed and defeated, he was pleading with my soul to understand him.

I quietly admitted, "Yes."

I was heartbroken, and in a strange way I could tell he was too. He didn't want me to know his secret. Because I had always adored him, and now I finally knew the truth.

It was a really sad moment. We both knew what the problem was for the first time. After fourteen years, finally I knew his secret.

So, very gently, as I would have during our marriage, I spoke lovingly to my husband, "Caleb, I can help you. God doesn't want you living like this, you can command it to come out of you in the name of Jesus, and it has to obey. It doesn't have a choice."

He looked down at his hands and shook his head slowly no.

He finally said, "It's too late for me."

I could not believe we were having this conversation. He was admitting what I had wrestled with in my thoughts; he did have a demon in him.

It was true.

I said, "Caleb, that is a lie from the depths of hell. God wants you and you can live in freedom with Him. You are His." He looked at me and shook his head no again. I stood there.

Quietly, but with anger and tears, I said, "Where did you get it from?" I was deeply mad at Satan and his demon—which I had been unable to put my finger on for years. They had wrecked and ultimately destroyed my marriage.

He sat there looking at me. I could see he was thinking about it, but he would not say a word.

"Was it the black panther that stalked you for years?"

He looked at me. I could see he was wrestling with what he was willing to reveal to me, so I stood in front of him waiting.

He said, "You will be better off without me." My eyes welled up with a few tears. They were tears of anger, tears of loss, tears from the years of sacrifice and destruction. Those few tears were the realization of what was true. It was as if a curtain had been drawn back and for the first time all the pieces of a puzzle I could not figure out came together. I was finally clearly seeing my husband in the light. I knew he had made his decision.

He was admitting it was his choice.

Caleb would not tell me where he had gotten it, or when he had allowed it to have control of him. It did not matter. It was over. He had made his choice.

He chose to allow this demon or demons to stay and give up a life with Jesus Christ as his Lord. He was walking away from God, and God was living in me. So, he was walking away from me also.

I said with tears in my eye, "Caleb, if you ever decide one

day in the future that you want help, that you want to get rid of the demon inside of you, I will help you. I will *always* be here to help you, no matter what." We just stared at each other. Both of us finally knew why it was over.

He sat there in silence. We were both sad.

"I need to go," I finally said.

In a concerned voice Caleb asked, "When are you coming back?"

"I don't know," I said, looking into his eyes once more. "Good night."

Then I walked out the office door, my tears rising then falling like waves.

CHAPTER 33
PUZZLE PIECES

But whoever denies Me before men, I also will deny before My Father who is in heaven.

—Matthew 10:33

Back downstairs, my cousin and I left. She had no idea what had just taken place. I went back to my mom and dad's and needed time to digest everything that had just happened. I thought, *Dr. Sanders was right. A person had to want to be free.* I was heartbroken that Caleb did not want to live the same life I had chosen to live. *How had I missed that? How had I not seen this demonic spirit before?* I believed the stuff I read in the Bible about people being affected by demons, but this was my real life. *When did Caleb start making these choices to walk away from God?* So many emotions and so many dreams shattered.

At that moment, I remembered something upsetting from the year before. Caleb and I were in Zimbabwe with his new business partner, Saul. The three of us had quickly

become good friends. I went hunting with Caleb everywhere, which meant I was with the two of them a lot. One
day Saul was driving the Land Cruiser single cab hunting
truck through the grassland with me sitting between him
and Caleb. We were out on a hunting trip in the bush driving, and we were just talking about anything and everything.
So, I asked Saul about his faith. He said he was Jewish, and
I asked what his beliefs were. He explained that his parents
were Jewish, and he was because his parents were. I commented that Caleb and I were Christians, and we believed
the Jews were God's chosen people. I explained that Jesus
was a Jew, and we believed that he was the Son of God, sent
to die for our sins so we could have a relationship with God.
We had asked Jesus to come live inside of us and be our
Savior, which was how we would be able to spend eternity
with Him in heaven when we died.

Saul seemed a little surprised by my declaration. He
casually asked if we were strong in our faith. I said confidently, "Oh yes. Caleb and I are both devout Christians. It is
the most important thing in our lives."

Saul said, a little curious, "Oh really. Caleb, I did not
know you are a Christian."

Caleb, who had not spoken the whole conversation
about Christianity said, "Well, Anne G. believes that, but
that's not what I believe."

My heart stopped. I turned and looked straight at Caleb,
"Caleb," I said in complete fear, "What do you mean? Don't
say that, Caleb." He did what he usually did in public if he
didn't agree with me and brushed me off, like it was no big
deal. I sat there, and my whole world went upside down.
As we drove through the wilderness, I felt as if I was going

through an internal wilderness as well, wandering through new terrain in my marriage. I did not want to fight in front of Saul because I thought that was inappropriate. I was quiet the rest of the drive; I was in my head. I kept thinking, *Why would Caleb say something so horrible? Our whole lives are based around our faith in Jesus.*

We got back to our camp that evening and at the first chance we had to be alone in our tent, I stood up to Caleb. "Why did you say you did not believe in Jesus today in front of Saul? The Bible says, 'Whoever denies me before men, I also will deny before my Father who is in heaven.' Why would you deny Jesus? Caleb, if you do that, He will deny you before God." I was fearful for both of us at his admitting to denying Jesus. "Why would you say something so horrible?" I was very upset.

Caleb brushed me off and said, "I don't feel the same way you do."

That made me mad, "Since when? We got married agreeing on all the same beliefs."

He got dressed and said, "You don't worry about me, you worry about you." That was his response more and more about the big issues in our marriage.

I was devastated, and it showed. He then explained that Saul would hold him to a higher standard if he claimed he was a Christian, and he did not want to be a bad witness. I thought that was hogwash and told him so. I wrestled for months over those words. Now they were coming back to me. I had signs that were upsetting, and it was as if they were coming together as a puzzle and all the pieces were finally making a picture I didn't want to see. It was becoming clear why God was ending my marriage. I got into the bed with the weight of why my marriage was over, praying and asking God to heal my brokenness. I kept thinking, *I can't believe this is really happening. This feels more like a movie I don't want to be a part of.*

I prayed that night, soberly realizing God had answered my prayer. I had asked him to show me what was true. I had wrestled with what I had experienced and heard over the last nine years of my marriage. And God had shown me something good—painful, but good. Tonight Caleb had admitted to me his darkest secret. Therefore, through Caleb's own words, God had given me a clarity that I could never doubt. I had the solid truth.

After my conversation with Caleb that night, I knew the truth, and he knew that I knew the truth. It was a strange feeling knowing a demon was living with me and was part of my marriage. I didn't understand what it was all about, and honestly, I didn't want to understand it all. I thanked God for pulling the curtain back and letting me see the reality of my life and the person I was married to. And why my marriage was over. I was trying to process all that was happening.

Begging the Lord to be my light in the darkness. It was very dark.

CHAPTER 34
GONE

If we are thrown into the blazing furnace, the God we serve is able to deliver us from it, and He will deliver us from Your Majesty's hand. But even if He does not, we want you to know, Your Majesty, that we will not serve your god or worship the image of gold you have set up.
—Daniel 3:17–18

Weeping may last through the night, but joy comes with the morning.
—Psalms 30:5

The next morning, I woke up. It was Tuesday, the day Caleb was leaving me forever. I felt peaceful and a quiet confidence. I had cried myself to sleep the night before, begging God for His mercy, asking Him to heal Caleb and our marriage. I was still hoping that God would intervene, that Caleb would tell me he wanted to go to Dr. Sanders to have that nasty demon commanded out of him so our marriage could be redeemed and we could live happily ever after. Yet now, in the new light of the new day, I felt refreshed. *Even if* God didn't answer my prayer, it would be okay, I would be okay. I knew that was only from God's grace. His mighty spirit was living in me.

Dressed in black jeans and a cute hot pink t-shirt, I pulled up to my house in my silver BMW at 8:00 a.m. and walked confidently in. The movers had just arrived. I greeted them as Caleb explained what was being moved and what was staying. When they started moving furniture, I helped answer any of their questions while keeping myself busy downstairs. At one point, Caleb came to me in the kitchen and asked if he could purchase the upstairs leather bonus-room furniture from me. Since I've always been happy to make a business deal, and because that furniture looked great in Caleb's trophy room (and would've reminded me of him if I'd kept it), I said, "Sure. How much?" We quickly agreed on a price, then the movers loaded that furniture into the box truck also. When they finally finished moving the animal heads, office supplies, furniture, and Caleb's boxes that were in the garage, Caleb confirmed the address of his storage unit in Texas where they would deliver everything.

Before leaving, the three young men came into the kitchen and said goodbye to me and told me it was very nice to meet me and that they hoped things went well for me in the future. It was clear what the situation was, and the young men had been kind to me throughout the day. I could tell it irritated Caleb; he was in an irritable mood. Frankly, he had been irritable for many years, and I had just grown accustomed to it. I tried to cover up his rude behavior in public, making excuses for why he was in a bad mood. I used to call him an ole grouch when he acted like that when we were alone, and I would tease him about how grouchy he was. I just kept my mouth shut and prayed God would give me strength to get me through this day. So far, so good. I bawled when he was not around, but anytime I was with him, I was in control of my emotions. That was important to me. I was too prideful to ever beg or cry for him not to leave me. The movers drove off with all Caleb's belongings. The house was looking vacant. It was just the two of us. After my confrontation with Caleb the night before, I was no longer afraid to be in the house alone with him, and so I started vacuuming where Caleb's furniture used to sit before moving to the kitchen to sweep.

Caleb came into the kitchen a few minutes later. "I have everything packed, and I think I'm ready to go."

I set the broom down and looked at him.

"Be sure to send me some pictures of Taz," he said as if he were going on a trip, not leaving for good.

I smiled sadly. I had already told him I was not going to communicate with him after he left, so I was not going to be sending him pictures. He looked at me and smiled sadly back. He knew once I decided to do something, I was usually determined to follow it through. Then he looked me straight in the eye and said something I didn't expect: "I swear to you, Anne G., I have never touched another woman since we've been married."

I just looked at him. I thought, *What about the one finger you held up?* But, it was not worth saying a word, it was just more lies. So I just looked at him. *This is really sad,* I thought.

After a heavy silence between us, Caleb said, "Well, after I'm gone, let me know if your nightmares go away."

I looked blankly at him. Those words were slowly sinking into the core of my spirit. I had never thought Caleb could be the reason for my night terrors. He actually must have thought he could be the reason. It caught me so off guard, I was a little stunned. I did not say anything. But his remark kept echoing in my heart. *Whoa, I thought. What? Could all those years of suffering with night terrors have been because of me living with a demon or demons inside of Caleb?* Then something else hit me. *Was the man in the hat and trench coat who stood at the end of my bed to kill me on the night of Caleb's birthday—the night no one could reach Caleb, who'd claimed to be working under-cover—not a man at all, but an evil spirit, a demon? Could it have been the demon of death?*

At that moment, it clicked in my heart as I resolved. *Yes. I believe that it was.*

My mind continued to spin. *Could the night of the demonic intruder have been a night Caleb cheated on me? Could it have been because he broke our marriage vows, opening the door for evil to enter our home? Was it a demon who hunted Caleb, and now Caleb had become the hunter?*

I have thought about that one statement a million times since he said it: After I'm gone, let me know if your night-mares go away.

"Bye," he finally said, pulling me out of my dizzying thoughts.

I was still thinking about his last remark.

"Bye," I said, grabbing the broom beside me and start-ing to sweep again. Caleb walked outside. I didn't even look up, I kept sweeping, not even knowing what I was sweeping, or caring. I was still lost in thought about that comment as I reflected, remembering all the suffering I had endured from nightmares over the last five years. *Caleb is why I could not get rid of my nightmares. Has he known all along?*

"I need you to move your car," Caleb came back into the kitchen to say, breaking my heavy train of thought once more. "You're blocking me in."

"My keys are in it. You can move it," I said.

"I need my credit card also."

I looked up and then set the broom down. His credit card was in my purse inside my car, so I walked outside, pulled my car out of the way, and got out his credit card. He was standing beside his 4Runner in the driveway when I hopped out of my car. For some reason he was determined that I was going to be out there when he left. I walked over to him and handed him his credit card, which I hadn't used since purchasing my ticket home from Tanzania, and he knew I would never use it without permission. The sun was shining brightly for such a terrible end to a sad marriage.

He said, "Well, enjoy your new-found freedom."

I thought to myself, *How immature, that is really what he has to say before he is leaving me forever?*

"I am not looking for freedom." I said.

"I know," he said. "But you might as well enjoy it."

I looked at him one last time, wondering how he could be the same boy I picked up from the airport fourteen years ago.

"Goodbye, Caleb," I said.

"Goodbye, Anne G." Then, to my surprise, he kissed me on the cheek. I was too dazed to realize what he was doing until after it happened. *Why would he do that?* I thought to myself. *He still is wavering from one side to the other.*

I started walking back into the garage and into the house

as he got into his 4Runner, not stopping until I reached the front door where I could see down the long driveway. Caleb backed up and turned around. When he reached the end of the driveway, his brake lights appeared. It was September 4, a month after I'd arrived at our hunting camp in Tanzania, and eleven days since I left Caleb in Africa. And now he was driving out of my life for good.

His brake lights vanished, and he turned out of our driveway.

I watched him drive down the street until he disappeared.

CHAPTER 35
A WAY IN THE WILDERNESS

Forget the former things; do not dwell on the past. See, I am doing a new thing! Now it springs up; do you not perceive it? I am making a way in the wilderness and streams in the wasteland.

—Isaiah 43:18–19

Staring out the front door, I said out loud, "Lord, Caleb is yours from here on. He is no longer mine. I trust You to take him." I went over to the couch we had cuddled on so many times and got on my knees sobbing. "Oh, God, have mercy on me. I don't think I can make it on my own. I need You." I cried out for God. I was broken. There was nothing inside me that was not shattered and crumbled. I cried as I was kneeling on the floor confessing it all to God.

I had started a divorce recovery class that my pastor had sent me to. I had been to one meeting, and it was about waiting on God to see if He wanted to restore your marriage. So, in that moment on the floor in my living room, I said out loud, "God, if You want me to wait on Caleb to come back to me, then You need to tell me clearly, if not, then I will obey You and move on with my life, although I don't know how." I picked up my Bible and opened it up. "God, speak to me. I have nothing. You have taken my entire life. What am I going to do?" I had been reading Isaiah. When I opened my Bible, I will never forget the first words that jumped out at me as I read Isaiah 43:18–19:

> Forget the former things; do not dwell on the past. See I am doing a new thing! Now it springs up; do you not perceive it? I am making a way in the desert and streams in the wasteland.

The verse matched what all the wise godly counselors around me were telling me. God was setting me free, although I did not want to be set free. "Forget the former things," I read again, "do not dwell on the past. See I am doing a new thing! Now it springs up; do you not perceive it? I am making a way in the desert and streams in the wasteland." The verse was washing over my spirit giving me a drink of living water. The hope of what I believed but could not see. I clung to the verse and read it over and over again as tears streamed down my face. My Heavenly Father was speaking loud and clear to my broken heart.

For the rest of that day and for many days after, all I could do was kneel at the foot of my chaise or lie on my bedroom floor asking for God's mercy. The pain I was experiencing was sharp and deep. It felt as if my heart had been physically cut out. It was excruciating. I was emotionally, physically, and spiritually drained. No one and nothing could comfort me. And although it hurt tremendously, I knew I needed this time alone with God to grieve. I needed to be able to cry out to Him. Which I did again and again, the only words I could speak were, "God, have mercy on me."

Caleb called the next day. When I saw it was his cell phone on caller ID, I did not answer it. He did not leave a message. Caleb called again the day after that, and I still didn't answer, but this time he left a message. He wanted to check on me, he said. I deleted the message after listening to it, knowing my extreme pain would only be made worse if I spoke to him.

My brother Frank called me the same week Caleb left. He said, "I have some bad news." I thought, *What now?* He said he remembered Caleb still owed my grandmother $30,000. My Granny had a "fund" that the grandchildren could borrow money from. We had to go talk to her about what we wanted to do with the money, and she would usually offer us a loan. We paid it back in monthly payments. It was a fabulous deal for the family. The grandchildren called it a "Granny Loan." Frank told me he was sorry, but I needed to call Caleb and ask him to pay it back. I broke out sweating.

"I told him I did not want to talk to him again, ever..." I groaned.

Frank said, "I know. I'm sorry. But, in this case, you need to call him. You need to only talk to him once. Just ask him to pay the loan off."

Defeated, I thought...*Noooooo.*

But, I agreed with Frank, I had married Caleb, and he had been given family perks because of me. It was my responsibility to the family and Granny. The loan was to start his new safari hunting company that he started with Saul a year and a half earlier. My Granny loved Caleb as if he was her own grandchild. I knew I had to take one for the team. Frank said Caleb would never pay it back if Frank asked him, but if I asked, I had a 50/50 shot of getting the money back. Down deep I knew Frank was right. It was a love loan. So, if he walked away, there was no recourse. So, I waited. I remember where I was when he called the next time. I was waiting at a red light in the town of Red Bank, at the bottom of the mountain. My cell phone rang and it was Caleb. My heart raced.

I answered. "Hello."

"Hey," he said. I could hear in his voice that he was a little surprised, because he had tried to call several times and I had not answered.

"Hi," I replied.

He said, "How are you?"

I knew I couldn't go there, so I said, "Fine." Then, "Did you get settled in?"

"Yes," he said.

"Good," I said. Then Caleb started talking. We exchanged a bit more small talk about his drive to Texas and his move into his travel agent's home before I cut to the chase. I said, "I'm glad you called. I wanted to talk to you. You know the loan you got from Granny?"

I felt the stiffness in his voice. He said, "Yeah."

I said, "Frank called and said it needs to be paid back. Now that you are gone, he is worried you might try to leave for Africa for good and never pay it back."

He said, "How am I supposed to pay it back now? I have all kinds of expenses." I could tell he was irritated.

I spoke softly and said, "Caleb, you can do whatever you want. Granny loves you. She has always treated you like her own flesh-and-blood grandson. Frank thinks you will not pay it back, but I believe you will do the right thing. To be honest, you and I both know there is nothing we can do if you decide not to pay it back. But I hope you will do the right thing. I hope you show me and my family you are a man of your word."

He took a deep breath before saying, "I'll try to get some money together to pay her back."

"Thank you," I said. "I believe you. I know you love Granny." Then I said quickly, "I need to go now. Goodbye."

"Goodbye," Caleb said, and that was that.

I hoped speaking to him would really work. I knew he still had a tender spot for me, I could hear it in his voice. I know it sounds crazy after he treated me so badly and after he had cheated on me, but I think I really was his good side.

Two weeks later, Frank called.

"You aren't going to believe it," he said when I answered. "I got a check in the mail. Caleb paid Granny back in full."

"Wow," I said. "I am glad he did it."

"I'm shocked," Frank said.

"Well, he loves Granny, and she loves him," I said. "I wonder where he got the money?"

"Who knows. I'm just glad he paid it back," he replied.

"Me, too." I smiled to myself. *He is still in there, somewhere down deep.*

After that phone call with Frank, I didn't put too much more thought into where Caleb got the money. Then three months later I received a phone call from Zimbabwe. It was Saul's wife, Rachel, calling to tell me that Caleb and Saul had had a major falling out and that Saul had come to her in tears. She said she had never seen Saul so upset and then went on to tell how Saul had discovered money missing from the bank account of the hunting company he and Caleb had started in Tanzania. Saul hired an accountant to try to figure out where the money had gone, and the accountant discovered Caleb had stolen $30,000 from the new company. Saul thought Caleb was his best friend and was devastated that Caleb had lied to him and had stolen from him. He confronted Caleb and told him he couldn't trust him as a friend or business partner anymore, and they had a big fight exchanging angry words.

Sitting on my front porch swing, I simply listened, wondering if this was my answer to where Caleb had gotten the money to pay Granny back, but not saying much except that I was so sorry Saul was hurt. Rachel said Saul spoke with his father about it, and his father said Saul should not be surprised and that, "If Caleb did what he did to Anne G., why would you think he would not do the same thing to you?"

Knowing what it was like to love and believe Caleb, I felt sympathy for Saul. Caleb was a master deceiver. I learned from Rachel that Saul and Caleb's friendship had ended, and the company had dissolved immediately. It was just more disappointment and sadness.

I never answered another phone call from Caleb again. We only spoke that one time after he left me. Oh, how I wanted to. He called often at first. He also emailed me. He was leaving my health insurance under his name and paying for it for the next three months so I would have time to find new insurance. He asked how I was doing. He said he missed me. I wanted to reply so badly, but I deleted the email. A month later, he emailed me again. He wrote that he'd left his 9mm police gun under his side of the mattress. He said he'd be happy to pay for shipping, that I could ship it Cash on Delivery, and he gave me his new address. He hoped I was well, he wrote. He missed me.

I did not respond to that email either, but I immediately went home and carefully packed the gun. With it I packed a lovely guest book engraved with Caleb's last name, which was no longer my name. I paid for insurance and shipped it to Caleb. I didn't include a note in the package because I didn't want to open up any doors of communication with him, I was still too weak for that, and I knew it. But I wanted to make sure Caleb never could say I was vindictive or in any way unfair. I still cared about how I treated him. It was important for me to treat him the way I wanted to be treated; sometimes I still wonder why.

As the months went by, slowly his calls came less and less. I am not going to lie, I liked it when he called and I saw his number on my caller ID. Even though I never answered after that one call, it meant he was thinking about me. I thought about him all the time. I was broken.

Every time he reached out, I wept. It felt like my insides were being pulled out when he emailed or called, and it deeply hurt.

The next days, weeks, and months were painful. I don't like any pain, not physical or emotional. I will do whatever it takes to *not* have to deal with pain. But, here I was. The pain was too much for me. I am the kind of person who wants to crawl into a hole and lick my wounds in private.

That is what I did. I struggled hard from being completely deceived by someone I loved and thought I knew. The mind games bombarded me as I fought the battles in my mind. My entire family gathered around me with protection and let me heal. My cousin, Tracy, who was ten years older than me with a family of his own, even offered to come spend the night on my couch so I could sleep without being afraid. My family knew I'd been scared, but they thought this was because of my night terrors and of living alone. They had no idea I'd also been afraid for my life. Wow. The mind games the devil tried to play; I clung to Jesus with everything inside of me.

It took me three days before I even told mom, daddy, and Bill what had happened with confronting Caleb's demon. I kept it in my heart and pondered everything. I was all in my head not speaking much for those first few days. It was strange even to me, and I experienced it firsthand. If someone had told me a story like what happened to me, I would have thought, *Are they nuts?* This stuff happened in the Bible, but this is today in the United States. I did not want to scare anyone with what the entire truth was. I was having a hard time with the truth myself. I didn't want to think about true evil. I just wanted it to all go away. I stayed at my house or my parents' for a good month, not going out in public except to church, where I sat on the back row weeping, leaving as soon as the service was over. Thirty days later, I met my lawyer, Walter, at the courthouse. The judge signed the divorce decree as tears streamed down my face. I went to my divorce care classes at a local Baptist church and that helped me a lot. Being with others who were hurting. It was a lonely time of great brokenness for me.

A male friend heard what had happened and called to see how I was doing. I told him thank you for calling, but my pastor told me I could not talk to any males except my family members, so I could not talk to him and quickly hung up the phone.

He then called my brother to see if he would tell me that it was okay to talk to him. My brother laughed and told the guy I was not going to change my mind. I was going to do whatever my pastor had told me to do, so he could call me after Christmas. My brother told him he was sure I would be happy to talk to him then. I was visiting my older brother at his house when he told me about this conversation. Apparently I hurt the guy's feelings.

"I just don't want to make another mistake to mess my life up more than it already is," I told my brother.

My big brother comforted me. "I know."

CHAPTER 36
IN JESUS' NAME

Then they are to take some of the blood and put it on the sides and tops of the doorframes of the houses where they eat the lambs.

—Exodus 12:7

On that same night I will pass through Egypt and strike down every firstborn of both people and animals, and I will bring judgment on all the gods of Egypt. I am the Lord. The blood will be a sign for you on the houses where you are, and when I see the blood, I will pass over you. No destructive plague will touch you when I strike Egypt.

—Exodus 12:12–13

I n October, I asked Dr. Bob Sanders if he would come to my house to pray over it and anoint it. I had read about God directing the Israelites to anoint their homes with the blood of the lamb, and the spirit of death passed over their homes. I wanted freedom. My night terrors were still keeping me up at night. I decided they had tormented me for long enough. Dr. Sanders told me to wait a while after Caleb had left and our divorce was finalized. So I was ready.

Finally, Dr. Sanders arrived at my house on a cool, sunny morning. On purpose, I didn't tell him anything about my house, I wanted to see what he picked up without any knowledge from me. He came into the house and started looking around. To be honest, it kind of freaked me out, but I told myself we all have different gifts (1 Corinthians 12), and this guy obviously had the gift of discerning spirits. I wanted any bad spirits out of my house. I had prayed by myself over my house and prayed the full armor of God in Ephesians 6 over myself, but I felt like I needed a little extra help.

He walked in and immediately after Dr. Sanders started examining my home he said, "There's a spirit here of another woman who had sexual relations with your ex-husband in this house."

My heart sank. I was hoping Caleb had been telling me the truth when he said he only cheated on me with one woman.

"Do I have your permission to command it to leave in Jesus' name?" Dr. Sanders asked.

I didn't hesitate to say, "Yes. Please."

He commanded that spirit to leave, followed by another, and then another as he and I walked through the downstairs. Surprisingly, there were several generational spirits from my family and from Caleb's family that Dr. Sanders discerned and drove out. We finished downstairs, and then we headed upstairs. At the top of the stairs, Caleb's office looked like a vacant bedroom. There was nothing there to indicate what it had been used for, so I was mightily impressed the second Dr. Sanders walked in and started looking all over and said, "Well, we have a lot going on in here." Then he got to work, commanding the spirit of pornography (that had come through the internet wires) to leave my house and never return. "In the name of Jesus," he said, then continued to cast out a long list of demonic spirits, including the spirit of death. As he did, I prayed along in agreement with him. I could not see a thing, but I knew in my spirit I had been living in the midst of something I could not explain, and it was exhausting. I wanted to get rid of anything that was not from the Spirit of God—which I knew from the Word of God was love, joy, peace, patience, kindness, goodness, gentleness, faithfulness, and self-control. Those were the only things I wanted in my house or anywhere around me.

We left the office and went into the other upstairs bedroom and bathroom. Dr. Sanders pulled back the shower curtain in the bathroom and said, "What do we have here?" I stood there as he absorbed what he was seeing. He turned and looked straight into my eyes and said, "Do you know someone plotted your murder in this shower?" A cold chill went down my spine. I had not told Dr. Sanders this was the room where Caleb decided to stay when he came back from Africa to sign our divorce papers. I was even surprised he did not stay in the master downstairs with the big master bathroom. I wasn't staying there, and we never discussed where he would sleep. He had the house to himself. There were five bedrooms in all, three downstairs, and two rooms with king-size beds, but he stayed in this one, which was a queen. I stood there looking at Bob Sanders. I knew with everything inside me, which I believe was the Holy Spirit,

Caleb had plotted my murder right there. All my nerve endings were standing straight up. I knew this man had a gift straight from God. We commanded the demonic spirit to leave my house and never return, followed by commanding the plot of murder over me to be dissolved. There were all kinds of thoughts swirling through my head.

Then I told Dr. Sanders, "Caleb stayed in this room when he came home from Africa."

He just nodded his head as if he was not surprised and said, "Let's keep going."

We finished upstairs and headed back downstairs. Dr. Sanders anointed my house, and we prayed over it together. Then he prayed over my night terrors and commanded in the name of Jesus nothing was allowed to stay in my house or be attached to me. I said, "Amen" along with him.

"How long will I keep having my nightmares?" I asked after we both said amen.

"They didn't come all at once," he said, "so they may not leave all at once either. It might take a little time." Then Dr. Sanders left. I was thankful for him and felt relieved that my house had been cleansed. I was curious to see how soon my night terrors would go away, especially with what Caleb had insinuated—that he'd been the cause of them.

The words Caleb spoke as he was walking out of my door for the last time kept echoing in my heart and in my mind, "Let me know if your nightmares go away after I am gone."

Now time would tell if the bad dreams would go or stay.

Little by little I will drive them out before you, until you have increased enough to take possession of the land.
—Exodus 23:30

I kept praying the new way I had learned to pray. I spoke out loud the verse God had given me about how the demons must submit to me in the name of Jesus. My night terrors became more like nightmares and they were happening less and less. Hallelujah!

Every night before going to sleep, I would pray out loud and ask God to fill my room with angels singing glory to God and worshiping Him. I am not sure why I prayed that, but that is what I wanted happening in my room to give me peace as I slept. I figured if angels were worshiping God, no evil spirits would want to be anywhere around there, and I would be at peace hearing them worship while I slept.

One night, I woke up, and instead of being awakened to fear and panic of something trying to kill me, I woke up and lay there completely relaxed. I opened my eyes, and I saw my room was completely filled with a multitude of angels singing and worshiping with the most amazing music I had ever heard. It felt like I was wrapped up in a cocoon of complete love and peace. I have never felt anything like it—it was truly perfect peace that surpasses all understanding. As I listened and watched, I worshiped God along with the angels in my own spirit for a while, and then I drifted off back to sleep.

I will give you hidden treasures, riches stored in secret places, so that you may know that I am the Lord, the God of Israel, who summons you by name.
—Isaiah 45:3

I think the Lord was giving me small little treasures along my dark journey to show me I was going to make it through the darkness (Isaiah 45:3). Seeing the angels in my bedroom was a treasure I clung to, just like seeing my guardian angel in Bob Sanders' office that day. I was walking in faith. I was hoping God would free me. Little by little my nightmares were going away, just like the verse in Exodus 23:30 when God is bringing his people to the promised land.

Little by little I started to have freedom. God was restoring me.

CHAPTER 37

FREEDOM AND
A FUTURE

*The steps of a good man are ordered by the Lord, and He
delights in his way.*

—Psalms 37:23

*At that very time Jesus cured many who had diseases,
sickness and evil spirits, and gave sight to many who were
blind.*

—Luke 7:21

Growing up, my mother told us my great-grandmother,
who was a mighty woman of God, said not to talk
about demons or evil spirits. So, we did not talk about anything like that. I understand why, because it can be scary.
However, as I dug into the Word of God as a light to find
my own way, the Bible clearly talks about demons over
and over. Jesus had *all* the authority. He cast demons out

of people as part of His healing ministry throughout the New Testament. He never pretended like they did not exist. He took authority over them, without fear. However, I also knew thinking about them too much was not healthy either, because it fed my fear. That is what Satan wants to do; control us with fear. I was done with sticking my head in the sand and pretending there was no evilness in the world. I had been tormented for five and a half years, and I wanted complete healing and nothing less. I also wanted complete peace. So, I prayed for God to heal me and give me the balance of being truthful to myself about the spiritual war we live in, but to keep my eyes on Jesus who is my deliverer.

Slowly, the weeks turned into months. I finally got freedom from the nightmares; I hardly had them anymore. One night my dog had a nightmare, and I got up and prayed over him; he was yelping and crying. I woke up sleepy and went out to my dog's bed in the hallway outside my bedroom. I got on the floor and comforted Taz as I prayed over him. I commanded those nasty demonic spirits to submit in the name of Jesus, because Taz was mine and God's. I said out loud, "You have no control over me anymore, so you think you can torment my dog, but you can't. You must leave my house and never come back. You have to obey me in the mighty name of Jesus." I knew what I had hoped for was coming, little by little.

One of Caleb's closest friends in the police department called. He told me Caleb always spoke so highly about me and how it was obvious Caleb loved me, and he was surprised Caleb left me. I told him briefly what had happened in Africa, and how Caleb wanted a divorce. He then told me there was something he wanted to tell me, and he never had. He and Caleb had made a drug traffic stop on the interstate together, driving separate police cars. The car they stopped had a duffle bag of money and scales to weigh drugs in the trunk. Caleb's police friend went and started writing up the report. Caleb moved the suspect to the back of his friend's police car. When this officer went back to count how much money was in the duffle bag, the duffle bag was gone, and so was the money. He went to Caleb's car and confronted him. Caleb said they could split it and no one would ever know. The guy got really mad and told Caleb he didn't want to work with a shady cop. They ended up turning the money in to the police with the report that night. He said Caleb came to him the next day and got choked up with tears in his eyes and said he didn't know what he was thinking, he didn't want to live his life like that, and he was really sorry. He didn't want the guy to tell anyone, and he promised he would never do anything like that again. The policeman never told anyone, but he wanted me to know now that Caleb had been gone for months. He said it had really surprised him Caleb had another side that had no remorse about stealing until he thought someone might tell on him. I was sad to hear this story that happened many years earlier. The guy said he always wondered if Caleb did stuff like that when he was alone. I wondered how many secrets Caleb carried during our marriage that I was unaware of and if I would ever find out about them all.

The next week, my mom and I were visiting together in her kitchen. At twenty-nine years old, I told her my desire to be married again and to have children of my own. She wanted me to have my own family too. As we sat in the kitchen, I was whining and admitted my fear of all the men my age already being married. Trying to offer encouragement, my mom said, "Yes, it seems like they are, but I'm hoping you can meet a nice forty-year-old widower to marry. You love kids, and you would make a great stepmom to his children. Maybe you could even have a baby of your own with him one day."

I didn't like that idea at all and said, "Yuck! That sounds horrible. I don't want to marry some old man."

That really scared me since Caleb and I had always been physically attracted to each other; that was never one of our problems. So I started praying regularly. *Oh, God, please let me think my future husband is handsome even if no one else does. Please let me be attracted to him physically, I cannot kiss someone I am not attracted to.* I also prayed, *Lord, if You want me to meet someone, You need to bring him to me, because I'm not going out to meet anyone.*

Christmas was coming.

CHAPTER 38
PAUL

The Lord is my shepherd, I shall not want. He makes me lie down in green pastures; He leadeth me beside still waters. He restores my soul...

—Psalms 23:1–3

I was finally feeling good again, as good as the crisp fall air. I was living with a confidence I had never experienced before, knowing deep in my spirit that God was on my side. It was invigorating; I felt lighter and stronger than ever. I was able to pay my bills on my own, which meant I got to keep my house, and it was empowering. For the first time in my life I was on my own, and it felt amazing. I would drive down the road with my sunroof back on my BMW with all the windows rolled down, singing as loud as I could to the stereo. I felt God's joy pouring out all over me.

I became a Young Life leader again, which brought me great joy and fulfillment. I also started spending even more time with my nieces, nephews, and their friends, who were between the ages of four and seventeen. They were my best friends; I had always adored them. We went bowling, roller skating, go-kart racing, or whatever sounded fun or adventurous to do. I kept myself busy, always having a good time.

On December 16, mom gave me two bushes to plant in front of my house and sent over her yard men to plant them for me. I needed to get a third bush to match the two free ones from my mom, since we are all about penny pinching in my family. So I called a fellow Young Life leader, Kim, whose parents owned a nursery about a mile away from my house. She said I could come by and she would help me match the bushes. I had on gray sweatpants, a red fleece, and no makeup when I arrived at the nursery with a leaf from the bush I was trying to match in my hand. I walked inside and asked the middle-aged woman at the front desk where I could find Kim.

"She went last-minute Christmas shopping with her mom," she said. "But you can walk out to the back greenhouse, and I'll radio Paul to help you." I was disappointed but headed to the greenhouse. As I entered it, this smoking hot guy who looked to be my age walked toward me. He was over six feet tall with brown hair and had the most beautiful green eyes I had ever seen. He wore a ball cap, a hoodie, and brown Carhartt pants. He was smiling and his eyes were locked in on mine.

My immediate thought was, *Oh, my. I'm in trouble.*

There was static electricity down my entire body. We just stood there staring at each other smiling. I had never responded to anyone that way in my life, especially a stranger. I could tell the feelings were mutual. We couldn't take our eyes off each other. As he smiled at me, looking straight into my eyes, he said, "Hi. Can I help you?"

I was flustered at my reaction to him. So I laughed and said, "Yeah, I need a bush to go with this leaf."

He started laughing. "You need a bush to go with your leaf? Well, let me see your leaf."

I handed it to him.

"Do you know what kind of bush this leaf is from?" he asked.

"No." I smiled. "My mom gave me two bushes to plant at my house, and I want to buy a third one to match the free ones from her."

His eyes twinkled with amusement. "Okay. This looks like a laurel. So, follow me." He turned and started walking.

I started to follow him, and I looked at the back of him and his faded brown Carhartt pants and thought, *Oh, Lord, help me...This one's either straight from heaven or straight from hell, and I am not sure which one.*

He led me over to the next green house and walked to the laurel bushes. Then he showed me all the leaves and picked out the closest match. He asked what I thought, and I knew nothing about bushes or plants, so I agreed that it was a match. I think I would have agreed to anything this boy said. He asked if I had something to pick it up in, and I said, "Yes, I have a truck."

"Okay, then after you pay at the front counter and get your truck, pull back here and I'll be looking for you to load your laurel," he said. "My name's Paul by the way."

I smiled and said, "Thanks, Paul. I'm Anne G."

My smile didn't fade from my face as I paid for my new bush, then drove back to my house to get my mom's old green F-150. An older model with some dents, it had been my daddy's farm truck that my mom now used for yard projects. I loaded Taz in the truck bed then drove back down the road to the nursery and went to the back. Paul walked out smiling, his green eyes dancing as I pulled up. I could tell he'd been waiting on me. (I later found out, he got on the radio after I left to pay and told everyone when the blonde came back, he was going to load her. No one else was to help her.)

Paul loaded up my new bush then started petting my golden retriever in the back of the truck. That got my attention even more. He was flirting with me, and I was liking it. He asked if I was new to the mountain. I didn't want to tell him I had lived up here all my life, and my family was enormous. So, I just laughed and said, "No, I'm not new."

"Well, I've lived up here for years, and I've never seen you," he said confidently. Which I thought was cute.

"I've never seen you either," I said, suddenly realizing that was odd considering how small and close-knit the mountain was. One thing I did know for sure is that if I had seen Paul over the years, I would have definitely remembered this boy. There was no question about it. He obviously felt the same way. I knew he was right; we had never laid eyes on each other.

"I don't ever come to the nursery," I said. "I'm not into plants and gardening. That's my mom's thing."

He asked if I lived close by, and I told him I lived on Northern Avenue, which was two streets away. He said, "I drive that way home every day. Do you need any help planting this bush?"

I said, "Oh no, I have some guys that can help me at my

house." I did not realize he was trying to see me again. Since I'd been out of the dating scene since college, it went right over my head. Then we chatted a little longer. In addition to being very handsome, Paul was funny and easygoing. He was comfortable to be around, like someone I could spend all day with even though we'd just met. When I said something funny, he responded instantly with something even funnier. It was refreshing to laugh so easily with someone. We both got tickled several times during our conversation, and there was no denying the sparks between us.

I didn't want to leave but needed to get back to help with my yard. So I thanked Paul then jumped in my truck and left, feeling giddy the whole way home. My oldest nephew pulled into my yard as I did. He had just gotten his driver's license, it was his sixteenth birthday, and he could finally drive over to my house—legally.

Once he left, I told my mom, who'd also come over to help in my yard, "Mom! I just met the hottest guy ever at the nursery."

"Really?" she smiled. "Did he have a ring on?"

"No. But who knows these days, he could be married," I said, remembering the number of married men who'd hit on me over the last few months, which had really ticked me off.

"Or maybe he's not married," my mom said.

Remembering Paul's sparkling green eyes, I hoped my mom was right.

CHAPTER 39
FLOATING ON SUNSHINE

You have stolen my heart, my sister, my bride;
you have stolen my heart
with one glance of your eyes,
with one jewel of your necklace.
How delightful is your love, my sister, my bride!
How much more pleasing is your love than wine,
and the fragrance of your perfume
more than any spice.
                    —*Song of Solomon 4:9–10*

New Year's Day was coming up. A few months before, a guy named David had asked me out. He had done some of my loans for my real estate clients, and while I was flattered he wanted to take me on a date, I told him my pastor had said I could not date or talk to any men besides family members until New Years. He was very attractive and teased me a few months before that he wanted to go out when I was "allowed to." I laughed, realizing it sounded like I was in middle school, but I didn't mind. Subconsciously, I liked the boundary.

Right before Christmas he called me as I was on a walk in my neighborhood. He said he was paying for a limo for New Year's and wanted to invite some people to go out on the town dancing and to celebrate. It was a fun group of people, and the limo would pick us all up and drop us all off at home at the end of the night. He asked if I would like to go as his date. I said, "That sounds like a blast! Thank you for inviting me. I need to talk to my pastor. Can I call you back?"

He said, "Sure."

I hung up the phone and immediately called Jim, my pastor. I was excited and I'm sure Jim could tell from my voice. I told him a guy who does my loans just asked me to go in a limo with him and some other people for New Year's to go dancing.

Jim asked me to tell him a little about him.

"He's a Christian, around my age, has never been married, and he's really cute."

Jim asked, "Do you want to go?"

"Well, I don't want to stay home by myself for New Year's. That would be *really* depressing."

"Then you should go," Jim said. "You waited the amount of time I told you to wait, so now you're free to date. Sounds like you have plans for New Year's!"

"Thanks, Jim!" I said, feeling like I finally had something to look forward to.

Then I called David back. "My pastor said I can go out

for New Year's," I said, feeling like a schoolgirl. "Thank you for inviting me. I'm excited."

So, almost four months after my divorce, on New Year's Eve, I went on my first date. It was refreshing to be out. My date looked like a GQ model, over six feet tall, blond hair, blue eyes, very attractive, and put together like a magazine. He was handsome and kind, perfect—just not perfect for me. I had always thought he was cute, and he was, but when it came to a romantic feeling, it was not there. I had no real attraction toward him and, honestly, I felt like I was still married. We danced all night, something I love to do, and at the end of the night he tried to kiss me. I didn't let that happen. When I returned home, I was thankful to have gone out, but it made me realize that even if someone was attractive and checked all the husband-material boxes on paper, it was going to take more than that for him to be my man. I had to *feel* it, that feeling greater than knowledge that you can't explain.

"Oh, Lord. Help me," I prayed that night. "I can't do this without You. Please let me be attracted to the man you have for me." I wondered what it was going to take.

Three weeks later, on January 21, Kim invited me and the other Young Life leaders on our team to the surprise thirtieth birthday party she was throwing for her husband, Mark, who was also a Young Life leader on my team. It was a cold January night at dusk. I arrived at the party, wondering if that cute Paul Lang might be there. He had popped into my mind several times since the day I met him. That amazing smile and those beautiful eyes.

Kim asked me at our weekly Young Life meeting the week after I bought my laurel bush, what I thought about

Paul. She said Paul had told her he met me and was asking her lots of questions about me. She also said he was separately questioning her husband, Mark, about me. I said, "He really is cute."

She smiled and said, "If you want to go out with Paul, you will have to ask him out. He doesn't ask any girls out, they ask him."

"Well, I guess we won't be going out then." I said. That was not a turn-on to me. Yet still, he was so cute, and here I was now at this surprise birthday party hoping he would be there. I went to the party with another girl, Jennifer, who was a Young Life leader with me. We arrived at the party and visited with everyone for a little while. Then I went to get something to eat where the food was at a buffet-style table.

I picked up my plate and started to serve myself. Then I heard a voice right beside me say, "Hello, Anne," followed by a long pause and then a distinctly pronounced, "G."

I turned and the cutest boy I had ever seen was smiling down at me with those amazing green eyes. It was Paul. He had grabbed a plate and was right next to me, smiling his cutest smile. My heart skipped and I gave a big smile back and said confidently, "Well, someone has been doing their homework, not many people know that is how my name is pronounced."

Paul said confidently, "Yes, I have."

Most people called me Angie and had no idea it was spelled Anne G., and they certainly didn't pronounce it correctly.

It caught me off guard how proud he was to admit he had been studying up on me. I actually did not know what to say then; he could stand up to me, and I liked it. So, I laughed. I was attracted to his courage, and I was attracted to him physically. He was big, towering over me like the men in my family, which I liked. Standing beside him I felt the same rush of attraction I did when I first met him a few weeks before. I was smitten with him already, and he was looking at me the same way back.

We made our plates, then Paul came and sat with me, and we talked the entire time. He didn't leave my side for the rest of the party, and when it was over, he asked if I wanted to go out to a pool hall. I told him another Young Life girl was with me. Paul replied, "Great! Ask her if she wants to go with us." Jennifer agreed to go, so the three of us left the party together—Paul in his car, me in Jennifer's—and went back to my house first, which was a mile down the road, so I could drive us all to the pool hall. Jennifer and Paul parked their cars in my driveway, then we all piled into my BMW.

"Nice car," Paul said. "I thought you drove that green F-150."

I laughed. "Sometimes I do. That's my mom's truck."

Thirty minutes later, we arrived at the pool hall downtown. Paul opened the door for Jennifer and me, then walked up to the bar. He was confident and kind, and as Jennifer and I followed him I thought, *Dang. I like everything about him.*

At the bar Paul ordered a beer, then asked what I wanted.

"May I please have a Diet Coke?" I asked the bartender.

Flustered, Paul quickly said to the bartender, "No, I mean, I want a Diet Coke too. We want two Diet Cokes."

The bartender said to Paul, "No beer?"

"No, no beer," Paul said. "Just two Diet Cokes." Then he asked Jennifer for her order, and she said Diet Coke also.

I thought that it was really cute—Paul was trying to be good in front of me. So I teased him and laughed, "I really don't mind you drinking a beer."

Paul replied, "No, I love Diet Coke."

(I found out later he'd never had Diet Coke before, and he'd hated it that night.)

After getting our drinks, we went to sit down. The three of us were there, but Paul and I could not take our eyes off each other. I was totally into him. He was totally into me too. It scared me a little how attracted I was to him. I kept thinking, *I'm not sure if this is a good thing or a bad thing. We might be too attracted to each other.* The three of us played darts and drank our Diet Cokes. David, who'd taken me out for New Year's, happened to be there and came over to speak to me. I introduced him to Jennifer and Paul, thinking how much more natural it felt to be around Paul than it had felt on my date with David.

A couple hours later, after a fun night out on the town, I drove Paul and Jennifer back up to my house, and Jennifer left. I invited Paul to come inside my house, and we sat down in the living room and kept talking. We could not get enough of each other. It was an easy conversation. He asked me a lot of questions about my life, my job as a realtor, and my family. We also talked about where he was from and his history, and after a while he admitted, "I've been asking around on the mountain about you since we met that day at the nursery."

"Oh, really?" I smiled, pretending to be surprised although I already knew he'd been asking around about me.

He grinned. "Yes. I *have* been doing my homework, and I know some stuff." He admitted proudly with no apologies.

Laughing, I said, "Well, what have you heard?"

"I know you're a *very* strong Christian, and I have heard you don't date. You only hang out with all your nieces and nephews." He looked at me and waited.

There was a short pause as I considered what he said. We lived in a small town, and word on the street, which was very true, was—I had no social life.

"Sounds like you know a lot about me," I admitted. "And you're right. In fact, last weekend I went roller skating with all of my nieces," I confessed through laughter.

Paul laughed and quickly replied, "Okay, Xanadu."

I laughed harder, thinking, *This guy is so funny.* (*Xanadu*, starring Olivia Newton John, happened to be one of the first movies I saw at the movie theater as a little girl. It was about roller skating, and I'd loved it.)

Regaining my composure after laughing, I went on to explain to Paul, "My faith and relationship with Jesus Christ are the most important things in my life. I have been through some hard times, and He is my constant, the only One who's always with me. I can't do life without God."

Paul nodded. "Do you mind me asking why you don't date?"

I took a deep breath. "My pastor advised that I wait until after Christmas to give myself time to heal from my past relationship. I actually just went on my first date on New Year's Eve. The guy I introduced you to tonight at the pool hall was who I went out with. He does some of my loans for the houses I sell, and for our date he hired a limo and everything to pick me up and drop me off; we went dancing."

"How'd it go?" Paul asked. "The date."

"It was fun going out dancing. But honestly, there was no attraction there. And then he tried to kiss me on the first date. Can you believe that? On the *first date*?" I emphasized.

Paul teased me, "Wow. The nerve of the guy. Trying to kiss you on a date after going through all that trouble and spending a *fortune* hiring a limo to take you out for New Year's, I can't believe it!"

We laughed and laughed. Paul made me laugh a lot, openly teasing me, which ironically made me feel comfortable around him.

"So, just to clarify," Paul eventually said, "Your pastor says you *can* date now?"

"Well, yes. It's after the New Year, so now I can."

He looked straight into my eyes and smiled his cutest smile then said confidently, "Good timing for me." It took my breath away and made me feel jittery inside. I wasn't sure what this was I was experiencing, but it felt good and right.

Then Paul became very direct, and his voice showed compassion. "I heard about your divorce, and I heard your ex-husband cheated on you, and he was a real jerk. I'm sorry."

Wow, I thought. *We're getting all this out in the open now.* At the same time, I dreaded having to actually tell anyone I was divorced, even if the reason was because of Caleb's infidelity. So it was a relief that Paul already knew this about me. It felt like a weight had been lifted off my chest, and I exhaled deeply. "Thank you. Yes, that's true," I said. Then I took a deep breath. "I have got a lot of baggage," I kind of laughed, and said truthfully and seriously, "and I mean *a lot*." Paul could sense my vulnerability.

He looked at me in all seriousness and said, "I don't mind baggage. But, I do have a question for you."

"Okay?" I said half hesitantly, half with curiosity.

"Do you hate all men now?"

Wow. I thought, *That is pretty insightful.*

I said. "No. I have great relationships with my daddy, my brothers, and my boy cousins. And I was very close to my PawPaw before he died. I don't hate men at all."

He smiled at me and said, "Okay. That's all I need to know." As if it was a done deal. He was so confident that it made me feel at ease.

Paul was pursuing me hard—and he was making it very clear. He was not shy at all about his intentions, and his straightforwardness was attractive to me.

I looked at him and said with a little attitude, "Okay, now I have a few questions for you." He had been grilling me for a while, and it was my turn.

He smiled and said, "All right, what are your questions?" raising his chin, as if he was up to the challenge.

"Are you a Christian?" I asked boldly and waited.

He said, "Yes," and we talked a little about his faith. He had asked Jesus to come into his heart when he was twelve and was baptized shortly after he gave his life to Christ at a Baptist church near where he grew up, in Buford, Georgia. He was now attending a Baptist Church close by to where I lived.

I was happy with his answer. He already knew I was a strong believer, so I figured he was looking for a Christian.

I then said as if I was interviewing him, and we both knew why, "Are you ever planning on moving from Signal Mountain?"

He smiled, "Nope. I am staying here for good." he locked eyes with me.

At that moment something clicked inside me. I smiled my biggest smile.

"Okay. That's all I need to know," I said, just as confident as he had said it.

He laughed at me, coining his remark. And for now, it was all I needed to know. The rest I could figure out with some time. If Paul was a Christian who was staying on the mountain, then I was interested. After chatting a few more minutes, he said he better go, and we said good night.

Although it was dark out, I felt like I was floating on sunshine as I slipped into bed.

That night I prayed, *Lord, please let me know if Paul is or isn't the one for me. I don't want to get hurt.*

CHAPTER 40
A NEW CHAPTER

*God can do anything, you know—far more than you could
ever imagine or guess or request in your wildest dreams! He
does it not by pushing us around but by working within us,
His Spirit deeply and gently within us. Glory to God in the
church! Glory to God in the Messiah, in Jesus! Glory down
all the generations! Glory through all millennia! Oh, yes!*
—*Ephesians 3:20–21*

The next morning was Sunday. I went to church downtown and then came home after lunch with my family.
I had a rose waiting on my mailbox. The rose included a
note from Paul. It read, "You really do have beautiful eyes
and a beautiful smile." My heart leaped, but I was also cau-
tious from my deep wound from Caleb. The next day at
our weekly Young Life meeting, I spoke to Kim, who told
me Paul had showed up at her church on Sunday morning
thinking I went to church there. Kim said he was looking
for me. I was excited that he was interested in me. He sure

did not seem like the type of boy I was going to have to ask out—which was not going to happen by the way.

The following week, as I was walking out of the restaurant where I'd had lunch with some of my realtor friends, I saw Paul on the sidewalk. Again, my heart skipped. He smiled and said, "I was wondering if I might run into you." (My office was a couple of stores down from the restaurant.) He asked if I was going back to my office.

"Yes, I am."

Then he asked if he could bring his brothers down to visit me, as they had come to town for a few days. "Of course," I said, "I would love to meet your brothers."

I returned to my office and a few minutes later Paul came in with his two brothers, Eric and Daniel. Paul introduced us, then we all sat down and talked for almost two hours. Like Paul, his brothers were attractive and funny. I instantly liked them and got a big kick out of all their stories. Near the end of our time together, Eric asked what I was doing that night.

"Well, I don't know," I said.

"Why don't you come over to my house and we'll cook you dinner?" Paul said.

I liked the sound of that. "How can I turn down three handsome guys cooking me dinner?"

"All right, we have a plan," said Paul, who then got my phone number, saying he'd call me with the details. He called a few hours later and said he and his brothers had decided to go out to dinner instead. "Is it okay if I pick you up this evening and take you out?" he asked.

I answered, "That sounds great!"

So, my first date with Paul was with his brothers too.

Eric and Daniel waited in Eric's new black SUV while Paul walked to my front door, rang my doorbell, then walked me out and opened the door to the back seat. His brothers both greeted me from the front seats as I got in. Then Paul closed my door, walked around to the other side, and slipped into the back next to me.

We had a fantastic first date. Paul and his brothers took me to the nicest restaurant on the mountain at the time, which was an Italian pasta place. The four of us talked easily and laughed a lot throughout the night. Paul and his brothers were hilarious with each other and very entertaining as they told their stories from their childhood and teenage years. Paul paid for my dinner, then everyone came to my house, where I served brownies and ice cream for dessert.

As we ate, Paul told his brothers the story of how he and I met at the nursery and how afterward he kept asking around about the blonde who drove the old green F-150 truck, and how no one knew who that was. However, he was determined, and he wouldn't give up, so he kept asking. We all laughed and then he followed it with another story I didn't know: he was invited to Mark's surprise party, he said, but wasn't planning on going. Instead, he had plans to go to a different party, on a date with another girl. Then he heard last-minute that I was going to be at Mark's surprise party, so he broke his date with the other girl and came to Mark's party specifically to find me. I thought it was adorable he was admitting his interest so openly to me, and it made me feel special. Not long after, I said good night to Paul and his brothers, feeling full from the good food and the good company.

Later I found out that when Paul and his brothers drove

out of my driveway that night, Paul told them, "I'm going to marry her." Eric and Daniel were apparently shocked because Paul had never spoken like that before.

Paul and I started dating, and it was serious from the start. We were both twenty-nine and we knew what we wanted. He had never been married. We saw each other every day after work, and on our days off we spent the entire day together. Paul was a blast to hang out with. He always had fun whatever he was doing, and he had a ton of energy like me. I was used to being the energetic one, so I loved Paul's zest for life and adventure. He was a natural leader and had a jolly, easygoing spirit. I noticed people wanted to hang out with him, and I was at the top of the list.

My attraction to Paul was a little frightening, and it scared me. Because of my past wounds, I was afraid I would have my heart hurt again. So, over the first few weeks of dating, I purposely told Paul all the things I would not do. I was not trying to sugar coat anything, and I wanted him to know what he was getting. In fact, to be completely honest, I acted like I was a lot more difficult than I really was. For example, I knew how much he loved his food. So one night I told him, "By the way, I don't cook." (Which was not true.)

He quickly replied, "It's okay. I do."

Another night, we were cooking dinner together at my house, and I told Paul he needed to know that I was not going to just date one person. Until I got married, I would be dating around.

He looked me straight in the eyes back and said, "Well, that is going to be hard for you to do. Because I will be here right after I finish work every day at five o'clock, and I won't leave until you go to bed." He did not say it mad or irritated at all, he was just stating the facts. I just looked at him smiling and thought, *He is the cutest man I have ever seen in my life.* As much attitude as I gave him, he never wavered. He was strong, and he made it clear—I was what he wanted and he was staying. I wonder sometimes why he continued to pursue me when I acted so badly.

The Lord really does work in mysterious ways.

Around this time, Mark from London called to check on me. He called once before right after the New Year, having been respectful to wait the amount of time my pastor had said for me to wait to speak to men I might potentially want to date. When he voiced his interest in me, I told him with compassion that I had started dating Paul. I told Mark a little about Paul, and he could tell by the way I spoke that I was falling in love with Paul. Everyone could tell.

Mark told me he was happy for me, although he was a little disappointed that I was dating someone already. He said he had always planned to come to Signal Mountain and take me on a date before I started dating anyone.

I said, "I always wondered if we would date also."

But I knew Paul was the one for me. I thanked Mark for his kindness and, after receiving one other phone call from him a few months later, we never spoke again. I will always love him, and he will be my forever friend. God used him in my life in a powerful way.

His heart was as beautiful as he was.

One week after Paul and I started dating, Paul said he wanted to tell me some things about his past. He said it was important that I hear everything from him and no one else; he wanted me to know everything and get it all out so there were no secrets between us. He was usually a lot like me, funny and lighthearted. So, I was a little surprised he was so serious. We sat down on my couch that evening and he started from childhood and explained his life and decisions. He asked Jesus to come into his heart at age twelve and was baptized. Then he told me everything he had ever done wrong, and any details to any questions I had about any event. It warmed my heart that he trusted me so much. He said, "I am serious about you, and I want you to hear about my past from me, so you know the truth. I do not want you to hear anything from someone else; I want you to hear it all from me." During his confession he revealed how he had been known to get into some fights over the years, even recently on the mountain where we lived. He told me he was not one to back down if another man provoked him, and he needed to be honest with me about it. Then he confessed, "To be even more honest about it, I like a good fight."

I was oddly attracted to what he was telling me. It reminded me of two of my brothers and my grandfather, who all had a history of fighting, and who all I adored. So I surprisingly liked that Paul had a rowdy side, and I admired that he stood up for himself.

As he went on and spoke about his past, I am not going to lie, there was a lot. But, because he was being vulnerable with me, it made me trust him because he trusted me to be honest about everything. It was the kind of honesty I had prayed for in my marriage to Caleb, but it just hadn't been there. At the same time, I kept my guard up, since it wasn't until after Caleb and I got married that his lying began. After Paul finished, I jokingly asked him if he always confessed his past mistakes with new girlfriends. He smiled gently and said, "I have never done this before, and I do not ever plan to ever do it again." He took my hand and held it. "I'm serious about you, Anne G., and I'm not going to screw this up. I'm going to make sure I do this right."

Simply, Paul was feeling more and more like an answered prayer.

Two weeks later, I came home from work to a weeping Japanese maple planted in front of my house. Paul had told me about this type of tree a few days before and how it would look beautiful in my yard. But when he'd told me how much it cost, I'd quickly said, "I don't need a tree that expensive."

Now here he was, surprising me with landscaping my yard. I knew the weeping Japanese maple was an extremely generous gift, so when I hopped out of the car I kissed him, then said, "Oh, Paul, it's beautiful! I absolutely love it. But it's way too expensive of a gift. If we break up, I'll give it back to you."

"We aren't breaking up," he said firmly.

I challenged him, "You're awfully sure of yourself."

"Yes, I am," he said, then kissed me again as if to seal the deal. When he drew back he said, "Do you really think the way we met was an accident? It wasn't an accident, Anne G. It was God."

It felt like my whole being smiled. He couldn't have known how soothing those words were to me. More than anything in the world, my heart hoped he was right.

During the first three weeks we dated, Paul went with me every Sunday to my big church downtown. He went happily, but one day when we were talking at my house he said, "I've gone to church with you for three weeks now. It's time you come to my church with me."

Paul had told me he attended the church down the street from my house, the tiny church that had always looked abandoned each Sunday as I'd driven by it on my way to and from my church. So, doubting him, I thought, *He doesn't really go to that church. He's not being honest with me. I'll tell him I'll go with him, and he's going to be in a mess.* (I was used to someone lying to me, remember, so I assumed that was the case here.)

"Okay, Paul," I said, smiling knowingly. "Let's go to your church this Sunday."

When Sunday morning rolled around, Paul picked me up for the one-minute drive down the road to his so-called church. As we parked I saw there were several cars in the small parking lot and also on the street. The door of the white wooden building was propped open, and the second we stepped in, a woman who was around eighty years old came up to us and said, "Paul! Where have you been?" She gave him a big hug. "We've missed you. I'm so glad you're back."

Paul introduced her to me then said, "I've been at Anne G.'s church the last three weeks, but I wanted to bring her to my church to meet all my friends and see why I love *my* church."

I stood there smiling outwardly, but inwardly thinking, *Oh, Lord, I am so bad and jaded. Here I thought Paul was lying to me because I'm so used to being lied to, when he's really been going to church all along.*

Soon other people gathered around us to tell Paul they'd been wondering where he'd been. Paul introduced me to part of the congregation—about eight people in all—who were the early arrivals, all of which looked like they had been getting social security benefits for a good twenty years. By the time the service started, there couldn't have been more than thirty people in that little Baptist church. As I sang along to the hymns, I was still surprised the church was operating. Even more shocked that Paul actually went here. So, sitting in the pew, I felt my guilt and confessed my sins silently to Jesus, asking for God's forgiveness of my suspicions against Paul. Soberly, I also asked God to somehow heal my jaded heart. I thought, *I really do have issues.* The sermon was fiery, and I ended up loving the pastor. "You have a great church," I told Paul when the service was over and we were back at my house. I laughed, "I thought I was going to catch you in a big lie. I could've sworn that church was abandoned. But I was wrong, and I confessed my sins to Jesus all during church."

Paul just shook his head and laughed. He knew it was going to take me a while to learn to trust again, and he was more than willing to prove to me he was a man for the job.

It was around this time I started thinking about Paul's honesty. I liked the fact he addressed what needed to be discussed head on and said it, and it was done. That had obviously never been my strength. So, the next week we were hanging out at my house after cooking dinner, and I told him I wanted to tell him about my past with Caleb. I thought, *I need to tell him the truth about my past, just like he told me.*

Nervously, I sat down with him on my living room couch and told him everything about meeting, dating, and marrying Caleb. I explained that I enjoyed being married and part of my marriage was good on the surface, but there had always been a dangerous undercurrent of deceit that I could not completely grasp, that was finally revealed at the dramatic end. I told him about how my daddy and Bill had both been worried Caleb would try to kill me. I told him about my vision of being shot by the river, and about seeing my guardian angel at Dr. Sanders' office. I told him about Abdul's warning call from Tanzania. And finally, I told him about hearing the voice of a demon from Caleb's mouth.

"I know it sounds unbelievable," I said with conviction, "but it's all true. I would think I was nuts if I heard my own story, but I lived it, and I know it's true."

Paul sat and listened earnestly and with compassion. When I finished speaking, he asked a few questions that I answered, then he left to go home. Later he told me when he got into his car that night he thought, *All right, she's either crazy or it's all real. But if she starts talking about demons and angels all the time, I'm out of here.*

With that done, I never mentioned demons again for a long time. To be perfectly honest, I didn't want to talk about it either. I just wanted Paul to know the truth about me and my past.

And even more importantly, about the God I serve.

Generationally, I come from a long line of strong women, who all married a long line of strong men. Over the next several months, I was clearly seeing Paul's strength—and I was drawn straight to him because of it.

One evening, in the early spring, Paul and I were out driving around on the back of the mountain in my mom's green F150 truck and he pulled into a scenic overlook pull off and parked. We sat looking at the lush green Sequatchie Valley below as the sun set, and the amazing Appalachian Mountains off in the distance.

Paul turned to look at me and said seriously, "We need to talk." Then he paused. I could tell it was going to be a serious conversation, because of his tone of voice.

Looking at me straight in the eyes he said, "I want to be very clear with you about my intentions. I am not dating you for fun, Anne G., I am dating you because I am serious about you. This is not a game for me. I want to get married, and that is what I am working toward."

I smiled. I loved hearing those words of truth from Paul and that he was sharing his heart with me.

Then he continued, "Is this relationship just a game for you? Are you dating me to have a little fun for a while, and then you plan to move on when you decide you're done—or are you serious about me?"

I was stunned at Paul's straight forwardness with me. I typically did not like to get locked into much. In fact, I had become an expert in the art of not making commitments, and here he was calling me out. Asking me directly what I was thinking. I got really uncomfortable, because I didn't want to reveal my heart to Paul. He was pinning me down and giving me no other option—but to tell the truth.

As he sat and waited for me to respond. My heart was thumping.

I said softly, "I am serious about you, I am not playing any games."

"Good," he said, obviously relieved, as he pulled me over to him on the bench seat and put his arm around me. "I was hoping you were going to say that—but I was a little worried. That is why I wanted to discuss it, so we are both clear where this relationship is going."

I smiled as Paul kissed me in the front of that old truck. *This boy knows exactly how to handle me*, I thought.

Oh Lord help me, I think I am in love.

CHAPTER 41
TRUTH BOMB

*Jesus said to the people who believed in Him, "You are truly
my disciples if you remain faithful to my teachings. And you
will know the truth, and the truth will set you free."*
—John 8:31–32

Around the three-month mark that Paul and I'd been
dating, we went out for dinner at an upscale restaurant in Chattanooga. As we waited for our table, I looked
up and one of Caleb's very closest friends from the police
department was standing there with his wife. Caleb and I
had double dated with this man and his wife, and they had
come to our house to visit in the past, so I knew them well. I
smiled and said I was glad to see them. Alex acknowledged
me happily, but I noticed that his wife could hardly look
at me. I thought that was strange, she had been friendly
enough on other occasions. I asked if they had heard Caleb
had a girlfriend and left me. The officer spoke and said he
had heard about that. I could not help but notice his wife

was physically uncomfortable and she went and held her husband's hand, trying to not make eye contact with me. We chatted for a few minutes, and I introduced them to Paul. Then, all of a sudden it was like the Holy Spirit just downloaded knowledge to me—and I knew it.

Our name was called and we were ushered to our table. I slid into the booth and said privately to Paul, "I think Caleb had an affair with that lady."

Paul said, "Who?"

I said, "That police officer's wife. I could tell by the way she was acting."

Paul looked at me, like, *Really?* He said, "How could you tell?"

I explained why I thought that was the case. I decided I did not want to look absurd, so we went on to talk about other things and enjoyed our date.

However, over the next couple of days I kept thinking and praying about the chance meeting with Alex and his wife. It was festering in my spirit. Caleb had been on the police force with Alex the entire time he was an officer, starting the year after we married. The two of them went through the police academy together and then were assigned to the same patrol team. They worked independently but backed each other up by answering calls and filling in for each other when necessary. They ate meals together; he was one of Caleb's two closest friends. However, as I mulled over Alex's wife's strange behavior toward me at the restaurant, I remembered Caleb mentioning at the end of his police career that he and Alex weren't such great friends anymore. "Why?" I'd asked, since it didn't make sense with how close they were for years. Caleb just shrugged my question off, and I didn't think much of the issue again.

Until now.

I kept thinking—*I know he had an affair with her.* It was like God just opened my eyes, and I knew it. I am usually not the type to confront. In fact, I make it a point not to confront people, unless I am backed into a corner. However, I was on a truth-track in my life, and in this case, I had to know the truth. So, I waited three days, then on Monday, I called Alex on his cell phone. I greeted him kindly, saying it was so good to see him and his wife the other night. "I called because something has been on my mind. I could not help but notice the way your wife acted when we saw each other at the restaurant. She was uncomfortable, and she could hardly look at me."

He said, "Yeah. I noticed that also."

I said, "I am sorry to say this, but I have a strong sense she and Caleb had an affair. Do you think that is possible?"

There was an uncomfortable moment of silence. Finally, he said, "I didn't until you called. But I noticed the way she was acting and thought it was strange too. I hope that is not the case, but I am going to talk to my wife. I will call you back later and let you know what I find out."

I said, "I do not want to start any trouble in your marriage, but have been praying to know the truth of all Caleb's lies and I would like to know if there was an affair. Caleb swore to me he never cheated on me with any other woman the entire time we were married. Then right before he left I asked how many other women there had been and he held one finger up. I would like to know the truth." The officer and I hung up the phone.

I guess we'll see what happens, I thought when Alex and I hung up. *Lord, I know You know the truth. Show me the truth.*

Therefore judge nothing before the appointed time; wait until the Lord comes. He will bring to light what is hidden in the darkness and will expose the motives of the heart.
—*1 Corinthians 4:5*

On Friday, my cell phone rang. It was Caleb's police friend, Alex. He said, "Hi, Anne G."

I said, "Hi."

"Well, you were right. I cannot believe it, but you were right." My heart stopped. He said, "I asked my wife if she had an affair with Caleb, and she denied it." He said, "I am sorry Anne G., but I told her you called me because you had a private investigator follow Caleb and you had pictures of them together. I told her when you saw us at dinner the other night, you felt like you needed to tell me the truth, so you called me, and I told her you had given me copies of the pictures of the two of them together from the private investigator.

"She continued to deny it, but after I told her about the pictures, finally she confessed everything. They had a long-term affair, mostly meeting for their 'hookups' at Caleb's sister's apartment while she was at work. We have been talking about it the last few days which is why I was waiting to call you back."

I was stunned that God really had just made that happen. For seven months I had wondered if there had been other women, and God was giving me truth. I told Caleb's friend I was so sorry, and that I knew what it felt like to be betrayed. He said they were going to try to work things out in their marriage. He then explained he would never tell on another policeman under any situation, but Caleb had betrayed him in the ultimate way by having an affair with his own wife. I thanked him for calling and being truthful with me, that was all I wanted. To know the truth.

As way leads on to way, so does truth lead on to truth. Shortly after my conversation with Alex—that same day—someone who I promised would remain anonymous called me and revealed that from the time Caleb started at the police academy, and for all the years he was a policeman, he had at least one girlfriend. He was always cheating on me, I learned, and was sometimes even cheating on his girlfriend with another girlfriend. The women were mostly strippers, and some were prostitutes. I couldn't speak. Never in a million years would I have thought that Caleb had been cheating on me the entire time we were married. I listened to everything the person who called had to say without saying much in return. I was stunned, as the blood drained out of my head. I sat there listening to what my marriage truly was for the entire time we were married. Life was happening in slow motion as I absorbed the words of truth being spoken to me out loud. The fact I felt like things did not add up in my marriage started making sense. The reason Caleb was not working on our marriage and did not care to, was because he was always busy working on a new girlfriend. The good times in my marriage were probably between relationships or when he thought he would lose me from neglecting me, then he decided he desperately needed me and pursued me with his all. It clicked in my heart. That missing piece in the puzzle that I could not put my finger on.

When the conversation came to an end I said sadly but with great conviction, "I know this is the Lord finally giving me the whole truth. I've prayed that I would no longer be deceived, and that I would know the truth about my marriage. You knew Caleb intimately, and I know I can trust what you have told me. God has used you in a powerful way to speak to me, and you will never know how much I appreciate your honesty."

"I'm sorry to be the one to tell you," he said. "I know it's hard to hear. But I hope you can move on and get remarried to a good guy who deserves you, and have a great life. You're a kind, good Christian, and you deserve better than Caleb."

I thanked him and wished him the best also. This person and I never spoke again. Neither did Alex and I. But I will always regard them as true friends. I found out all I needed to know about my diseased marriage from our conversations.

In one day, God filled in all the missing blanks.

Although necessary, this was an outrageously painful experience. I went to the Lord alone and grieved hard, and, taking the rest of the day off work, I stayed in bed. My entire marriage had been a lie. What an awful truth to swallow. Especially since Caleb promised me that he'd only had an affair with Layla. The mind games overwhelmed me along with all the unknowns. It had been more than seven months since Caleb left. Now, I finally knew the truth. God was merciful in his timing. And it was God's way of setting me free for good. Because for nine years I wondered why it felt like something wasn't right in my marriage and I wondered why the extremes. Now, finally through God's amazing grace,

He gave me the answers. Not at the time of my divorce, but in His perfect time.

One day I was sitting on my back porch with the Lord after reading my Bible. All was quiet and still and, in my mind's eye, the Lord showed me a beautiful red apple. As I gazed at it, it looked perfect. I felt the Lord say to my heart, "I had to end your marriage to Caleb quickly. You were carrying around this red apple that represented your marriage. You saw it as beautiful, and you were proud of it." Then a large knife came down and split the apple in half. As it was cut open I could see the entire inside was rotten completely with maggots. The Lord said, "This is why I had to end your marriage, you had no idea what your marriage was in truth. It was rotten to the core. I love you and I would not allow you to stay in a marriage like that."

I continued to date Paul, and he was amazing, but the truth about my marriage to Caleb made me question if I was so naïve that I would never see people for who they truly were. I never wanted to live in suspicion of other people the way Caleb seemed to live his life. But I did want wisdom.

I told Paul everything; he was shocked I was correct about the affair in the first place, and all the other new information I discovered was even more astonishing. I told him my concerns about how I would know if I could really trust him, and he reassured me greatly by saying, "You have to remember, I'm not Caleb. I'll show you that you can trust me."

CHAPTER 42
DESERT STREAMS

*Instead of your shame you will receive a double portion,
and instead of disgrace you will rejoice in your inheritance.
And so you will inherit a double portion in your land, and
everlasting joy will be yours.*

—Isaiah 61:7

The last week of March, I went to meet with my accountant who had done my and Caleb's taxes for nine years. I sat down alone with him for the first time. He told me he had some bad news. Caleb had deferred his taxes on his business last year and since we had filed jointly, the taxes were my responsibility also. Unless I wanted to take the chance of the taxes being multiplied with interest by not paying the full amount, I needed to pay them off. I sat there. I had no idea he had deferred the taxes; I did not know that was even an option. Another lie coming to surface. I asked how much I owed. He said Caleb owed $20,000 from the last year that he deferred. Then he gave me the amount I owed for my own business. I sat in that chair in that high-rise office in downtown Chattanooga and thought I was going to be sick. I had felt so good and empowered about paying my bills and making enough at my job. Now, so quickly, I felt like I had been hit by a Mack Truck. He said he was very sorry, but to represent me well, he needed to advise me to pay them so I would be done with Caleb for good and not be tied to him if he defaulted and didn't pay the taxes and took off to Africa or wherever. I was choked up and I thanked him for doing my taxes. I got up and drove home. I got home and immediately crawled into my bed. I pulled the covers over my head and wept. *Oh God here I am again, when is this going to stop?* I thought, *The worst part is, I am never expecting it.* That was the truth of my pain.

About 5:30 my doorbell rang. I went to the door with no makeup on and swollen eyes. Paul was standing at my door. He took one look at me and asked what was wrong. I told him Caleb didn't pay the taxes the year before and I just found out from my accountant I owed $20,000 plus what I owed for the year from my own job. I burst out in tears just telling the story out loud. Paul came in and hugged me. He told me we would figure something out. I told him it wasn't his responsibility, it was my mess. He said, "I am not in a full-time position yet, but I'm working on it." I was feeling very defeated, and I asked if he even wanted that position. He assured me he did as he hugged me and wouldn't let me go. It made me feel better knowing he was not running away from me and all my problems.

Paul left and I went to sleep that night bummed out, praying for the Lord to help me. I woke up the next day and got back to work. I had to get things settled and figure out what I was going to do. As I began my day, all of a sudden, I remembered that I had sold a rental home I owned, and I had set closing to be April 15. I sat there thinking, *No way.* I went and figured out what I was going to net from that closing. I am not kidding you when I tell you it paid for all my taxes. I could not believe it. I was selling the property to have some extra money so I would not be stressed out. I just happened to set the day of closing for the exact day I had to pay the IRS for the deferred taxes Caleb had not paid the year before. The Lord was making streams in the desert for me. I knew it was God and walked around in awe and wonder for the next week at what He had planned without me even realizing why I was selling that rental house, but Jesus knew.

I shared with Paul that evening when he came over after work how God always takes such good care of me. He was blessing me and walking with me. That was a ton of money for Paul and me. We both were completely relieved. I sold my rental house the morning of April 15 and mailed my check to the IRS that afternoon. It was all paid in full. Hallelujah! It was a gift straight from heaven.

Interestingly, it seemed my tax ordeal got Paul thinking about our future. The week after my meeting with my accountant, Paul and I were getting gas on the mountain and, instead of getting back on the main road after filling up, he pulled into the parking lot of the grocery store beside the gas station and put his car in park. He turned and looked at me seriously. I wondered, *What's this all about?* Then he took a deep breath and said seriously, "I think I need to get a new job to support you. I know you want to be a stay-at-home mom, and that you want a whole litter of kids."

I laughed. (The week after we had started dating he asked how many children I wanted, and I had told him four. When I'd asked how many he wanted, he'd replied, "I guess a whole litter!")

Now smiling, I said, "I think that's a good idea. I'm expensive."

"I know," he smiled. "That's why I wanted to talk to you about it."

"Well, what do you want to do?" I asked. "What do you love?"

He said he'd always wanted to start his own landscaping company. So we started talking about what would be involved and spent the rest of the week coming up with ideas. I was his biggest cheerleader who encouraged him to go for his dream, knowing he could accomplish it. When we went to my parents' house that week, I told them Paul was considering starting his own business, and they encouraged him too, telling him they thought it was a wise decision. And so after several long discussions, Paul decided to go for it.

He started his landscaping company in April 2002. A hard and determined worker, he was successful from the start. And it worked out well that our businesses overlapped with each other on our small mountain. We would meet for lunch almost every day at the shopping center I worked in. Paul and I both did well working independently, but we also enjoyed working as a team. I was drawn to Paul's work ethic and drive to make his business a success. I had the same fiery drive, and I could see us building our future together easily.

One summer night in June, Paul gave me the nicest compliment anyone has ever given me in my life. We were driving down a mountain backroad heading to my house and he said, "I never realized until now how lonely I was before I met you."

Wow, I thought. *I finally have what I've been waiting for.* I understood at that moment Paul had lived enough life to have been broken like I had been. And because of that, he appreciated me as much as I appreciated him.

It was a beautiful realization.

CHAPTER 43
DIAMOND TREE

For this reason a man will leave his father and mother and be united to his wife, and the two will become one flesh. Therefore what God has joined together, let no one separate.
—Mark 10:7–9

My parents loved Paul from the start and welcomed him into our family with open arms. He had a close relationship with both of them, and they said he seemed like a good, trustworthy man. They also trusted me as I dated him to decide for myself if he was the man I wanted to marry, and if I felt like he was the one God had picked out for me. It was encouraging that they didn't try, out of fear from my past, to discourage me to pursue my dream of having my own family, which had been a deep desire in my heart since I was a little girl.

Slowly, I began to learn to trust Paul. I am not going to lie, it took a while. Honestly, years. But little by little I began to heal from the pain of my past. Paul has been a steady rock of encouragement and has loved me as I have grown in my relationship with the Lord.

He would tell me when I made him mad or if I hurt his feelings, and we dealt with our problems directly, which was how I was raised. He was simple to understand, and there were no mind games. I remember when we fought the first few times, I was so relieved he told me why he was upset. I didn't even care about the argument or who won it.

In August of 2002, seven months after Paul and I started dating, Paul told me he had always wanted to see the Opryland Hotel gardens. He heard they were amazing, so we planned a trip on August 23, to Nashville, our plan being to explore the city and visit the Opryland Hotel, then to stay the night with my sister, Mary Lee, and her family.

At the hotel, as Paul and I walked through the extensive garden, I wandered off for a minute just gazing at the beautiful flowers and trees.

Paul said he wanted to show me a diamond tree, and he led me to the tree. He had already shown his excitement by pointing out several species of plants before.

He pointed. "Look at the root. If you look closely, you'll see a diamond."

I looked at where he was pointing. At the root of the tree, tucked within a fern, was a black jewelry box that was open to reveal a gorgeous three-stone diamond ring. The middle stone, which had to be over a carat, and two side stones all shimmered in the bright daylight beaming inside the large glass conservatory. Surprised, I looked from the ring back up at Paul. He immediately got down on one knee. *Is this really happening?* I thought. *Is this too good to be true?* "Anne G. Powell," Paul said. "I love you. Will you marry me?"

Smiling brighter than the day and engagement ring combined, I said, "Yes!"

Both of us were thrilled. We left the garden to go share our good news with Mary Lee and her family. The next day we went home and showed my parents my ring. Paul had already asked my daddy for his permission to marry me, and they were thrilled for us. We discussed the wedding with my parents, who were only engaged for two weeks themselves. They asked, "Why would you wait?" Paul and I agreed, and as a result set a wedding date for less than two months out.

After all, I only needed a little time to find a dress and to send out invitations.

On October 19, 2002, nine months after we started dating, I married Paul Bryan Lang. We spent very little on our wedding ceremony, which was at the Little Brown Church in Summertown, followed by a wedding reception in my backyard. We waited to sleep together until our wedding night. And, yes, it was well worth the wait! After saying, "I do," we went on an outstanding two-week honeymoon that I planned to the Greek Islands of Mykonos, Santorini, Crete, and then to Athens, Greece. It was probably the best two weeks of my life, filled with romance and adventure. I thank God we have a good marriage. Especially because I know more than anyone, you can do your absolute best and still not have a good marriage. And when that happens, it is devastating. This life is far from perfect. We all have to battle to lay down the idol of ourselves, trusting Jesus and God's word to heal the everyday wounds that do come and affect all of us who live in this world.

CHAPTER 44
A LIGHT SHINING

*In Him was life, and that life was the light of men. The
light shines in the darkness, and the darkness has not
overcome it.*

—John 1:4–5

*He settles the childless woman in her home as a happy
mother of children. Praise the Lord.*

—Psalms 113:9

P aul and I have two simply amazing children who are our
delights, Paul Bryan Lang, Jr. who we call Bryan, and
Laurel Anne Lang. We named Laurel Anne after the laurel
leaf that led me to meet Paul. Our children are brilliant
and funny and both of them are strong and independent
like their parents. I could not be more proud of both of
them. We are doing our best to raise our children up in the
way they should go so when they are old they will not depart
from it (Proverbs 22:6). Just the way my parents did. I want

my children to see me reading God's word daily as I saw both of my parents do. It equipped me for the battles that do come, living in this world. I knew what my parents held in the highest regard: their personal relationship with a living God. When my life fell apart, that is who I also clung to. My Father who holds me close and is fiercely protective over me. Jesus, my friend and my deliverer, and the Holy Spirit, my counselor and my guide. A Holy Trinity of perfect balance. I want my children and all of my descendants to know who they can turn to when they have nothing else.

I am so thankful my parents, siblings, and my entire family walked with me through a dark and painful time in my life. Apart from mom, daddy, and my brother Bill (and Paul on the night I told him everything), I didn't speak to anyone else about seeing and speaking to the demon (or demons) in Caleb, or about him wanting to kill me. In fact, only now are my siblings, the rest of my family, and my best friends reading my entire story for the first time. Over the years, I revealed bits and pieces of it if I felt like God was encouraging me to share or encourage someone, but I never gave all the dark details. I didn't want to speak about it, and I was afraid everyone would think I was nuts. I could always share my heart with my parents. They were pillars of faith in my life, steady and full of truth, holding up the Word of God as a light for me to see when I needed the extra light of Jesus on the dark path I walked. My brother Bill, who is quiet in spirit, loves Jesus and has a simple faith. To this day, anytime I tell him what's on my heart he says, "If you think it's God, you need to obey Him. And if it's not, you'll figure it out." I think God gave Bill those specific gifts for me, as well as the others that he loves. Love and faith are the mighty gifts God gave Bill. Those Bill loves, he loves fiercely. I'm fortunate to have been one of those people since the moment I was born his baby sister.

I stopped having nightmares completely about a year after Paul and I married. Little by little God healed me. Hallelujah—all the glory goes to God.

Paul and I built a house on our family property in 2008 and moved onto the land that sits above the barn that I have always loved. I lost both of my parents when my children were young. They do not remember my mother at all, who was a mighty woman who walked with God. I lost her in March of 2009 to multiple myeloma, a cancer of the blood, when Bryan was barely four and Laurel Anne was twenty-two months old. They only remember my father with advanced Alzheimer's, which breaks my heart. He died in September of 2017 after a long battle that took his mind. Both of my parents showed me until their deaths on this earth what it looks like to walk with God and trust Him, even when the road ahead seems dark and confusing. They showed me that their hope was not in this world. That this world is not our eternity, and one day we will be in eternity with a Father who loves and adores us more than we could ever think or imagine. And there are some things we will simply never understand, but we can make the choice daily to trust God, *even if* we never get the answers.

Life has had some major bumps in the road. Paul has been a faithful and loving husband, and I appreciate him more every day. We are very similar in personality, and he makes me laugh harder than any person I have ever met. We enjoy each other and spend most of our free time together with our children and their crew of friends. My children are now in Young Life and for over five years we have hosted the Young Life Club of about forty kids weekly at our house, plus some Young Life Bible studies another two nights of the week. Our home is always open to our children's friends and Christian groups that need a place to gather. Our home and our family life are filled with joy and peace.

Sometimes Paul and I fight and there are fireworks. We are both strong and can hold our own. However, when we do fight, it's usually worth the battle. Our lives are not perfect, and we are not perfect, but who wants perfect? That would be boring.

The Lord has not supernaturally healed me from my sassy mouth yet. I am still a work in progress, and unless it is a miraculous healing—I realize I might be struggling with my tongue until the day I see Jesus in glory. But I think Paul secretly likes my feisty side. I tell him, "I am the spice in your life, baby. Life would be boring without me."

He just laughs, because he is a smart man.

Both Bryan and Laurel Anne prayed and asked Jesus Christ to be Lord and Savior of their own personal lives. I had the privilege of praying with both of them individually, which remains one of my greatest joys in this life, knowing my children will be with me in eternity. My children have been two of my greatest pleasures on this earth. They have brought me tremendous joy and fulfillment. God gave me my greatest desire: to be a wife and mother.

It is well with my soul.

I will always hold Africa in a tender place in my heart. The first time I traveled there I saw it with fresh young eyes and an open and untamed heart. Each trip I experienced exquisite and exciting countries full of God's creative masterpieces, beautiful people, and spectacular animals. It filled my soul to see those animals in the wild, living and breathing, especially with their babies. It touched me deeply. One day my desire is to go back and bring Paul, Bryan and Laurel Anne and share with them all the beauty of that lovely continent. But truthfully, more than that, I want to go back and reap good. It is a deep desire in me to do God's work there to bring healing to others in supernatural ways that only God can do. When I am weak, He is strong. I want Satan to remember what he did to me and see the good that will be done because of it.

I *will* overcome evil with good. To God be the glory.

Do not be overcome by evil, but overcome evil with good.
—Romans 12:21

I never spoke to Caleb again after that one phone call about the Granny loan. I have heard through the grapevine he is married to his third wife and still lives in Texas. He still goes to Africa for long periods of time without his wife.

I hope he is in heaven one day.

I thought I had healed from my past, and did not speak about it for more than twenty years. Which I guess was a coping and survival mechanism. I did not want to speak about my experience with demons or about standing against the devil's schemes. Now I know, with everything in me, the Word of God is true. My prayer is that all the generations who come after me will be a people who walk with God. The Lord gave me Isaiah 54 the week Caleb left. It was a love letter from the Lord that I have read often and have prayed as I was waiting on Him. It is my life chapter that I treasure and have held close to my heart, believing

in faith what is said—for the things I hoped for, but could
not yet see:

"Sing, barren woman,
you who never bore a child;
burst into song, shout for joy,
you who were never in labor;
because more are the children of the desolate woman
than of her who has a husband,"
says the Lord. [...]
"Do not be afraid; you will not be put to shame.
Do not fear disgrace; you will not be humiliated.
You will forget the shame of your youth
and remember no more the reproach of your
      widowhood.
For your Maker is your husband—
the Lord Almighty is His name—
the Holy One of Israel is your Redeemer;
He is called the God of all the earth.
The Lord will call you back
as if you were a wife deserted and distressed
      in spirit—
a wife who married young,
only to be rejected," says your God.
"For a brief moment I abandoned you,
but with deep compassion I will bring you back. [...]"
"Afflicted city, lashed by storms and not
comforted, I will rebuild you with stones of turquoise,
your foundations with lapis lazuli.
I will make your battlements of rubies,

your gates of sparkling jewels, and your walls of
    precious stone.
All your children will be taught by the Lord,
and great will be their peace.
In righteousness you will be established:
Tyranny will be far from you; you will have nothing
    to fear.
Terror will be far removed; it will not come near you.
If anyone does attack you, it will not be my doing;
whoever attacks you will surrender to you. [...]
...no weapon forged against you will prevail,
and you will refute every tongue that accuses you.
This is the heritage of the servants of the Lord,
And this is their vindication from me,"
declares the Lord."

                —Isaiah 54:1,4–7,11–15,17

What is stated in this chapter did come true in my life as
I write these holy words down over twenty years later.

EPILOGUE

Then Jesus asked them, "Would anyone light a lamp and then put it under a basket or bed? Of course not! A lamp is placed on a stand, where its light will shine. For everything that is hidden will eventually be brought into the open, and every secret will be brought to light. Anyone with ears to hear should listen and understand."

—Mark 4:21–23

In 2008, while on vacation in the Great Smoky Mountains, I was out sitting next to a river reading my Bible and spending time with God, when suddenly out of the blue, I was overwhelmed by the way I treated Tim Finnegan back in college. I felt clearly the Lord wanted me to apologize for my actions. So, after some prayer, I called him after 16 years of no communication at all. Dialing his office phone number, I was secretly hoping he would not answer—but he answered the phone at 8:15 am, before his office opened. His voice confirmed he was clearly surprised I had called. Blurting out my convictions, I told him I was calling to apologize to him. Confessing Caleb and I had divorced, I was happily married now to Paul and had two beautiful children. I started to cry, and told him I was heavily weighted down with remorse that I had not treated him with respect. I had just disappeared out of his life without explanation because that was easier than having to choose between him and Caleb. I ran away from both him and my inability to choose. Now, the Lord was calling me to humble myself and ask for his forgiveness. I felt clearly that God loved Tim, and I owed him an apology. As I spoke through my tears, I told him it was difficult for me to call to apologize, especially after so many years. However, the heavy conviction I felt from God was so strong, that I knew I needed to obey Him. Tim was generous and told me he knew it must be from God because he knew me well, and for me to call after so many years—it must be miraculous. Graciously he received my apology with humor and forgiveness. Tim updated me on his life; he was also happily married with children of his own, his life was good, and God had been good to him. Through our conversation I could hear he was clearly walking close to the Lord. Then he actually ended up encouraging me in my walk of obedience with God. I told him we would probably never speak again, and he asked if I would tell Paul about our conversation, which I told him I absolutely would. And I did, immediately. I will always appreciate Tim, and consider him a forever friend, who encouraged me in my walk of faith.

He loves Jesus, and his heart is pure.

Believe it or not, that same vacation is when I had my first thought, that one day I would write a book. Then I laughed to myself, thinking that would surely be a miracle of all miracles.

Many years later, when I felt like the Lord was telling

me to write this book, I grieved. I didn't want to deal with my past or remember my pain. I had stuffed my past down deep and hidden the truth for so many years, even in my own heart, and I didn't want to tell my story of darkness. I thought, *Come on Lord, I want to write about rainbows and blessings, not about demons and torment. Are you kidding me?* However, the Lord continued to speak to my heart. So, after praying about it, I spoke with Paul. He reminded me, "You've been telling me for years that you thought you were going to write a book about God one day." He had a good point, so after my and Paul's conversation, I spoke to my children separately. They've always known about my divorce, but for the first time I told them the whole story of it that you now know. I brought my secrets to light and told them of God's amazing grace and provision over my life. They both thought I should share my story, which encouraged me to continue on toward the calling I felt I was hearing from the Lord.

As you know I was a horrible student, and I have never been a writer. But since that vacation in 2008 I have had the thought hundreds of times, *I think I will write a book one day—about God,* so I would casually try to write in faith, but nothing ever came. I would put whatever I was working on to the side, not worrying about it, then try again months later. Still nothing.

Then on September 4, 2021, I was out on a walk by myself and the Lord said to me, "It is time. What you learned in the darkness, I want you to share it in the light. I want to heal you and my people. Write your story of darkness and I will make it a light." I knew then what the Lord wanted me to write about. It was clearly something I did not feel comfortable sharing. But I figured God knew what He was doing, and I would take a step of faith and get out of my boat and keep my eyes on Jesus (Matthew 14:22–33).

Then on September 28, after my husband left for work and my children left for school, I sat down and began to write. And to my surprise, my story poured out of me. It was like a faucet within me had been turned on, and I could not stop. I had to get it all out. "Not by might, nor by power, but by my spirit says the Lord" (Zechariah 4:6). Because I had tried to obey over the years and it never flowed, I knew it was not me, but the Holy Spirit in me. I wrote for months which turned into years, laughing as I'd tell my family at dinner, "I wrote all day, seven or eight hours." One night at dinner I asked Paul, Bryan, and Laurel Anne if they had any reservations about me writing this book. "If you do," I said, "I won't write it." Without hesitation, all three said I should continue to write. So I did, and as I wrote God performed a deep and supernatural healing in me, in spite of my pride. He has always been so good to me.

I have written the truth of my life, the good, the bad, the godly, and the evil. The things I have pondered in my heart for over twenty years, I am finally speaking out in the light. And what Satan tried to tell me were skeletons in my closet, God has spoken to my heart—they are simply dry bones (Ezekiel 37:4–14). I will trust Him as the bones rise up and come to life, forming a mighty army joined together for His powerful purpose. The details are not my responsibility, my job is simply to trust and obey.

Now I reflect and I allow God my Father to meet me through the power of His Holy Spirit. I am very thankful that God spared my life and raised me out of the darkness and set me in the presence of His glorious light. In His light is where I have been able to heal through the truth of the Word of God, and equally as important—being truthful with myself. Which has honestly been the hardest part for me. Only God knows the pain in the depths of our souls, even more clearly than we ourselves can comprehend. And He knows precisely how we need to receive healing, specifically and individually. He will bring us truth deep into our innermost being, and in the inner parts He will make us know wisdom.

Only He can do it.

"Behold, You desire truth in the innermost being, and in the hidden part You will make me know wisdom."
—Psalms 51:6 NASB 1995

I will never forget my past. And I do not think God wants me to. I think he wants me to use it for His glory. To use it as a light in this dark world. My testimony and your testimony are one of the most powerful things God gives us. We are changed because of them. When I am struggling, I go back to my own story of how I walk with God and what he has already done in my past to meet me in my pain and confusion. Then I know in my heart, in his timing he will help me, as he also changes me through the hard times. I want to tell my children, my descendants, and my family of Christ about the miracles God has already done in my life, so that we will never forget that we are children of the Most High God, Abba, Father.

Everyone who lives on this earth will at some time or another experience a hard or dark season. The good news for believers is, we don't have to walk through it alone. Jesus tells us that in this world we will have trouble, but have peace and know that He has overcome the world. So use the name *Jesus*—it is the most powerful word we can speak. Everything must submit to His name.

Furthermore, it's important to not isolate yourself if you are walking through a dark season, because Satan wants to isolate you and build lies in your mind to confuse you. The Bible tells us the enemy wants to kill, steal, and destroy us. I encourage you to find someone or a few people you can trust to share your heart with, who can hold the Word of God up as a light to help you see God's truth and His promises that are for *all* of His children. We need each other, that is how God designed us. Many times we heal in supernatural ways through sharing with others our wounds and our heartbreaks. God tells us in His word, in 2 Corinthians 1:3–4:

> Praise be to the God and Father of our Lord Jesus Christ, the Father of compassion and the God of all comfort, who comforts us in all our troubles, so that we can comfort those in any trouble with the comfort we ourselves receive from God.

One powerful treasure I received in my darkness was discovering that one of the most successful ways to battle spiritual warfare is to continually have gratitude and praise rising up to God from my heart and out of my lips. Another treasure I received was the Lord teaching me to speak His truth out loud. That's what Jesus did in the wilderness when He was being tempted by Satan. He didn't allow Satan's lies to enter into His spirit. Now I look up verses about what I'm struggling with, write them on note cards, and put them on my bathroom mirror or beside my kitchen sink, and I speak these verses out loud, which is the sword of the spirit. We have the greatest example of what to do, God in flesh: Jesus. "He that lives within us *is* greater than he that lives within this world." It doesn't get any better than that.

Now, I dress spiritually, just as I put my clothes on for the day, I also put my spiritual armor, which are verses I feel prompted from the Holy Spirit to speak over myself. Because of the Father, Son, and Holy Spirit, as believers, we do not live by a book of rules—we are set free to live by the spirit of God that lives and dwells in us. I know I do not have to live in fear. God is in control and He is my stronghold—I do my part and God does His.

I am sobered and thankful for my parents' and all my grandparents' prayers over me. Parents, your prayers over your children are full of power. Look at the Old Testament and the powerful prayers the parents prayed over their children that changed generations. Please think about what you speak over yourself and your children. God's Word tells us in Proverbs 18:20-21: "Death and life are in the power of the tongue, and those who love it will eat its fruits."

Words are powerful.

After writing this book, I looked back at my journal to confirm dates. I flipped to my journal entry from the day Caleb drove out of my driveway for the last time. The date was September 4, 2001. I was stunned. The Lord had spoken to my heart about writing my story on September 4, 2021, as I mentioned at the beginning of this book. It was exactly twenty years later to the day. I have no idea what God's timing means, and I'm okay with not knowing.

Anne G. Lang

I know it's significant, and I know His timing is perfect.

It is a hard thing for me to lay down my pride and write about the truth in my life, but I am trusting God for his continual healing in me every day and to bring healing to many others through my story of hope. In the mighty name of Jesus, I am a living testimony of His amazing grace! Amen.

> *"Forget the former things; do not dwell on the past. See I am doing a new thing! Now it springs up; do you not perceive it? I am making a way in the desert and streams in the wasteland."*
> —*Isaiah 43:18–19*

This is my life verse. Hold on my fellow believer in Christ. Do not dwell on the past, God is doing a new thing! Now it springs up. He is our living water for our thirsty souls in the desert.

The story is not over.

Hallelujah!

He lives.

328

Dugg and Eleanor Powell, my parents.
Kirawira Tented Camp, Serengeti Tanzania
June 2000

Anne G. with Maasai Tribe. Ngorongoro Crater Rim, Tanzania
June 2000

Dugg and Eleanor Powell purchasing a knife from
Maasai Warriors. Ngorongoro Crater Rim, Tanzania
June 2000

Paul and Anne G. Santorini, Greece
Our Honeymoon
October 2002

Paul, Anne G., Bryan and Laurel Anne
Signal Mountain, TN
2010

Paul, Anne G., Bryan and Laurel Anne
Stirling Castle, Scotland
April 2023

Bryan and Laurel Anne (family vacation)
Athens, Greece
June 2024

Paul, Anne G., Bryan and Laurel Anne
Mykonos, Greece
June 2024

ACKNOWLEDGMENTS

For the ones closest to me, you know who you are. I asked you to read my story before publishing it. Thank you to those who encouraged me to continue what I believe was the Holy Spirit guiding me to do. God bless each one of you.

Don Franklin, I cannot think of you without a heart full of gratitude. I am thankful God used you to save Paul's life, so I could reap the future God had in store for me and my children. You are a man of wisdom, and a doctor of faith. But to me, you are my real life superhero. God bless you.

Claire Miller, my editor. God used you to take my story and polish it into a treasure, bringing God all the Glory. Thank you for being easy to work with and always open to the Holy Spirit's leading. God bless you.

David Nichols, my friend. You created the most beautiful book cover I could have ever imagined. Thank you for this precious gift—God bless you.

Made in USA - Kendallville, IN
38153_9798321948040
01.02.2025 2208